AF449166

Glossae – Scholia – Commentarii

Warsaw Studies in Classical Literature and Culture

Edited by Mikołaj Szymański and Mariusz Zagórski

Volume 2

Mieczysław Mejor / Katarzyna Jażdżewska /
Anna Zajchowska (eds.)

Glossae – Scholia – Commentarii

Studies on Commenting Texts
in Antiquity and Middle Ages

Bibliographic Information published by the Deutsche Nationalbibliothek
The Deutsche Nationalbibliothek lists this publication in the Deutsche
Nationalbibliografie; detailed bibliographic data is available in the internet at
http://dnb.d-nb.de.

Library of Congress Cataloging-in-Publication Data
Glossae, scholia, commentarii : studies on commenting texts in antiquity and
Middle Ages / Mieczysław Mejor, Katarzyna Jażdżewska, Anna Zajchowska (eds.)
   pages cm
 ISBN 978-3-631-65250-3
 1. Criticism, Textual. 2. Classical literature–History and criticism. 3. Literature,
Medieval–History and criticism. 4. Bible–Commentaries–History and criticism.
 I. Mejor, Mieczysław. II. Jażdżewska, Katarzyna. III. Zajchowska, Anna.
 P47.G56 2014
 801'.95–dc23

                                                    2014026779

This publication was financially supported by the Institute
of Classical Philology and Culture Studies,
Cardinal Stefan Wyszynski University.

ISSN 2196-9779
ISBN 978-3-631-65250-3 (Print)
E-ISBN 978-3-653-04312-9 (E-Book)
DOI 10.3726/978-3-653-04312-9

Table of Contents

Introduction

"The commentary-tradition, indeed, is so rich and varied in itself that we cannot claim to be comprehensive even in dealing with it alone."

Medieval Literary Theory and Criticism c.1100-c.1375. The Commentary-Tradition. Ed. by A.J. Minnis, A.B. Scott with assist. of D. Wallace, Oxford: Clarendon Press, 1991, vii.

A need to comment on a text arises when its contents is concealed before the eyes of the recipient and one must unveil it in order to ensure the text's understanding. This applies especially to sacred, revealed books, the understanding of which is not possible without proper commentaries and explanations, and also to philosophical, scientific, and medical writings which require continual clarification and elucidation of their contents.

Commentaries are also indispensable tools when a text is archaic and therefore remains obscure without the aid of explanatory comments. These types of commentaries were composed since antiquity, since the Hellenistic period in which the language of Homer and Hesiod was already archaic and in large part incomprehensible.

A commentary is the most characteristic scholarly form of the Middle Ages. It is closely connected with the medieval scholarly methodology which relied on the practice of shared reading and commenting on a text, the aim of which was to reveal the work's hidden meaning and to express one's own attitude towards it.

The present collection of studies, titled *Glossae, Scholia, Commentarii*, focuses on commentary literature coming from diverse cultural and intellectual circles and attempts to appraise similarities and differences between them in regard to methods and techniques employed. We have invited eminent specialists – orientalists, medievalists, and historians of medieval philosophy – from different Polish universities to participate in this project. This book, which is a result of their joint efforts, only partially answers the questions raised. The subject matter is extensive and insufficiently researched; therefore, despite existing previous studies[1], a comprehensive synthetic overview of various forms

---

1 Cf. e.g. *Le Commentaire – Le Commentaire entre tradition et innovation. Actes du Colloque international de l'Institut des Traditions Textuelles* (Paris Villejuif, 22 – 25 sept. 1999). Publ. sous dir. Marie-Odile Goulet-Cazé, avec coll. édit. de T. Dorandi, R. Goulet [et al.], Paris 2000, *Der Kommentar in Antike und Mittelalter. Beiträge zu seiner Erforschung.* Hrsg. von Wilhelm Geerlings, Christian Schulze. Clavis commentariorum

and genres of commentary literature is still a long way off. The present volume is a *collectanea* of studies focused on the practice of commenting in different cultures and periods; perhaps it will lead to further interdisciplinary meetings and projects devoted to commentaries and isagogic literature.

The Editors of the book would like to thank the authorities of the Faculty of Humanities at the Cardinal Stefan Wyszyński University in Warsaw for granting funding that enabled the publication of this volume.

Separate thanks go to Dr Katarzyna Jażdżewska from the Institute of Classical Philology and Culture Studies, Cardinal Stefan Wyszyński University in Warsaw, who has undertaken the task of editing the contributions written in English.

Mieczysław Mejor

---

antiquitatis et medii aevi, t. 1. Leiden–Köln: Brill, 2002, *Der Kommentar in Antike und Mittelalter. Neue Beiträge zu seiner Erforschung*. Hrsg. von Wilhelm Geerlings, Christian Schulze. Clavis commentariorum antiquitatis et medii aevi, t. 2. Leiden: Brill, 2004.

Qumran Pesharim as an Example
of an Accommodative Commentary

Dorota Muszytowska

Chair of Old Polish Literature and Rhetoric,
Cardinal Stefan Wyszyński University in Warsaw

The term 'pesher' (*pēšer*) has three different meanings in modern scholarship: it is used in reference to texts found in scrolls which were discovered near the Dead Sea, to a form or a genre of commentary literature, and to a method of textual exegesis. The term, then, has a fairly extensive semantic field, as it can refer to specific texts, more broadly to a commentary type they represent, or to a procedure of explaining and clarifying texts, not necessarily limited to a specific literary form. All three meanings, however, relate somehow to the community living at the turn of the first century in the neighborhood of today's Qumran. This community employed a particular form of text interpretation which it considered sacred, and which can be seen at work both in organizational writings of that community and in commentaries interpreting books of the Bible. Their hermeneutical approach was influenced, on the one hand, by the specific situation and self-awareness of the Qumran community, and on the other hand, by other exegetical traditions of Judaism, in this period not restricted to biblical exegesis. I have in mind, primarily, the impact of understanding and assessment of current and past events in the Old Testament prophetic literature and influence of religious traditions which evolved in close relationship with texts acknowledged as sacred; both influences were increasingly significant during the rabbinic period in halakhic and haggadic midrashes.

The distinction between commenting styles of midrash and pesher is not sharp. They have the same aim: actualization of the message of the interpreted text. However, the methods of the two types of commentaries are not identical. They are founded on different hermeneutical premises, which allow the pesherists to customize interpreted texts in a peculiar way, relevant to current circumstances.

1. Circumstances of pesharim development

As I indicated above, the origin of the commentary literature referred to as pesharim (*pēšārîm*) is associated with the community living in Qumran, in the

Judean Desert, between around 150/130 BC and 68 AD.[1] Archaeological research led in 1947–1965 in Khirbet Qumran and its surroundings, in Wadi Murabba'at, in Khirbet Mird (identified as Hyrcania), as well as in Nahal Hever, Nahal Tse'elim, Nahal Mishmar, and Masada confirmed inhabitation of the area at various times, including the turn of the eras. Numerous scrolls were discovered there, usually made of some sort of parchment, among which there were manuscripts of the biblical texts and commentary literature. Findings discovered in other places of the Judean Desert are not considered as directly connected with the cave findings from Qumran and its neighborhood because of their different dating and character. The latter, however, are commonly associated with the settlement in Qumran itself.[2]

Yet, the origin of the Qumran scrolls is not clear. One cannot with certainty ascribe them to the population inhabiting the area. There is no proof that the scroll collection belonged only to inhabitants of this settlement, even though the vast majority of researchers recognize a close relationship between the settlement and the manuscripts.[3] So far, there is also no satisfactory evidence

---

1 See Józef T. Milik, *Ten Years of Discovery in the Wilderness of Judaea*, transl. from French John Strugnell (London–Naperville, Ill., 1959), 54; Roland de Vaux, *Archeology of the Dead Sea Scrolls* (London, 1973), 19.116–117. Today, the Essene settlement in Qumran is dated to not earlier than the last quarter of the second century BC. Cf. Christoph Dohmen, "Zur Gründung der Gemeinde von Qumran," *Revue de Qumran* 11, 41 (1982): 88; Philip R. Callaway, *The History of Qumran Community: An Investigation* (Sheffield 1988), 50; and so-called Groningen Hypothesis, formulated by Florentino García Martínez, Adam S. Van der Woude, "A 'Groningen' Hypothesis of Qumran Origins and Early History," *Revue de Qumran* 14 (1990), 521–541. For even later dating, the mid-first century BC, cf. Jean-Baptiste Humbert, *Fouilles de Khirbet Qumran et de Ain Feskha*, (Fribourg 1994), 1: 175, 210.

2 For a history of discoveries made in various archaeological sites in the Judean Desert and their specifications, see e.g. Lena Cansdale, *Qumran and the Essenes: a Re-evaluation of the Evidence*, Texte und Studien zum antiken Judentum, 60 (Tübingen, 1997), esp. 5–11, 87–97.

3 There are two major trends in scholarship here. Most scholars believe that the scrolls from around Qumran belonged to a library of a religious community, though they differ as to the purpose and origin of the collection. See e.g. Frank M. Cross, *The Ancient Library of Qumran and Modern Biblical Studies* (New York, 1958); Hartmut Stagemann, *Die Essener, Qumran, Johannes der Täufer und Jesus* (Freiburg, 1994). Others think that the scrolls were stored in caves near the village, but were not produced and used by the inhabitants of Qumran; here the most famous hypothesis is the one proposing Jerusalem as the origin of the scrolls (see Norman Golb, *Who Wrote the Dead Sea Scrolls? The Search for the Secret of Qumran* (New York, 1995).

enabling us to identify the settlement[4] and the community living there at the turn of the eras. Scholars operate on a working hypothesis developed by the first researchers which identified the Qumran people with the Essenes or members of their radical faction.[5] This hypothesis is based mainly on interpretation of ancient writings mentioning the *Essenoi*, their way of life, and places inhabited by them (the main sources here are Pliny the Elder's *Historia Naturalis* and the works of Josephus: *The Jewish War, Against Apion*, and *Antiquities of the Jews*).[6] The Essene hypothesis was constantly modified since the eighties of the twentieth century. As a result, many of its original proposals were rejected, as were some alternative hypotheses (e.g. Qumran association of Zadokites).[7] Two issues in particular have been discussed and revised: the connection between the origins of Qumran and the beginnings of the Essene faction and the quasi-monastic character of Qumran community.[8]

Whether we accept the Essene hypothesis or not, the Qumran scrolls reveal that the community depicted in them held unusual views, which were different from the mainstream opinions of the so-called official Judaism of that period, or at least from the politicized Judaism of the Hasmoneans. Characteristic of the Qumran society are apocalyptic views, which, however, should be distinguished from both the mainstream Old Testament eschatological apocalyptics and the mainstream mystical Enochic apocalyptics. Both these trends are manifest in the Qumran writings, though in a modified form, mainly influenced by sapiential tradition and its way of seeing history (as can be clearly seen in *Ages of Creation* – 4Q180 and 4Q181). When we take into account the specific political

---

4   Qumran as a place of settlement is considered here in the broader context of time. Beginnings of the colonization are associated with a military character of the place. Some researchers (e.g. N. Golb) are of the opinion that even at the turn of eras the settlement functioned as a fortress. For an overview of current research on identification of the settlement see e.g. Piotr Muchowski, *Komentarze do rękopisów znad Morza Martwego* (Kraków, 2000), 14–17; Timothy H. Lim, John J. Collins, "Introduction. Current Issues in Dead Sea Scrolls Research," in *The Oxford Handbook of the Dead Sea Scrolls,* ed. by Timothy H. Lim, John J. Collins (Oxford, 2010), 3–4.

5   Such identification is attributed to Roland de Vaux team. It was independently developed by E. L. Sukenik and M. Burrows; and explained in details and documented by F. M. Cross, Józef T. Milik i Geza Vermes. See Lim, Collins, "Introduction", 5.

6   For a discussion of these ancient sources, see Eugeniusz Dąbrowski, *Odkrycia w Qumran nad Morzem Martwym a Nowy Testament* (Poznań, 1960). See also *The Essenes according to the Classical Sources, ed. by* Geza Vermes, Martin D. Goodman, (Sheffield, 1989) and Cansdale, *Qumran and the Essenes,* 19–41.

7   See *The Essenes,* 15–17.

8   See Muchowski, *Komentarze,* 13–14.

and religious situation of the community, its views and its conception of "a realizing eschatology" become understandable.[9]

The main text, the so-called *Rule of the Community* (1QS) – a compendium of rules governing the community and its life, which influenced other Qumran writings[10] – focuses on the biblical idea of the Covenant. The purpose of the *Rule* was to prepare community members for the eschatic fulfillment of the Covenant, which would consist of the coming of God's messiah (or messiahs: prophet, king, priest) and his victorious battle over the forces of evil.

The conviction of the Qumran community that they are living in the final times is strongly noticeable in the texts.[11] The figure of the Teacher of Righteousness played a significant role in crystallizing such views. In the scrolls, he is contrasted with characters of his opponents – the Wicked Priest, the Man of Lie – and the community named Ephraim or the House of Absalom. Qumran scriptures indicate that the community considered the authority of the Teacher of Righteousness to be unquestionable. A more realistic image is conveyed through documents which are attributed to him, such as the *Rule of Community* (1QS), the *Rule of Congregation* (1QSa), the *Blessings* (1QSb), or hymns called *Lehrerlieder* from the collection of *Hodayot* (1QH).[12] Although the image in these texts is diversified, it indicates someone aware of his mission and confident about his God-given vocation; someone who is forced to confront opponents who distort God's intentions and who has to endure false accusations, insults, and persecution.[13] The *Damascus Document* emphasizes in particular the role of the Teacher of Righteousness as the founding leader of the association: "...for twenty years they were like blind men groping for the way. And God observed their deeds, that they sought Him with a whole heart, and He raised up for them a Teacher of Righteousness to guide them in the way of His heart to give later generations the knowledge of what God has done for the last

---

9   See Sylwester Jędrzejewski, „Peszer jako metoda egzegetyczna," *Seminare* 24 (2007): 114; Lim, Collins, "Introduction", 7–8.

10 The *Rule of Community* was found in multiple copies and in different versions in the I, IV and V cave. The oldest text is dated to the second century BC. Many transcriptions retain features of Qumran spelling. See Muchowski, *Komentarze*, 59–66.

11 See Elisha Qimron, James H. Charlsworth, *Rule of the Community and Related Documents,* vol. 1 of *The Dead Sea Scrolls. Hebrew, Aramaic and Greek Texts with English Translation* (Tübingen, 1994), 3.

12 See Stanisław Mędala, "Alkimos historii i autor 1 QH X–XVII," *Ruch Biblijny i Liturgiczny* 54 (2002), 77.

13 For the figure of the Teacher of Righteousness based on Qumran community doctrinal writings, see F. M. Schweitzer, "The Teacher of Righteousness", in *Mogilany 1989. Part II: The Teacher of Righteousness: Literary Studies,* ed. by Zdzisław J. Kapera (Kraków, 1991), 53–97.

generation, assembly of traitors and infidels. Indeed, they were the ones who strayed from the path" (CD-A 1,9–13).[14] Pesher Ps 37 (4QpPs[a] 3,15–17) takes up this thread by clearly calling the Teacher of Righteousness the founder and leader of the community. In pesharim, however, the person of the Teacher of Righteousness is idealized. First of all, he emerges as the sole legitimate interpreter of prophets' words. Only he can properly explain the meaning of community experience and current events which have been foretold by earlier prophets. In pesharim prophetic texts, the Interpreter-Teacher of Righteousness makes references to the contemporary situation in Jerusalem and Judah, to the association which he leads, and also to himself. The type of idealization we observe in pesher texts clearly shows the direction of the evolution of the eschatological views of the community, as well as the possible process of identifying the experience of the Qumran community with the experience of the Teacher of Righteousness.[15]

The conviction that the time is being fulfilled created a noticeable tension in the community and generated certain behaviors. Reading and meditating on the sacred books was considered one of the most important phases of the preparation. "In any place where is gathered the ten-man quorum, someone must always be engaged in study of the Law, day and night, continually, each one taking his turn. The general membership will be diligent together for the first third of every night of the year, reading aloud from the Book, interpreting Scripture." (1 QS 6, 6–7).[16] An extensive literature considering different ways of interpreting of and commenting on sacred texts was a result of this command. It included paraphrases of entire books (e.g., *Paraphrase of Genesis and Exodus* – 4Q42) and of smaller units of biblical texts in the form of didactic considerations or narrative midrashes (e.g. *Meditation on Creation* – 4Q303, 304, 305), as well as targumic translations. But the most significant form of commenting, characteristic for the Qumran community, are continuous and thematic pesharim.[17]

---

14   Geza Vermes, *The Dead Sea Scrolls in English* (Sheffield, 1995[4]), 97.

15   See Steven D. Fraade, "Interpretative Authority in the Studying Community at Qumran," *Journal of Jewish Studies* 44 (1993): 46–49.

16   Vermes, *The Dead Sea Scrolls in English*, 77.

17   See Wiliam H. Brownlee, "Biblical Interpretation among the Sectaries of the Dead Sea Scrolls," *Biblical Archeologists* 14 (1951): 54–76; Devorah Dimant, "Qumran Sectarian Literature: Biblical Interpretation", in *Jewish Writings of the Second Temple Period,* ed. by Michael E. Stone (Assen, Philadelphia, 1984), 2: 503–508; Stanisław Mędala, *Wprowadzenie do literatury międzytestamentalnej* (Kraków, 1994), 66–69.

2. Pesharim characteristics

2.1. The etymology and semantics of the word pēšer

The Semitic root *pšr* has an Akkadian origin.[18] In the Hebrew Bible, the root does not exist in the form of a verb, but as a noun *pšer* (פֵּשֶׁר).[19] In Book of Ecclesiastes 8:1, it was used to describe the ability of the wise man who knows the essence of things and therefore can provide an explanation of the meaning of words (מִי כְּהֶחָכָם וּמִי יוֹדֵעַ פֵּשֶׁר דָּבָר), which LXX referred to as τίς οἶδεν λύσιν ῥήματος. In the Aramaic biblical texts the root *pšr* occurs several times in the Book of Daniel: for example, *pəšar* (פְּשַׁר) in Dn 4:3 (דִּי־פְשַׁר חֶלְמָא יְהוֹדְעֻנַּנִי) means "explanation of the meaning of a dream", and in Dn 5:15.26 (פְּשַׁר־מִלְּתָא) "explanation of a written text".[20]

We find analogous meanings of the root *pšr* in a Hebrew pesharim from Qumran. In 1QpHab 2.8, the verb 'to explain' appears in relation to the activities of the Teacher of Righteousness. It is most noticeable, however, in commentaries on biblical texts as well as in legal and doctrinal texts of the community, where the word 'explanation/interpretation' becomes a technical term, used in some sort of a formula. In most biblical commentaries it appears in introductory statements (in the form of פשר אל 'explanation applies to', פשרו אל 'his explanation [i.e. the Teacher of Righteousness] in relation to', etc.). In doctrinal texts, where the biblical text is not dominant, such formula is not always present, although the contents of a comment is analogous to such formula[21]; also, if the formula appears, it is either of introductory character (*pišrô al*), or, more commonly, of summarizing and informative one, indicating that the interpretation has the highest authority, whereas the biblical quotation serves to reinforce the argument.[22] It should be noted that often this model of

---

18 It appears in the cuneiform records from the Old-Babylonian period, from the first half of the second millennium, in basic form of the verb *pašaru* and forms derived from it, and it means 'to release' (e.g. from bonds), 'to appease' (e.g., dispute), 'comment' (e.g., on an oath or a spell), and 'to explain' and 'interpret' (e.g., dream); the noun *pišru* means 'solution' (e.g., of a riddle), 'explanation' (e.g., of a dream, oracle). See Wolfram von Soden, *Akkadisches Handwörterbuch* (Wiesbaden, 1969), 842–843.

19 For example in an analogous context, in Genesis 40:16, where reference is made to Joseph clarifying the Pharaoh's Dream, it is expressed by the verb פָּתַר.

20 More about etymology of *pēšer* see, for example, Małecki, *Peszery*, 46–50.

21 See Jonathan G. Campbell, *The Use of Scripture in the Damascus Document 1–8, 19–20* (Berlin–New York, 1995), 21.

22 See e.g. Fred L. Horton, "Formulas of Introduction in the Qumran Literature," *Revue de Qumran* 7 (1971): 505 – 514; Moshe J. Bernstein, "Introductory Formulas for Citation and Re-citation of Biblical Verses in the Qumran Pesharim: Observations on a Pesher Technique," *Dead Sea Discoveries* 1 (1994): 30–70.

argumentation is used not only to provide instruction, but also to interpret events and characters.[23] However, the formula which includes the term *pēšer*, and which influenced the name of current Qumran commentaries, has a meta-sense and does not merely serve to distinguish formally between the text and the commentary. The semantic range of this term is equivalent to the meaning of the Aramaic *pəšar* as it appears in several passages in the Book of Daniel. The first of them (in chap. 2) is associated with Daniel's explanation of the meaning of his dream of a mysterious statue which he gives to Nebuchadnezzar. In the text, the explanation is preceded by an eager prayer of Daniel and his three companions to God, who request that he reveals the meaning of the dream. Daniel is thus the mediator through whom God reveals the mystery (*rāzā^h*). In the book he is portrayed as a man of God, who was given the ability to solve and explain complicated things (Dn 5:12 מְפַשַּׁר חֶלְמִין וַאַחֲוָיַת אֲחִידָן וּמְשָׁרֵא קִטְרִין). In the context of the book, calling Daniel an interpreter (pael participle: *məpaššar*) 5:12 takes on a special meaning. It is not simply that he has an ability to explain something, even exceptional; the ability that he has is not something that can be learned, but is a gift of extraordinary nature, which allows the recipient to get in contact with the supernatural reality. Qumran texts indicate that the Teacher of Righteousness' ability to interpret the words and the reality is understood in the same way. His interpretations, introduced by a formula containing *pēšer* or derivatives, were treated as explanations revealed by God. Hence, pesharim were recognized not only as commentaries on the inspired message, but also as authoritative texts. Their value was not much lesser than that of commented texts.[24]

2.2. Pesher as a literary genre and a method of commenting

Despite the prevalence of a formula with the root *pšr* in many Qumran documents, not only in biblical commentaries[25], not many texts were recognized as pesharim. The pesharim come from four caves: the first, fourth, fifth, and

---

23 See Isaac Rabinowitz, "Pesher/Pittârôn: Its Biblical Meaning and Significance in the Qumran Literature," *Revue de Qumran* 8 (1972–1975): 222–225.

24 Some scholars do not agree that the particular status of pesher in the community was a result of a belief in their inspired character. They believe that Qumran pesharim were not considered as divine revelation, but as texts inspired by the Scripture. However, one should distinguish between two understandings of inspired texts: 1) direct words of God, transmitted by prophets; 2) explanations of the meaning of texts originating from the divine inspiration. In either case there is God's action present, but in different ways. However, the word of God always has a superior position in relation to its explanation.

25 Such instances are documented for example by Timothy H. Lim, *Pesharim* (Sheffield, 2002), 16–18.

eleventh. Their classification takes as the basis few important elements, which at best should occur together and are all significant in determining the genre: the form, content, purpose, and method.[26] The pesher commenting method can also be found in the New Testament: an example, though not literal, is provided in chapter 12 of the Gospel of Mark, often referred to as quasi-pesharim.[27]

The form of Qumran pesharim can generally be reduced to citations from biblical text followed by relevant comments (introduced by a formula) explaining the meaning of the quoted words. This reflects the pattern: *lemma + formula + glossa*. Quoted and commented passages sometimes come from one book and are quoted in order, unit after unit (*pesher continuus*)[28]; sometimes there is a thematic selection, in which case the quotations can be taken either from one or from several books (*pesher thematicus*).[29]

The content of pesharim is primarily dictated by the content of the cited biblical text. Despite its atomization, the biblical text is the base and the skeleton of a pesher. It should be noted here that as the biblical text is split into small fragments and provided with commentary, it becomes qualitatively and

---

26 See George J. Brooke, "Qumran Pesher: Toward the Re-definition of a Genre," *Revue de Qumran* 10 (1981): 483–503.

27 For an analysis of the pesharim characteristics of these texts see e.g. Jędrzejewski, *Peszer*, 122–125.

28 To continuous, best-preserved pesharim belong Pesher Habakkuk (1QpHab), Pesher Nahum (4QpNah), and also Pesher Psalms (1QpPs and 1QpPs a), although not every psalm is covered in it. Two different commentaries on the Book of Isaiah are preserved in fragments. The older one (scrolls 4QpIs c and 4QpIs e) can be considered thematic because it also refers to books of other prophets; more recent ones (scrolls 4QpIs a, 4QpIs b, 4QpIs d, and probably also 3QpIs) seem to be of a continuous character, for instance the pesharim to the Book of Hosea (4QpHos and, 4QpHos b), Pesher Micah (1QpMic), and Pesher Zephaniah (1QpZeph). For introductions to continuous and thematic pesharim see e.g. Stanisław Mędala, "Peszery qumrańskie i midrasze judaizmu," *Collectanea theologica* 63 (1993): 3, 29–38; Idem, *Wprowadzenie*, 68–75; Muchowski, *Komentarze*, 129–164.

29 These include: 4QTest – *Testimonia*, a commentary which provides the scriptural basis of the association's messianic expectations (it makes use of the Book of Deuteronomy, of Numbers, of Joshua, and of apocryphal *Psalms of Joshua*); 4QTanh – *Tanhumim*, commentaries focused on a consolation (draws mainly from Dt-Isaiah and the Psalms); 11Q Melch – *Melchizedek*, presenting the last, the tenth part of the time in which messenger carrying the forgiveness of sins is to sent to earthly exiles (draws from the Pentateuch, the Psalms, the Book of Isaiah and of Daniel); 4QAgesCreat – commenting on the passages of Genesis; 4QMidrEschat (five documents marked 4Q174, 4Q177, 4Q178, 4Q182, 4Q183) – *Midrash on Eschatology* (draws from 1 and 2 Chronicles, Psalms, the Pentateuch and the prophetic books; it reflects on the upcoming end of time, which is considered in the context of the situation of the community and its opponents).

semantically a new text, quite different from the base text.[30] Explanations of the biblical text become an integral part of the new text which they provide not only with form but also with new meaning. The pesher text should be read as a whole, not as a gloss next to the existing text.[31] However, by analyzing the content of explanations from different pesharim, which focus on different base texts, it is easy to notice some repeated themes which stem not only from the contents of the commented texts, but also from the community's theological interpretation and its specific socio-religious situation.

There are two main hermeneutical principles which influence the content of pesharim. Firstly, prophetic announcements refer to the end of times; secondly, the end of times has already occurred. The books of the prophets are treated in pesharim as a code which needs to be decoded. Pesherists believe that prophets' aim was not to analyze their own times; rather, the prophets speak of God's salvation plan for those who are faithful and obedient to God and of total extinction planned for those who disobey God. The time and place of these events, however, remains uncertain. Pesherists believe and argue that the prophets announced the events which will become fulfilled during the life of the Teacher of Righteousness and that their words relate to the life of the congregation and its opponents. Such views reveal the aim of pesharim authors whose task is not only to demonstrate that the eschatological fulfillment is happening, but also to prepare their recipients and give them certainty that they will be saved and will see the triumph of God's reign after the victorious eschatological battle.[32]

To achieve this goal, pesherists applied specific methods of reading and interpreting the commented biblical texts. Most common techniques are paraphrase, allegory, semantic polyvalence, and recontextualization[33]; they are used to adapt a commented text so that becomes relevant to the current conditions. They are also employed in midrashes, where a commented text is appropriately divided and interpreted according to certain rules, which were later classified as seven rules of Hillel, thirteen rules of Yishma'el, or thirty two rules of Eliezer ben Yose ha-Gelili, which take into account also allegory and ambiguity.[34]

---

30 See Bilha Nitzan, *Megillat Pesher Habakuk: mi-Megilot Midbar Yehudah (1QpHab)* (Jerusalem, 1986), 39–54.

31 Cf. Lim, *Pesharim*, 54.

32 See Timothy H. Lim, "Eschatological Orientation and the Alteration of Scripture in the Habakkuk Pesher," *Journal of Near Eastern Studies* 49 (1990): 2, 191–193.

33 See Shanni L. Berrin, *The Pesher Nahum Scroll from Qumran: An Exegetical Study of 4Q169* (Leiden, 2004), 11.

34 See John Bowker, *The Targums and Rabbinic Literature* (Cambridge, 1969), 315–318.

Interpretation of biblical texts by paraphrasing them appears mainly in thematic pesharim, where commented texts are not always quoted literally; this strategy allows an interpreter to suggest the reader a proper understanding of the text. Here it is necessary to draw attention to a certain difficulty. The biblical text in pesharim sometimes diverges from the later Masoretic text. We must remember that when pesharim were being created, not only the canon of the sacred books in Judaism was not yet recognized, but also the wording of these texts was not clearly established. The differences therefore are not necessarily caused by commentators' adaptation of the text so that it fits their needs. Such conclusion is not justified even when there are discrepancies between Qumran-versions of biblical texts and versions quoted in pesharim. The differences between citations in pesharim and MT in most cases do not significantly change the meaning of the text. This suggests that pesharim authors did not manipulate the base text, which, moreover, one can assume, was well-known to the recipients. Significant changes in meaning occur only at the level of the commentary. The question whether different variants of the base text influenced its interpretations or different interpretations generated new variants of the text and what impact pesharim had on the wording of the biblical text established later by Masoretes is open.[35]

Recontextualization is the most useful technique for the purpose of accommodation of a text's message. It is manifested in different ways in pesharim. First, a new division of the base text into smaller units is introduced. Such deconstruction of an existing text provides it with a new meaning: a pesherist can next add an explanation of each unit according to his plan. The second stage of recontextualization consists of placing words of a biblical text in a new context which is created by pesherist's comments. Authors of pesharim in general were not interested in compositional features of the biblical texts. For example, the phenomenon of structural parallelisms was of no interest for them. Their methodological procedure for commenting is rather consistent with a literal reading, but it is focused not so much on words as on arbitrarily chosen units of text.[36] Decontextualization and relocation of words to a new context, one reflecting experience of the pesharim recipients, allows pesherists to combine biblical words with the reality of the readers' life.[37]

---

35   Cf. Lim, *Pesharim*, 18.

36   See Nitzan, *Megillat Pesher*, 29–79; Berrin, *The Pesher*, 12; Alex P. Jassen, "The Pesharim and the Rise of Commentary in Early Jewish Scriptural Interpretation," *Dead Sea Discoveries* 19 (2012): 371–379.

37   See Lou H. Silberman, "Unriddling the Riddle: A Study in the Structure and Language of the Habakkuk Pesher (1QpHab)," *Revue de Qumran* 3 (1961–1962): 342.

3. The technique of recontextualization in selected examples from 1QpHab

The Pesher Habakkuk (1QpHab) found in Cave One is the best preserved commentary pesher. It dates to the last decades of the first century BC and is now the oldest known and preserved interpretation of this book. The manuscript was created in the Herodian script with a typical Qumran spelling system. It was copied by two scribes: the first one copied paragraphs from 1.1 to 12.13, and the second one – from 12.13 to 13.4. The biblical text quoted in 1QpHab essentially overlaps with the Masoretic text, although there are some discrepancies.[38] They are not significant enough to be recognized as a purposeful adaptation by the pesherist but rather indicate that a slightly different version of the Book of Habakkuk was used. The text of the discovered document (a complete scroll) contains a commentary on the first two chapters of the Book of Habakkuk; the third chapter is omitted for unknown reasons.

The Book of Habakkuk, belonging to the collection of the Twelve Prophets, was probably written between 609 and 597 BC, as suggested by its reference to the appearance of Chaldeans on the historical scene. They gained dominance in the region after the fall of the Assyrian Nineveh in 612 and built the Neo-Babylonian Empire. The Book of Habakkuk, however, in no way refers directly to the destruction of Jerusalem in 597 and 586, probably because it was created before these events.[39]

The Book has the form of a dialogue between the prophet and God. It is based on the liturgical scheme of lamentation, oracle, and thanksgiving. In lamentations, the prophet complains to God about pervasive evil in Judah, about prevailing wickedness, and oppression of the poor. He eagerly awaits the divine intervention which will bring God's kingdom and righteousness. In response to prophet's complaints there comes an announcement of destructive expansion of the Chaldeans who will conquer nations, including Judah. The prophet recognizes the need for a purifying punishment; those who are faithful to God will survive and live to see the triumph of God's reign, whose kingdom will come in designated time. Main theological topics of the Book are God's lordship over the history, a punishment awaiting the wicked, and a reward for the faithful and righteous, who will be able to see God's glory.[40]

---

38 See e.g. Muchowski, *Komentarze*, 131–133.

39 See David W. Baker, *Nahum, Habakkuk, Zephaniah. An Introduction and Commentary* (Leicester 1988), 43–47. For various views on dating, see e.g. Kenneth L. Barker, *Micah, Nahum, Habakkuk, and Zephaniah* (Broadman & Holman Publishers 1998), 266–268.

40 See Frederick F. Bruce, "Habakkuk", in *The Minor Prophets*, ed. by Thomas E. McComiskey (Grand Rapids, 1992), 831–896.

Pesher Habakkuk refers the prophet's poetic visions to current events and situations of the community. A comment on the first verse provides the key to the exegesis of the book: "The explanation of this relates to the beginning of the last generation [...]". According to other writings of the community, Qumran inhabitants considered themselves as the generation living at the end of time; it is therefore indicated to the recipients that the commentary refers precisely to the contemporary times in which the prophet's words reach fulfillment.[41] Since the beginning of the pesher is preserved only in fragments, we do not know whether the author explicitly called the members of the association "the last generation" or expected them to be able to make this connection. However, it should be observed that such understanding of Hab is possible only if the sentence is separated from the original context and provided with a suitable comment. Let us look at the text collation[42]:

Biblical text	Pesher biblical text	Pesher explanation
Hab 1:2 LORD, how long shall I cry for help, and you will not hear? Or cry to you 'Violence!' and you will not save?	Col. 1.1–2 How long, YHWH, must I cry and you will not hear, I will shout to you: rape! and You will not save me?	Col. 1.2–3 The explanation for this relates to the beginning of the last generation.

In Hab 1:2, the prophet's lamentation begins with a series of complaints in which Habakkuk complains to God about the situation in the country and urges Him to take action. The text does not specifically say against whom the prophet's words are directed, but the context makes it clear that the prophet talks about current situation in the place where he resides.[43] The separation of the passage its context allows from the change of meaning which is introduced in the explanation.

The remaining parts of 1QpHab commentary are more literal and concrete. It seems that the first the recipients of pesher had no problem with identifying individuals or groups indicated in the text. This is suggested by the fact that the author uses specific names without explanation. For example, there are two groups identified in the comments: a good one, defined as the 'chosen ones'

---

41   See Berrin, *The Pesher*, 13.
42   In all tables below the biblical text in the first column is quoted from English Standard Version. The second and third column contain my own translation of 1QpHab text, which is based on the edition of Bilha Nitzan, *Megillat Pesher Habakuk: mi-Megilot Midbar Yehudah (1QpHab)* (Jerusalem, 1986).
43   See Barker, *Micah*, 288–289.

(5.4) and a bad one, referred to as 'poor ones' (12.3); these groups can be identified with community members on one hand, and 'traitors' on the other; the latter are clearly accused of treason in the commentary, although they do not seem to form a unified group.

Biblical text	Pesher biblical text	Pesher explanation
Hab 1:5 Look among the nations, and see; wonder and be astounded. For I am doing a work in your days that you would not believe if told.	Col. 2.1 [...] talk about him.	Col. 2.1–7 The explanation for this relates to the traitors being with the Man of Lie who lies, who did not listen to the words of the Teacher of Righteousness from the mouth of God, and to the traitors of the new covenant, who did not believe in the covenant of God, and despised his holy name. And so this clearly applies to all the traitors in the last days. They are allied mighty men who do not believe when they hear about everything that has to fall on the last generation.
Hab 1:13 You who are of purer eyes than to see evil and cannot look at wrong, why do you idly look at traitors and are silent when the wicked swallows up the man more righteous than he?	Col. 5.8–9 Why do you look, traitors? You are silent when the wicked devours a man more just than he?	Col. 5.9–12 This explanation relates to the house of Absalom and his council of people who remained inactive when the Teacher of Righteousness was punished and did not support him against the Man of Lie, who rejected the law amid their whole congregation.

The quote from Hab in col. 2 was not fully preserved and we do not know how the biblical text was cited. In Hab this fragment belongs structurally to the speech of God, who promises His intervention: an arrival of a frightening Chaldean army. Its expansion will be the God's answer to the prophet's complaints and a punishment for the committed wickedness. This context indicates that the word of God is addressed not only to the prophet, but also to those who will not believe in what is to come.

Pesherist's clarification – very well preserved (2.1–7) – quite precisely defines those who did not believe and are therefore traitors. It seems that the author of the pesher considers them as the recipients of the quoted biblical text. His comment is a good example of the polyvalence technique. The author's comment refers the quoted words from the Book of Habakkuk to three different types of traitors at the same time, guiding the addressees of the pesher to a threefold understanding. The distinction between the traitors is based on chronology – their betrayal is seen basically in the same categories and assessed in the same way.

Those who were with the Man of Lie (2.2) are referred to as traitors and are later called "the house of Absalom" (5.6). This phrase refers probably to a specific, relatively narrow group of people. The pesherist accuses them of not listening to the Teacher of Righteousness. Then the "traitors of the new covenant" are mentioned (2.3); the phrase presumably refers to people who took the same attitude as those who follow the Man of Lie. The objection against them is that they did not believe in the new covenant with God and in the teachings of the Teacher of Righteousness. The third group of traitors is the most general – the words of the prophet concern "all the traitors in the last days", i.e. those who do not believe that the fulfillment of the time is happening now and in all consequences of this.[44]

The content of the pesher is primarily focused on the conflict between the Teacher of Righteousness, the Man of Lie, and the Wicked Priest.[45] Recontextualization allows the author of the pesher to associate these characters with the text of the commented book. This is well illustrated in the following excerpts:

---

44   See Muchowski, *Komentarze*, 130–131.

45   There have been many attempts to identify the Teacher of Righteousness with historical figures, for example with the High Priest Onias III, with a staunch opponent of John Hyrcanus – Zadok, with Judah from among the Essenes (mentioned by Josephus), with Onias the miracle worker stoned to death in 65 BC, with Alkimos, and with a high priest exercising power after Alkimos and removed from the office by Judah Maccabee. On the Teacher of Righteousness, see a publication edited by Zdzisław J. Kapera, *Mogilany 1989*, 7–147. For identification of Alkimos, see Stanisław Mędala, "Alkimos Nauczycielem Sprawiedliwości?," *Filomata* 429–430 (1995): 74–92 and idem, "The Character and Historical Setting of 4QMMT," *The Qumran Chronicle* 4 (1994): 1–2, 1–28. For hypotheses about the unnamed high priest, see Hartmut Stageman, *Esseńczycy z Qumran, Jan Chrzciciel i Jezus*, transl. Zdzisław Małecki, Antoni Tronina, (Kraków, Mogilany 2002), 173. Analogous attempts were made to identify the opponents of the Teacher of Righteousness. An argument for the identification of Ephraim as a group of Pharisees was developed by Jean Carmignac, "Les éléments historiques des 'hymnes' de Qumran," *Revue de Qumran* 2 (1959–1960), 205–222. Adam S. van der Woude discusses attempts to identify the Wicked Priest with several high priests of the Hasmonean dynasty ("Wicked Priest or Wicked Priests? Reflections on the Identifications of the Wicked Priest in the Habakuk Commentary," *Journal of Jewish Studies* 33 (1982): 351).

Biblical text	Pesher biblical text	Pesher explanation
Hab 1:4 So the law is paralyzed, and justice never goes forth. For the wicked surround the righteous; so justice goes forth perverted.	Col. 1.10 Therefore law disappears Col. 1.12 [and judgment never falls], as the wicked cornered the just. Col.1.15 Therefore,[unfair] judgment falls	Col. 1.11 [Explanation of the one ...] who rejected the law of God. Col. 1.13–14 The explanation for this: the wicked – is the Wicked Priest, the just – is the Teacher of Righteousness
Hab 2:12 Woe to him who builds a town with blood and founds a city on iniquity!	Col. 10.6 Woe to him who builds a town with blood and founds a city on iniquity	Col. 10.9–10 The explanation for this relates to the Preacher of Lies who deceived many by building a city of vanity in blood and by raising a gathering in fraud for his glory.
Hab 2:15 Woe to him who gives drink to his neighbors, pouring it from the wineskin till they are drunk, so that he can gaze on their naked bodies!	Col. 11.2–3 Woe to him who gives drink to his neighbor, adding own poison! Or let's drink to watch their festival periods!	Col. 11.4–7 The explanation for this relates to the Wicked Priest, who oppressed the Teacher of Righteousness to engulf him in his furious anger in the place of his exile. At the end of the festive period, [during] the resting of the Day of Atonement, he came to them to engulf them and cause them to fall.
Hab 2:16 You will have your fill of shame instead of glory. Drink, yourself, and show your uncircumcision! The cup in the LORD'S right hand will come around to you, and utter shame will come upon your glory!	Col. 11.8–11 You are filled with more shame than glory! You drink as well and lurch! Against you the cup in the right hand of YHWH will turn, and disgrace will be over thy glory.	Col. 11.12–15 The explanation for this relates to the priest, whose shame surpassed glory, because he did not circumcise the foreskin of his heart and walked the ways of drunkenness to quench the thirst. The cup of God's wrath will consume him, gathering disgrace over him.

We can see that the prophet's words in Hab, though uttered in response to a particular situation, have a universal dimension, and there is no reference to specific people in the biblical text. The prophet's complaints (1:4) and threats (2:12–16) are addressed to all who act improperly and have inappropriate attitude towards others.[46] This universality disappears in the pesher; instead, specific characters and current events from recipients' experience are indicated.

---

46   See e.g. Barker, *Micah*, 293.

The pesherist applies the words of the prophet to individuals named the Man of Lie and the Wicked Priest, who are known to the recipients and therefore do not have to be explicitly identified. For us, however, it is not clear who these characters were – were they different people or, what seems more likely, do they represent the same opponent of the Teacher of Righteousness? The Wicked Priest who rejected the interpretation of the Scripture given by the Teacher of Righteousness and who persecuted his followers is often identified with Jonathan.[47] He is the one who at the beginning of his activity, in the days when he fought to regain the independence from the Seleucids, "was called with the name truth" (1QpHab 8.8–9). He was, however, recognized as an apostate when he usurped the office of the high priest and removed the legitimate high priest who opposed him. Jonathan died later from the hands of his enemies. Because the comment of the pesher indicates some passage of time – some events have already taken place – such identification can be possible. For our analysis, however, the identification of a historical figure hidden under the name is not important. What is important is that the change of context and the pesherist's references to specific characters in the commentary allowed the recipients to perceive the present events as the fulfillment of the punishment announced in the prophecy of the Book of Habakkuk. At the same time, the author's comment guided the readers to see the punishment as the beginning of the last phase of God's purifying action against traitors. This could convince the readers that they are on the right side and that they will be saved, as promised by the prophet.

The potential of the recontextualization technique to change the meaning of a text is clearly visible in the passage in which the Chaldeans from the Book of Habakkuk are identified with the Kittim in pesher.

Biblical text	Pesher biblical text	Pesher explanation
Hab 1:6 For behold, I am raising up the Chaldeans, that bitter and hasty nation, who march through the breadth of the earth, to seize dwellings not their own.	Col. 2.10–11 Behold, I will establish the Chaldeans, fierce and impetuous nation.	Col. 2.12–15 This explanation relates to the Kittim, who are quick and valiant in battle and will lead to the destruction of many. The whole world will get into the power of Kittim. They will take possession of many countries, but will not believe in the law of God

47 Jonathan Maccabee is not the only hypothesis. Other scholars propose his brother Simon or Aristobulus' brother Hyrcanus, whom Romans entrusted with power after 63 B.C., in exchange for loyalty to Pompey the Great. For the possible historic identification, see e.g. Michael O. Wise, "The Origins and History of Teacher's Movement," in *The Oxford Handbook*, 92–121.

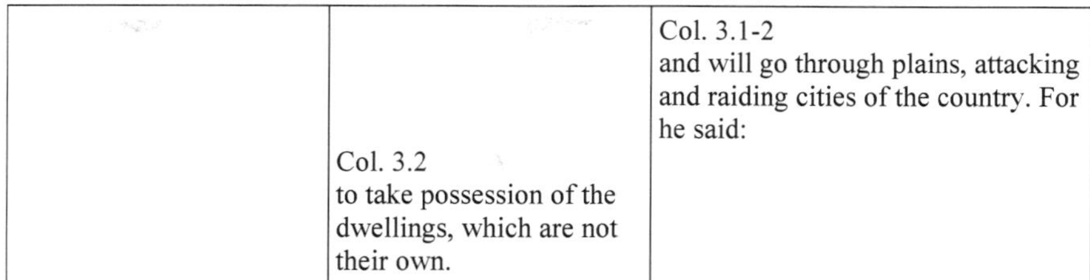

	Col. 3.2 to take possession of the dwellings, which are not their own.	Col. 3.1-2 and will go through plains, attacking and raiding cities of the country. For he said:

The Chaldeans appearing in the prophetic text are allegorized by the pesherist. The name Kittim appears in the Hebrew Bible (e.g. Gen 10:4, 1 Ch 1:7; Is 23:1, Jr 2:10; Ez 27:6; Dn 11:30) and generally means invaders arriving from the sea, from the islands.[48] It appears many times in 1QpHab (e.g. 2.10,12,14; 3.4,9; 4.5,10,13; 5.14, 6.12, 9.2,7). Historical allusions in this pesher (to captures of fortresses, style of fighting, subordination of conquered territories, political decisions, etc.) allow us to identify the Kittim-invaders with the Romans.[49]

The original historical sense of the commented text is therefore rejected. A recipient of the pesher can no longer relate the words of the prophet Habakkuk to the past events, namely to the well-known destruction of Jerusalem, which occurred in the sixth century as a result of the Babylonian invasion. According to the pesherist, the Book of Habakkuk does not speak about a punishment which has already occurred, but about a punishment which is about to be fulfilled. The Romans become an instrument of God's punishing action for apostasy and wickedness. Although they are put among the wicked who eventually will be destroyed, they are seen as the right hand of Yahweh who punishes the opponents of the Teacher of Righteousness. Combining the technique of recontextualization with allegory opens new possibilities for interpretation. On one hand, as a result of changes in the historical context, a development of the prophetic message occurs. The recipient reads the text of Habakkuk as being fulfilled now, before his eyes. On the other hand, as the author also makes use of allegory, the recipients of pesher can at the same time refer to the original context of the events, which he knows from the sacred

---

48   The term Kittim comes from the sea port of Cyprus – Kition. According to Josephus, the Hebrews used the term 'Kittim' in reference to islands and coastal lands (*Ant.* 1.128). See Marek Parchem, "Peszer do Księgi Nahuma (4Q169) z Qumran – aluzje do wydarzeń historycznych z I w. przed Chr.," *Collectanea theologica* 81 (2011): 4, 69.

49   See George J. Brooke, "The Kittim in the Qumran Pesharim", in *Images of Empire*, ed. by Loveday Alexander, (Shieffield, 1991), 135–159; Bilha Nitzan, "The Continuity of Biblical Interpretation in the Qumran Scrolls and Rabbinic Literature,", in *The Oxford Handbook*, 337–350.

scripture. This intertextual relationship allows the recipient, by analogy, to imagine how God's promise will be fulfilled.

Conclusion

Qumran pesharim, literally meaning 'explanations', were preserved in very few copies. In spite of it the texts are considered to be representative for one of the currents of biblical exegesis within the Second Temple Judaism. This study shows that the method of commenting on the biblical texts which was developed in Qumran was not, in its precise form, subsequently taken over and spread beyond the Qumran community, though this does not mean that later exegesis, whether rabbinic or Christian, did not share certain elements, methods, and hermeneutics with pesherists.

The limited audience and influence and of the pesharim were a result of the texts' hermeneutical assumptions, which had a significant impact on their final shape. The method of commenting they employed, relying primarily on techniques of paraphrase, allegorization, polyvalency, and recontextualization, was less important and was subordinate to hermeneutical assumptions. The main goal of this kind of literature was to adapt the biblical message, especially of the prophetic texts, to circumstances of the life of the first recipients of the pesharim.

Summary

The first part of this study explores the most important problems of identification of pesharim in literature and outlines the situation of Qumran community and its religious views. The second part is focused on literary aspects of the pesharim literature. It deals with problems of their classification, structure, characteristics, and methods of commenting. The third part of the study is devoted to a brief analysis of selected passages from 1QpHab; the aim of my examination is to show the function of the technique of recontextualization which allowed pesherists to adapt the biblical text to the current situation of their recipients.

Buddhist Tradition in Quest of the Authenticity and the True Meaning of the 'Word of the Buddha' (*buddha-vacana*)

Marek Mejor

Research Centre of Buddhist Studies, University of Warsaw

§1. Buddhism is the most ancient of the great universal religions of the world, and it is both religion of the (spoken) Word and the (written) Scripture. For the believers, the Buddha, or the 'Awakened One', the Dharma, or his Doctrine, and the Saṅgha, or his monastic Order, constitute the so-called Three Jewels (*tri-ratna*), the triple foundation of their faith. The recitation of the triple formula of 'taking refuge' in the Three Jewels ('I take refuge in the Buddha, etc.', *buddhaṃ śaraṇaṃ gacchāmi, dharmaṃ śaraṇaṃ gacchāmi, saṅghaṃ śaraṇaṃ gacchāmi*) has been always regarded as a confession of faith.

§1.1. The Buddha, the founder of the religion, whose secular name was Siddhārtha Gautama (ca. 566–486 B.C.), became a *buddha* or 'the awakened one' ('enlightened one') after long and strenuous ascetic and spiritual efforts, when in a series of deepest meditations he attained the absolute 'awakening' (*anuttara samyak-saṃbodhi*), the highest and perfect knowledge. He discovered the ultimate truth (*paramārtha-satya*) and cognized the real nature of things (*dharmatā*).

§1.1.1. Vasubandhu (5th cent.), one of the greatest Buddhist thinkers, at the very beginning of his famous treatise *Abhidharmakośa* ('Treasury of Higher Doctrine') praised the glory of the Teacher as follows:

> "I make obeisance to the one who destroyed all darkness in an absolute manner, who has pulled out the world [of sentient beings] from the mire of transmigration, the Teacher of the Truth, before I compose the treatise called the 'Treasury of Higher Doctrine'."[51]

§1.2. In his first sermon delivered in Sarnath to the group of five ascetics, the Buddha promulgated his Doctrine (*dharma*) of the Four Noble Truths (*ārya-satya*), in which he declared the existence of suffering (*duḥkha*), its cause (*samudaya*), its annihilation (*nirodha*), and the path leading to annihilation of

---

51 *Abhidharma-kośa* I.1., p. 4.1–4: *yaḥ sarvathā sarva-hatāndhakāraḥ saṃsāra-paṅkāj jagad ujjahāra / tasmai namas-kṛtya yathārtha-śāstre śāstraṃ pravakṣyāmy abhidharma-kośam //*.

suffering (*mārga*). He called his doctrine the 'middle one' (*madhyama*) since it refrains from the extreme positions (*anta*). This sermon was later called the *Dharma-cakra-pravartana-sūtra*, or 'Discourse on setting in motion the wheel of the Doctrine'. Out of great compassion (*mahākaruṇā*) he revealed the Dharma to suffering sentient beings who are bound to the beginningless circle of birth and death (*saṃsāra*) in order to bring them to final liberation (*nirvāṇa*).

§1.2.1. *Dharma* is eternal, but it is not a divine revelation. The Buddha discovered the Dharma anew, for it is said,

"Whether the Tathāgatas, or the Perfect Ones, appear in the world or not, the true essence of things remains unchanged."[52]

The doctrine of the Buddha was summarized in a popular stanza which became regarded as a kind of Buddhist *credo*:

"Phenomena which have arisen due to causes, their cause and [that which is] their cessation – [all this] was declared by the Tathāgata (himself); the Great Ascetic is the one who said [this] in such a way."[53]

§1.3. According to the Buddhist tradition, the Buddha taught the Dharma as a wandering teacher for forty-five years. He gathered a circle of disciples and faithful followers and established a monastic order (*saṅgha*) of monks (*bhikṣu*) and later also of nuns (*bhikṣuṇī*). The everyday life and formal proceedings of the monastic order were regulated by a code of discipline (*vinaya*) which was prescribed by the Teacher.

§2. The Buddha's doctrinal teachings (*sūtra*) and monastic instructions (*vinaya*) were carefully remembered and preserved by his disciples thanks to mnemonic methods, which were highly developed in ancient India. After the demise (*parinirvāṇa*) of the Buddha, the disciples undertook the attempt to codify and systematize the teachings of the Master. According to the Buddhist tradition, soon after the Buddha's *parinirvāṇa* a congregation of five hundred learned monks met and recited together (*saṅgīti*) the corpus of doctrinal texts (*sūtra*) and monastic instructions (*vinaya*). It is said that in this way two collections of texts originated, which received canonical sanction: the so-called *Sūtra-piṭaka* ('Basket of Discourses') and the *Vinaya-piṭaka* ('Basket of Discipline'). Some time later the third collection was added, the 'Basket of Higher Doctrine' (*Abhidharma-piṭaka*). The oral transmission of the texts has continued for many generations.

---

52 *utpādād vā tathāgatānām anutpādād vā sthitaivaiṣā dharmāṇāṃ dharmatā* /. For the references see Lamotte 1988: 25 n. 25.

53 *ye dharmā hetu-prabhavā hetuṃ teṣāṃ tathāgato hy avadat / teṣāṃ ca yo nirodha evaṃ-vādī mahā-śramaṇaḥ* //. Mejor 1998: 123, 130; cf. Lamotte 1988: 495 n. 67.

§2.1. The oldest and the most complete canon of Buddhist scriptures has been preserved in the Pali (*pāli*) language. All texts have been arranged into three big collections called 'baskets' (*piṭaka*); therefore, the Buddhist canon is traditionally called *Tipiṭaka* (in Sanskrit *Tripiṭaka*), or 'Three Baskets'. The *Tipiṭaka* in Pāli was written down in Ceylon in the 1ˢᵗ century B.C. and became the scriptural authority for the school of Theravādins, which dominated the region of South East Asia. The Hīnayānistic school of Sarvāstivādins, influential in Northern India and Central Asia, as well as the schools of Mahāyāna, used Sanskrit as the means of propagating the word of the Buddha.

§2.2. According to the tradition, the Buddha ordered the monks to promulgate his teachings by means of local languages, and not in the language of the Brahmins, i.e. Vedic Sanskrit. However, due to the cultural role of Sanskrit, in the course of time also the Buddhists began to compile their canonical texts in Sanskrit. Therefore, the canonical texts in vernaculars and in Sanskrit were circulating side by side. It is, however, difficult to reconstruct the process of Sanskritization of Buddhist scriptures. The missionary activity of Buddhist monks in India and beyond has been attested from the middle of the third century B.C. From the beginning of our time reckoning, the Buddhist scriptures in many languages were in use both in India and outside. A process of translating the Buddhist scriptures into different languages, like Chinese, Tibetan, Khotanese, Sogdian, Uighur, Tokharian, etc., has lasted for hundreds of years.

§3. The corpus of Buddhist canonical texts has become very vast in the process of compilation. It contains now thousands of texts of different types and of various dimensions, including sermons, or doctrinal lectures (*sūtra*), monastic instructions and rules of discipline for monks and nuns (*vinaya*), philosophical discourses and scholastic elaborations of the doctrine (*abhidharma*).

§3.1. Buddhaghosa, a great Buddhist commentator active in Ceylon in the middle of the 5ᵗʰ century, explained that the *Buddha-vacana*, or the 'word of the Buddha', is subject to a sevenfold classification:

> "It should be known that the Word of the Buddha is single in flavor, twofold by reason of the doctrine (*dharma*) and discipline (*vinaya*), threefold by reason of the initial, intermediate and final (words of the Buddha), also threefold by reason of the Baskets (*piṭaka*), fivefold by reason of the collections (*nikāya*), ninefold by reason of the constituent parts, finally, of 84,000 kinds because of the articles of the Law (*dharmaskandha*)."⁵⁴

---

54 *evaṃ etaṃ sabbaṃ pi Buddha-vacanaṃ rasa-vāsena ekavidham, dhamma-vinaya-vāsena duvidham, pathama-majjhima-pacchima-vāsena tividham, tathā piṭaka-vāsena, nikāya-vāsena pañcavidham, aṅga-vāsena nava-vidham, dhamma-kkhanda-vāsena caturasiti-*

§3.2. In the Sanskrit *Mahā-parinirvāṇa-sūtra* (§40.62), the Buddha gave dispositions to monks concerning the admission of the followers of other schools to the Order, and on that occasion he recommended the twelve divisions of teachings (*dharma*) which bring to salvation –

> "These are [the texts of] discourses, versified narrations, expositions, stanzas, solemn utterances, giving the circumstances, exploits [of Buddhist saints in their former lives], [texts which begin with the words] "thus it was said", stories about the former births [of the Buddha], developed texts (of great extension), marvels, and instructions. These are the teachings, which bring the visible world to salvation, which (...) lead [to happiness] of gods and men."[55]

§3.3. A systematic explanation of the notion of *dharma-viniścaya*, or 'determination (discrimination) of the Doctrine' was provided by Asaṅga's (4th century) treatise 'Compendium of Higher Doctrine' (*Abhidharma-samuccaya*). It is said that the Noble Teaching (*ārya-śāsana*) of the Blessed One consists of twelve parts or divisions (*dvādaśāṅga-dharma*),[56] viz.:

1. *sūtra* – discourse	7. *avadāna* – exploits
2. *geya* – verse narration	8. *itivṛttaka* – "thus it was said"
3. *vyākaraṇa* – exposition	9. *jātaka* – birth-stories
4. *gāthā* – stanza	10. *vaipulya* – development
5. *udāna* – solemn utterance	11. *adbhutadharma* – marvels
6. *nidāna* – circumstance	12. *upadeśa* – instructions

§4. The 'word of the Buddha' (*buddha-vacana*) alone should be the highest and ultimate authority for all believers, both members of the monastic order and lay followers. The Buddha promulgated his teaching, his Dharma, for the benefit of all sentient beings to show them the path towards liberation from the suffering (*duḥkha*) of the circle of transmigration (*saṃsāra*). Therefore he emphasized the highest position of the Dharma as the sole basis, an 'island', a 'refuge' for the believers.

§4.1. The *Mahā-parinirvāṇa-sūtra*, in which the last months of the Buddha's worldly life are described, contains, among others, a very important passage in

---

sahassa-vidhan ti veditabbaṃ. (*Samantapāsādikā* p. 16; *Sumaṅgalavilāsinī* p. 15; *Atthasālinī* p. 18) quoted in: Lamotte 1988: 141ff.

55   Waldschmidt III 1951: 386; Weber 1999: 241f.

56   Cf. *Mvy* 1267–1278.

which the Buddha, asked about the future of the Order (Saṅgha) after his passing away, summoned the monks:

> "(...) you should live as islands unto yourself (*ātma-dvīpa*, Pāli: *atta-dīpa*), being your own refuge (*ātma-śaraṇa*, Pāli: *atta-saraṇa*), with no one else as your refuge, with the *Dharma* (Pāli: *Dhamma*) as an island, with the *Dharma* as your refuge, with no other refuge."[57]

§4.2. Candrakīrti (c. 600 – 650) in his commentary (*vṛtti*) entitled *Prasannapadā* ('Clear-worded') on Nāgārjuna's *Mūla-madhyamaka-kārikā* substantiated the statement that the 'word of the Buddha' (*buddha-vacana*) has the ultimate value as *pramāṇa*, or the means of valid cognition, and *āgama*, or the authoritative canon:

> "Therefore the wise men declare the words of the Blessed Buddha the means of valid (authoritative) cognition (*pramāṇa*) because they are conforming to logic (*sopapattika*, 'having a justified ground') and are free from contradictions (*avisaṃvādaka*). And therefore for the word of the Buddha there is established the status of 'authoritative canon' (*āgamatva*), since [it possesses three good qualities implied by the etymology of the word *āgama* (lit. 'coming to, acquisition [of knowledge]'), viz.] it has come (*āgatatvāt*) from the trustworthy men (*āpta*), entirely free from all faults; since it leads (*āgamayati*, 'makes come near to') to a complete cognition of *tattva* ('reality, truth'); and since it is 'bringing forwards [those] directed towards the goal' (*abhimukhyād gamarād*), i.e. the people (*loka*) who rely on this [Buddha's word], to advance their going to *nirvāṇa*. The other systems [with the exclusion of Mahāyāna] remain thoroughly disjoined with logic and therefore their lack of valid cognitive norm (*prāmāṇya*) as well as their lack of authoritativeness (*āgamatva*) is established."[58]

§5. The teachings of the Buddha have been transmitted in a long and continuous tradition, proceeding from a master to a disciple. The contents of these teachings, however, were subject to scrutiny as regards their consistence with the existing and acknowledged canonical texts. In later times, there arose a controversy among the representatives of the Hīnayāna and the Mahāyāna schools about the criteria of acceptance of the texts according to their doctrinal standpoint.

§5.1. Śāntideva's (fl. first part of the 8th century) great poem *Bodhicaryāvatāra* ('Introduction to the practice of Awakening') argued against the Hīnayānist:

> "41. [Hīnayānist] Surely Mahāyāna scripture is not established!
>   [Mādhyamika] In what way is your scripture established?
>   [Hīnayānist] Because it is established for both of us.
>   [Mādhyamika] It was not established for you at first!

---

57 Walshe 1995: 245 (with modification). Cf. Waldschmidt 1951: I, 200 (§ 14.22, 26) for the Sanskrit, Pāli, Tibetan and Chinese versions of the passage.
58 *Prasannapadā* p. 268.1–269.3; transl. after Schayer 1931: 68–69.

42. Apply your criterion for its acceptance also to Mahāyāna scripture. If something is true because accepted by two different parties, even texts such as the Vedas would be true.

43. If your objection is that Mahāyāna scripture is controversial, reject your own scripture since it is contested by non-Buddhists, and any part in that scripture contested by your own people or others.

(...)

49. You accept that whatever text might be in accordance with the Discourses was spoken by the Buddha. So why are the Mahāyāna scriptures not accepted as equal in value to your own Discourses?"[59]

§5.2. Prajñākaramati (c. 9th cent.) in his commentary (*pañjikā*) on Śāntideva's poem characterized the position of the Hīnayāna followers thus:

"That which has come by means of tradition in a succession from a teacher to a disciple as the Buddha's word, and that which descends into the discourse, which is discerned in the discipline code, and which does not go against the true essence of things, i.e. the dependent arising, that is [verily] the word of the Buddha, and not any else." [60]

§5.3. On the controversy between the followers of the so-called Śrāvaka-yāna, or the Vehicle of Disciples, and the followers of the Great Vehicle (Mahāyāna) about the authenticity of the Mahāyāna scriptures, Vasubandhu in his *Vyākhyāyukti* said:

"[…] *sūtras* such as the *Mahāparinirvāṇa Sūtra* are recited differently. Hence... it is clear that even in the Śrāvakayāna the word of the Buddha is incomplete. Even the authorized editions (*yang dag par bsdus pa'i gzhi ba*) which are composed by the four arhants such as Mahākaśyapa, etc. have degenerated, for the various sects (*sde pa*) have disparate ways of setting forth the scriptures, of dividing them into chapters, and so forth... What is more, even in one sect, one and the same *sūtra* will oftentimes have different passages and chapters... Hence, when the authorized versions have degenerated, how can we know that the word of the Buddha exists in its entirety? (P. 116b, D. 99b)."[61]

§5.4. The problem of the authenticity of Buddha's teachings as preserved in the transmitted texts was of great importance for the later Buddhists. An interesting remark is found in Vasubandhu's *Abhidharma-kośa* (ad III.12d), where the author complains sadly:

---

59 *Bodhicaryāvatāra* 1996: 119–120, cf. also Notes on pp. 183–185.

60 *Bodhicaryāvatāra-pañjikā* p. 313.16–19: *yad guru-śiṣya-paramparayāmnāyāyātaṃ buddha-vacanatvena, yac ca sūtre' vatarati, vinaye saṃdṛśyate, dharmatāṃ pratītyasamutpādaṃ ca na vilomayati, tad buddha-vacanaṃ nānyat /*.

61 Cabezon 1997: 227.

"And what, they [i.e. our adversaries] do not transmit these Discourses too... What shall we do now when the Teacher has gone into *nirvāṇa* and the Teaching, left without guide, is set in variance in many ways; and also now the texts and meanings are being changed according to wish... ."[62]

§5.5. In another place of his treatise Vasubandhu argues vigorously against the Pudgalavādins, the Buddhist school which advocated the doctrine of existence of 'person' (*pudgala*):

"[Alas,] they do not regard this text (*grantha*) as the authoritative norm of valid cognition (*pramāṇa*). Why so? [They say:] 'Because in our school (*nikāya*) we do not recite this [text] (*na paṭhyate*).' What then is for them the authoritative norm of valid cognition, [their own] school or the word of the Buddha (*buddha-vacana*)? If their own school then the Buddha is not their Teacher! And they are not the followers of the Buddha (*Śākya-putrīya*) [any more]. Now, if the word of the Buddha is the authoritative norm, why not recognize this text as a norm [too]? Because, it is said (*kila*), that [the text] is not the word of the Buddha. Why? 'Because in our school we do not recite this text.' This [argument] turns to be illogical (*anyāya*). What is illogical here? 'Because the text which is recited in all other schools, and which does not oppose the Discourses (*sūtra*) nor the real essence of things (*dharmatā*), we do not recite it in our school and therefore it is not [accepted as] the word of the Buddha' – such a statement is merely inconsiderate (*sāhasa-mātra*)."[63]

§6. The Dīpakāra, an anonymous author of the treatise *Abhidharma-dīpa* ('Lamp of Higher Doctrine') from the 5th century, mentioned four different doctrinal standpoints prevalent among the Buddhist philosophical schools:

"There are four disputants with regard to the teaching. Which four? It is explained: [V.299] All exists (*sarvam asti*); limited extent (*pradeśa*) [of time] exists; all does not exists (*sarvam nāsti*) – says another; one claims existence of indeterminate (*avyākṛta*) [objects] – there are mentioned four disputants.

Here, (1) for the *sarvāsti-vādin* the three times (*adhva-trayam*) do exist (*asti*) and these three [times] are eternal (*dhruva*); (2) for the *vibhajya-vādin* and the *dārṣṭāntika* [there exists] a limited extent [of time] called present time [moment]; (3) for the *vaitulika* who declares the emptiness of non-application (?) (*ayoga-śūnyatā-vādin*) nothing exists [in reality]; and (4) for the *paudgalika* who declares indeterminate points (*avyākṛta-vastu-vādin*) a *pudgala* 'person' exists as an entity (*dravyatas*)."[64]

§6.1. Farther it is boldly stated by the Dīpakāra that only the first from the list of disputants, called *sarvāsti-vādin*, is the advocate of truth (*sad-vādin*), because he

---

62 *Abhidharma-kośa* ad III.12d, p. 415.1–3: *athaitānyapi sūtrāṇi tair nāmnāyante / kim idānīṃ kurmo yacchāstā ca parinirvṛtaḥ śāsanaṃ cedam anāyakam bahudhā bhinnam [/] bhidyate cādyāpi yathecchaṃ granthataś cārthataś ca /.*

63 *Abhidharma-kośa* IX, p. 1203.11–1204.2.

64 *Abhidharma-dīpa* ad V.299, p. 257.1–258.2.

is expressing his opinions furnished with (logical) arguments (*yukti*) and scriptural authority (*āgama*). Other three disputants, i.e. *dārṣṭāntika, vaitulika,* and *paudgalika,* do not speak in conformity with *yukti* and *āgama,* but are self-conceited with speculation (*tarka*), and therefore, because of speaking falsehood (*mithyā-vāditva*), they should be placed on the same side as the materialists (*lokāyatika*), destructionists (*vaināśika*), and naked mendicants (*nagnāṭa*), i.e. Jainas. Therefore, the author declares that he will demonstrate (*upadarśayiṣyāmi*) that all is omnipresent (*sarvaṃ sarvagataṃ*), i.e. that all dharmas, the ultimate factors of being, exist in all three times.[65]

§7. Later a controversy arose between various Buddhist schools concerning the real authority of the Abhidharma. The Sautrāntikas, or 'those relying on the authority of the Sūtras', questioned the authority of Abhidharma as the Buddha's direct word, whereas the Ābhidharmikas, on the contrary, were much in favour of it.[66]

§7.1. Vasubandhu in his *Abhidharmakośa* (I.3) emphasized that without the thorough investigation (examination) (*pravicaya*) of the dharmas (*dharma*), i.e. the ultimate factors of being, there is no other means (*abhyupāya,* 'super-means') of bringing the defilements (*kleśa*) to extinction, and it is precisely due to those defilements that the world (of sentient beings) is wandering about (*bhramati*) in the ocean of existence (*bhavārṇava*). Therefore, it is said, the Teacher (*śāstṛ*), i.e. the Blessed One, promulgated the teaching of the Higher Doctrine (*abhidharma*), since without the teaching of Abhidharma a pupil (*śiṣya*) would be unable to examine the dharmas. However, the teaching of the Higher Doctrine was promulgated by the Buddha only in parts (*prakīrṇa*), not as a whole, and therefore it was later put together by his great disciples, like Bhadanta Kātyāyanīputra, Sthavira Dharmatrāta, and others.[67]

§7.2. A controversy between the Buddhist schools of the Vaibhāṣikas and the Sautrāntikas was concerned also with different understanding of the real nature (*svabhāva*) of the word of the Buddha – whether these are material sounds of speech or immaterial 'heavenly sounds'. It was discussed in connection with the question of the exact number of Buddha's utterances and their classification either as a 'voice' (*vāk*) or as a 'name' (*nāma*). Some schools, like the Sautrāntikas, regard the word of the Buddha to be a 'voice' by its nature (*vāk-svabhāva*) [i.e. vocal sounds, material], while for other schools (*nikāyāntarīya*), i.e. the Vaibhāṣikas, it is a 'name' by its nature (*nāma-svabhāva*), [i.e. words,

---

65   *Abhidharma-dīpa* ad V.300, p. 258.6–259.2.
66   *Abhidharmakośa-vyākhyā* p. 15.18ff., 27f.
67   *Abhidharmakośa* I.3, p. 14.3–6.

non-material].[68] And since there exist in the world eighty thousand sentient beings which are subject to all sorts of afflictions, the Blessed One taught eighty thousand *dharma-skandha*s, or 'teaching-constituents'.[69]

§7.3. Vasubandhu in his *Abhidharma-kośa* (I.25) said:

> "25. The eighty thousand *dharmaskandha*s that the Muni promulgated, depending on whether one regards them as 'voice' [*vāc*] or as 'name' [*nāma*], are included within the *rūpa-skandha* ['aggregate of material form'] or the *saṃskāra-skandha* ['aggregate of formations']."[70]

§7.4. The Dīpakāra in his commentary (*vṛtti*) on the *Abhidharma-dīpa* quoted in this connection a significant passage from a canonical scripture (*āgama*)[71]:

> "While the Lord lived, his words were of the nature of speech (*vāk*) as well as of the nature of *nāma* ['name'], respectively in a secondary and primary sense. After his *parinirvāṇa*, however, his words are only of the nature of *nāma* and not of *vāk*. For the Lord of the sages had a 'heavenly sound', not comparable to any mundane speech."[72]

§7.5. Yaśomitra (7th century) in his commentary (*vyākhyā*) on Vasubandhu's *Abhidharma-kośa* quoted two passages from the *Jñāna-prasthāna*, a canonical work of the Sarvāstivāda Abhidharma, which is the basis of the views of the Ābhidharmikas, who accept the inclusion of the Buddha-vacana both in the *rūpa-skandha* and the *saṃskāra-skandha*:

> "What is a Buddha-*vacana* ['Buddha's word']? The speech (*vāk*), speaking (*vacana*), talk (*vyāhāra*), voice (*gīr*), utterance (*nirukti*), range of speech (*vāk-patha*), sound of speech (*vāg-ghoṣa*), action of speech (*vāk-karman*), vocal expression (*vāg-vijñapti*) of the Tathāgata is Buddha-*vacana* ['Buddha's word']."[73]

Moreover, it is stated there that the 'word of the Buddha' is included into three collections, 'bodies' (*kāya*) of words (names), sentences (phrases), and letters (phonemes), respectively:

> "What is this *dharma* ['factor'] called Buddha-*vacana*? The arrangement in regular order (*anurūpa-racanā*), the establishment in regular order (*anupūrva-sthāpanā*), the uniting in regular order (*anupūrva-samāyoga*) of the *nāma-kāya* ['collection of

---

68 *Abhidharma-kośa* ad I.25, p. 70f. Cf. *Abhidharma-dīpa* ad I.12, p. 11.7–8.

69 *Abhidharma-kośa* ad I.26, p. 72.5–6.

70 Pruden, *Kośa* I, 1988: 86 (modified).

71 *Abhidharma-dīpa* ad I.12, p. 11.9–11: *jīvato bhagavato vāṅ-nāma-svabhāvaṃ buddha-vacanaṃ gauṇa-mukhya-nyāyena / parinirvṛtasya tu nāma-svabhāvam eva, na vāk-svabhāvam, brahma-svaratvān munīndrasya, loka-vācāṃ tatsadṛśyānupapatteḥ //.*

72 Jaini 2001: 202.

73 Jaini 2001: 202f. (with modifications).

words'], *pada-kāya* ['collection of sentences'], and *vyañjana-kāya* ['collection of letters'] (is called Buddha-*vacana*)."[74]

§8. The basic type of a doctrinal text is *sūtra*, or 'discourse'.

"What is a discourse (*sūtra*)? It is a prose account explaining a point of view. The Tathāgata, seeing ten advantages, expounds, explaining the teaching in this way: (1) he sets out and expounds easily; (2) the listener also understands easily; (3) through respect for the teaching he rapidly acquires the equipment with a view to Awakening (*bodhi-saṃbhāra*); (4) rapidly penetrates the teaching; (5) obtains serene joy based on the conviction (*avetya-prasāda*) with regard to the Buddha, (6) his Teaching (*dharma*), and (7) the Order (*saṅgha*); (8) experiences supreme happiness in this very life (*parama-dṛṣṭa-dharma-sukha-vihāra*); (9) delights the minds of sages through vigorous discussion; and (10) is recognized as a sage (learned, *paṇḍita*)."[75]

§8.1. The *Artha-viniścaya-sūtra*, or the 'Discourse on Discriminating the Meanings'[76], begins with the words which constitute a typical opening phrase of a *sūtra*:

"Thus have I heard: The Blessed One was once staying in the Eastern Park in the large palace of Mṛgāramāta at Śrāvastī, together with a large assembly of monks numbering 1250.

Then the Blessed One addressed the monks, his voice firm, deep, sweet, lofty, and faultless:

'The Dharma, monks, that I shall teach you is virtuous in the beginning, virtuous in the middle, virtuous in the end. It is good in sense and letter, most perfect, pure, and clear, and leads to the highest path. Such is this Dharma discourse on the Compendium of Categories. Listen and fix your mind well and rightly on, and I shall speak.'

'Well said, Lord' the monks answered the Blessed One, giving their assent."[77]

§8.2. Vasubandhu (c. 400–450), famous for his great treatise 'Treasure of Higher Doctrine' (*Abhidharma-kośa*), composed also many other treatises and commentaries. In his *Vyākhyā-yukti* ('The Logic of Explication')[78], a unique in the Buddhist tradition manual of commentarial exegesis, he set the five rules which should be regarded as guidelines for a commentator-to-be. These are the following:

1. *prayojana* – 'purpose',
2. *piṇḍārtha* – 'concise meaning',

---

74   Jaini 2001: 203 (with modifications).

75   *Abhidharma-samuccaya* p. 178f.

76   Or 'Gathering the Meanings' as translated by Samtani (Samtani 2002).

77   Samtani 2002: 48.

78   See Schoening 1995: 38–43; Nance 2012: 100–122 and Appendix A (annotated translation of the *Vyākhyā-yukti*, Book I).

3. *padārtha* – 'meaning of words',
4. *anusandhi* – '(logical) connections',
5. *codya-parihāra* – 'objections and responses'.

Vasubandhu put these rules into a well-known stanza:

> "The purpose, together with the summary meaning, the meaning of phrases, connections, and objections and responses; [These five aspects] should be stated by those who propound the meaning of sūtras."[79]

In his explanation of the above stanza Vasubadhu said:

> "How should one discuss the sūtras? [One should do so] via five aspects. One should state the purpose of the sūtra; the summary meaning; the meaning of the phrases; connections; and the two – objections and responses... Why are these [five aspects] expressed? When one hears the greatness of the sūtra's meaning, one is spurred on to listen to and grasp [the text]; for this reason, the purpose is expressed. Moreover, the purpose may also be understood from the summary meaning of the sūtra, and the summary meaning from the meaning of the phrases. From the connections, [one may understand] that the meaning of the phrases is sequentially noncontradictory. From the objections and responses, [one may understand] that [the text] does not contradict reason and that there is no contradiction between those [texts] that are earlier [and] later. Thus, the summary meaning and so on should be stated."[80]

§8.3. A detailed explanation of the structure of a *sūtra* text can be found in Vīryaśrīdatta's (8th century?) commentary (*nibandhana*) on the *Artha-viniścaya-sūtra* ('Discourse on Discriminating the Meanings'). It is said that the 'body of sūtra' (*sūtra-śarīra*), or the framework of doctrinal discourse, consists of six parts, viz. (1) *nidāna* 'introduction', (2) *upodghāta* 'preface', (3) *prayojana* 'purpose', (4) *uddeśa* 'list of topics' (or statement in brief), (5) *nirdeśa* 'exposition (in detail)', and (6) *anusandhi* '(logical) connection'.

> "1. The Introduction here consists of the words beginning 'Thus have I heard' and ending with 'monks numbering 1250'.
>
> 2. The Preface consists of introductory words explaining the topics of the Sūtra. It is not auspicious to speak without prefatory words (...).
>
> 3. The Purpose is for getting [the audience] actively involved. One who desires to expound Sūtra should tell [the purpose] in order to command the respectful attention of those who will listen to the Sūtra. (...)

---

79 Nance 2012: 132. The stanza is quoted in Haribhadra's *Abhisamayālaṃkārālokā* p. 277.16–18: *prayojanaṃ sapiṇḍārtham padārthaḥ sānusaṃdhikaḥ / sacodyaparihāraś ca vācyaḥ sūtrārthavādibhiḥ // iti pañcabhir ākāraiḥ sūtraṃ vyākhyātavyam iti Vyākhyā-yuktau nirṇītam /* ("...a sūtra should be explained by means of the five aspects, so it was declared in the *Vyākhyā-yukti*").

80 Nance 2012: 105f.

4. The List of Topics is presented for the student's ease of comprehension. When one knows the general topics, one can easily learn the detailed parts. (...)
5. The Exposition is given to analyze in detail what has been briefly listed. It is like a commentary (*vṛtti*) on an aphorism (*sūtra*)...
6. The Logical Connection (*anusandhi*) shows the relation between the preceding words and those that follow."[81]

§8.4. Even a more detailed analysis of a commentary of a *sūtra*, or a 'teaching uttered from the mouth of the Buddha', was provided by Kamalaśīla (c. 740–795) in his learned explanation of the *Śālistamba-sūtra*, or 'Discourse on a Young Rice Plant'. Kamalaśīla follows the guidelines set out by Vasubandhu in his *Vyākhyā-yukti* and says that one should first mention the following five elements of a commentary:[82]

1. the concise meaning (*piṇḍārtha*),
2. purpose (*prayojana*),
3. meaning of the words (*padārtha*),
4. connections (*anusandhi*),
5. response to objections (*codya-parihāra*).

These are farther divided into the following seven parts:
1.1. prologue (*nidāna*),
1.2. introduction (*upodghāta*),
1.3. subject to be comprehended (*parijñeya-bhāva*),
1.4. comprehension (*parijñāna*),
1.5. result of comprehension (*parijñāna-phala*),
1.6. how it is to be comprehended (*tat kathaṃ parijñeyaṃ*),
1.7. purpose of the sūtra (*sūtra-prayojana*).

§9. The Buddhists elaborated the means of hermeneutics in order to ascertain the authenticity and correct interpretation of the Buddha-vacana. Therefore two sets of rules were elaborated:

1. *mahāpadeśa* ('great authorities') – rules of assessment of textual authenticity of the texts ascribed to the Teacher (*śāstṛ*), which were explained in the 'Discourse on the Great Authorities' (*Mahāpadeśa-sūtra*);

2. *pratisaraṇa* ('refuge, reliance on') – rules of assessment of correct interpretation of the texts regarded as the 'word of the Buddha', which were explained in the 'Discourse on the Four Refuges' (*Catuḥ-pratisaraṇa-sūtra*).

Both texts do not exist independently but are only included in other larger texts.

---

81   Samtani 2002: 45–47 (abbreviated).
82   After Schoening 1995: 193ff.

§9.1. In the *Mahā-parinirvāna-sūtra*, in a long discourse of the Buddha to Ānanda, it is said that the Buddha himself formulated the four 'great authorities' (*mahāpadeśa*). Accordingly, a text can be recognized as a 'word of the Buddha' if –

(1) it was obtained directly from the Buddha, or
(2) from the established regular Buddhist community (*saṅgha*), or
(3) from the group of the 'elders' (*sthavira*), i.e. learned and respected monks, or
(4) from a single learned and respected monk.

However, such text must be confronted with the acknowledged doctrinal texts (*sūtra*) and the monastic code of discipline (*vinaya*) in order to ascertain its full agreement with the spirit of the Buddhist Dharma. Only after having proved that the given text fully conforms to the Discourses and the Code of Discipline one can conclude:

> "Assuredly this is the word of the Buddha, it has been rightly understood by this monk."[83]

§9.2. The *Catuh-pratisarana-sūtra* introduced the following four rules:
1. *dharma-pratisarana* – 'reliance on dharma', i.e. the true essence of things (*dharmatā*),
2. *artha-pratisarana* – 'reliance on meaning',
3. *nītārtha-pratisarana* – 'reliance on explicit scriptures',
4. *jñāna-pratisarana* – 'reliance on (direct) knowledge'.

The relevant passage form the Sūtra was quoted by Yaśomitra in his *Abhidharma-kośa-vyākhyā*[84]. Its content was rendered by Etienne Lamotte as follows:

> "The *Catuh-pratisarana-sūtra* posits, under the name of refuges (*pratisarana*), four rules of textual interpretation: (1) the dharma is the refuge and not the person; (2) the spirit is the refuge and not the letter; (3) the sūtra of precise meaning is the refuge and not the sūtra of provisional meaning; (4) (direct) knowledge is the refuge and not (discursive) consciousness."[85]

---

83 For the full translation of the Pāli version (*Dīgha Nikāya* I.16 §4.8–11) see Walshe 1995: 255.f.; for the translation of the Sanskrit version see Weber 1999: 161–167 (§24).

84 *Abhidharma-kośa-vyākhyā* p. 1202.25-28. *catvārīmāni bhikṣavah pratiś(s)aranāni / katamāni catvāri / dharmah pratiś(s)aranam na pudgalah / arthah pratiś(s)aranam na vijñānam / nītārthasūtram pratiś(s)aranam na neyārtham / jñānam pratiś(s)aranam na vijñānam, iti //.* See LVP, *Kośa*, IX, p. 246 r. 2 (references). Long explanation in *Akṣayamati-nirdeśa-sūtra*, Braarvig 1993 (I: 114–119, text; II: 440–456, translation).

85 Lamotte 1993: 12.

§10. The Buddhist exegetes introduced, as we have seen above, two categories of texts, viz. those having a 'definitive meaning' (*nītārtha*), and those which have only a 'provisional meaning' (*neyārtha*) and need to be interpreted.

§10.1. In Vasubandhu's *Abhidharma-kośa* it was said that "the Blessed One declared the scriptures with explicit meaning as the authority; therefore they need not to be examined again," in search of another meaning (*nītārthaṃ ca sūtraṃ pratisaraṇam uktaṃ bhagavatā / tasmān na punaḥ parīkṣyate*).[86] Moreover, it was specified that the definition in the Sūtra is intentional (*ābhiprāyika*) whereas the definition in the Abhidharma has a strict character (*lākṣaṇika*).[87]

§10.2. This topic was explained in detail in the *Akṣayamati-nirdeśa-sūtra* (X.28–31):[88]

"Which Sūtrāntas[89] are of provisional meaning and which of definitive meaning? Those Sūtrāntas taught to introduce to the Path (*mārgāvatāra*) are termed 'of provisional meaning'. Those Sūtrāntas taught to introduce to the Fruit (*phalāvatāra*) are termed 'of definitive meaning'. [...] When in Sūtrāntas there are taught Emptiness (*śūnyatā*), the signless (*ānimitta*), the desireless (*apraṇihita*), absence of conditioning effectuation (*anabhisaṃskāra*), the unborn (*ajāta*), the unoriginated (*anutpāda*), absence of entity (*abhāva*), the non-substantial (*nirātman*), no sentient being (*niḥsattva*), no ensouled entity (*nirjīva*), no person (*niḥpudgala*), no master (*asvāmika*), and the Gates of liberation (*vimokṣamukha*), these are termed 'of definitive meaning'. This, Venerable Śāradvatīputra, is termed having recourse to a Sūtrānta of definitive meaning, not having recourse to one of provisional meaning."[90]

§10.3. Similarly it was said in the *Samādhi-rāja-sūtra* (VII.5):

"The particularity of a Sūtra of definitive meaning one knows as Emptiness taught by the Sugata.
  And one in which, on the contrary, a person, being or soul [are taught] one knows all [these] things as having a provisional meaning."[91]

---

86 *Abhidharma-kośa* IX, p. 1202.9; cf. LVP, *Kośa*, IX, p. 246 n. 2 (references).

87 *Abhidharma-kośa* ad VI.3, p. 887.6 (*ābhiprāyikaḥ sūtreṣu nirdeśaḥ / lākṣaṇikas tv abhidharme /*); cf. LVP, *Kośa*, VI, p. 137 n. 2 (reference to Yaśomitra's *Vyākhyā*: *abhiprāye bhavaḥ, abhiprāyeṇa vā dīvyatīty ābhiprāyikaḥ sūtreṣu nirdeśaḥ /; lakṣaṇe bhavo lākṣaṇiko nirdeśo 'bhidharme /* [p. 887.23,25]).

88 Sanskrit quoted in Candrakīrti's *Prasannapadā* p. 43.4–9.

89 Cf. BHSD p. 604: *sūtrānta* m. (Pali *suttanta*), a Buddhist *sūtra* text; *sūtra* 'discourse'.

90 Ruegg 2002: 81.

91 Ruegg 2002: 81. Stanza quoted in *Prasannapadā* p. 44.1–5: *nītārtha-sūtrānta-viśeṣa jñānati yathopadiṣṭā sugatena śūnyatā / yasmin punaḥ pudgala-sattva-puruṣā neyārthato jñānati sarva-dharmān //.*

§11. These categories of textual exegesis were not only the subject of erudite arguments and speculations of learned commentators, but also were regarded as indispensable elements of the Buddhist practice on the path to realisation of the highest truth. It was emphasised that the study of scriptures and knowledge of their proper interpretation are important steps in the bodhisattva's practice.

§11.1. Thus in chapter 17 of the *Bodhisattva-bhūmi*, on the elements favourable to enlightenment (*bodhi-pakṣya-paṭala*), the following methods have been prescribed in detail under the headings of [XVII.4.] *śāstra-jñātā* 'knowledge of scriptures' and [XVII.6.] *pratisaraṇa* '(fourfold) reliance'.

> "[§4.] What is the 'knowledge of scriptures' (*śāstra-jñānatā*) by a bodhisattva? Here, [it is meant] the teaching attached to the collection of words (*nāma-kāya*), collection of sentences (*pada-kāya*), and collection of letters (*vyañjana-kāya*), beginning with the five subjects of knowledge (*pañca vidyā-sthāna*), which is well grasped (*sugṛhīta*) from another (*paratas*) by a bodhisattva, and which is well practised by speech (*vacasā suparicita*). The meaning of the teaching is well heard (*suśruta*) from another, or it is well considered by himself (*svayaṃ suvicintita*), and well inferred (*svabhyūhita*).
>
> So also the purpose (*prayoga*) is not pushed away (*anirākṛta*) by a bodhisattva, who is knowing the teaching and knowing the meaning, in order not to forget (remember) the meaning of the teaching, [as well as] for the sake of knowledge of another new (*abhinava*) and [even] newer and newer special meaning(s) of the teaching.
>
> [Thus,] the maturity (*paripāka*) [and] tranquility (*prasāda*) with respect to that teaching and meaning which was brought about in the intermediate time (*kālāntara-kṛta*) is acquired by a bodhisattva who has gone to the perfect knowledge, coming from hearing and reflection (*śruta-cintā-niṣṭhā-gata*).
>
> By means of these forms one should know the bodhisattva's immesurable (*apramāṇa*), complete (*paripūrṇa*) and unperverted (*aviparīta*) 'knowledge of scriptures'."[92]

§11.2. Now, the so-called four refuges or reliances (*pratisaraṇa*) are explained under four headings; one who is aspiring to the state of a buddha should have reliance on 1. the true meaning of the teaching (*dharmārtha*), and not on that which has been formed by the letter(s) (*vyañjanābhisaṃskāra*); 2. one's (own) reasoning (*yukti*), and not on the words adopted from other person(s) (*pudgala*), learned as they are; 3. the *sūtra* with definitive meaning (*nītārtha*), and not on the *sūtra* with provisional meaning (*neyārtha*), which requires interpretation; 4. the knowledge of spiritual realization (*adhigama-jñāna*), and not on the cognition arising from listening and reflecting alone (*śruta-cintā-vijñāna-mātraka*).

---

92 *Bodhisattva-bhūmi* p. 172.13–21.

"[§6.] How the bodhisattva applies himself to the 'four refuges' (*caturṣu pratisaraṇeṣu prayujyate*)? – Here, the bodhisattva who is seeking [to gain] the [true] meaning (*arthārthī*) listens (*śṛṇoti*) to the teaching from another [i.e. teacher]; he is not seeking [to gain] the accomplishment of the letter (*na vyañjanābhisaṃskārārthī*).

He who is seeking [to gain] the [true] meaning when listening to the teaching is not seeking [to gain the accomplishment of] the letter; the bodhisattva having reliance on the [true] meaning carefully (respectfully) (*satkṛtya*) listens to the teaching even when it is communicated by natural speech (*prākṛtyāpi vācā*).

And again, the bodhisattva knows in accordance with reality (*yathā-bhūta*) the 'timely expressions of authority' (*kālāpadeśa*)[93] and the 'great expressions of authority' (*mahāpadeśa*) and having known [them] he has reliance on [his own] reasoning (*yukti-pratisaraṇa*).

He does not have reliance on a person (*na pudgala-pratisaraṇa*) [who claims:] 'these teachings have been uttered by a knowledgeable elder or a [single] person or the Tathāgata or the community [of monks]'. He who has placed reliance on the reasoning and not on the person, does not deviate (*na vicalati*) from the truth (*tattvārtha*).

And there exist also different conceptions (*anya-pratyaya*) with regard to the teachings.

The bodhisattva having put his faith and belief on the Tathāgata (*tathāgate niviṣṭa-śraddha, niviṣṭa-prasāda*), exclusively (*ekāntika*) believing in [the Buddha's] words (*vacasyabhiprasanna*), has reliance on the sūtra with definitive meaning (*nītārtha*) [as given by the Buddha], and [does] not [place reliance] on the sūtra with provisional meaning (*neyārtha*).

[When the bodhisattva] has reliance on the sūtra with definitive meaning, he becomes irresistible, not to be diverted (*asaṃhārya*) from our [Buddhist] teaching and discipline (*asmād dharma-vinayāt*).

For so, the different meanings of the sūtra with provisional meaning put forward in various directions, are unascertained (*aniścita*) and making doubt (*saṃdeha-kara*). And again, if the bodhisattva would not be devoted solely to the sūtra with definitive meaning, he would then become diverted from our [Buddhist] teaching and discipline. The bodhisattva regards the knowledge of spiritual realization (*adhigama-jñāna*) as the essence (*sāra-darśī*) and does not [rely] merely on the cognition of the meaning of teaching [arising] from listening and reflection (*śruta-cintā-dharmārtha-vijñāna-mātraka*).

Having realized that what is cognizable (*jñātavya*) by means of the knowledge arising from meditation (*bhāvanāmaya jñāna*) cannot be cognized merely by cognition arising from listening and reflecting, [the bodhisattva,] having listened even to the most profound (*parama-gambhīra*) teachings (*dharma*) spoken by the Tathāgata does not reject nor denies [them] (*na pratikṣipati, nāpavadati*).

In this way the boddhisattva applies himself to the four refuges (reliances)."[94]

---

93   BHSD p. 180.

94   *Bodhisattva-bhūmi* p. 175.14–176.2. Cf. Lamotte 1993: 12 n. 4; 20 n. 43; 23 n. 46.

And in short it is declared in the *Bodhisattva-bhūmi* – "The bodhisattva who resorts to the meaning and not to the letter penetrates all the enigmatic words of the Bhagavat Buddhas."[95]

§12. With the rise of the Mahāyāna Buddhism about the beginning of our era, the role of the Buddhist sacred texts written in the form of a book (*pustaka*) is more and more increasing. The Buddhists were probably the first religious group in India which used on large scale written books in order to spread the teachings of their Master. Some of the early Mahāyāna sutras, like 'The Perfection of Wisdom in Eight thousand Stanzas' (*Aṣṭasāhasrikā-prajñāpāramitā*), or 'The Lotus Sutra' (*Saddharmapuṇḍarīka*), or 'The Diamond Sutra' (*Vajracchedikā*), contain characteristic passages in which a sacred text in the form of a book is made an object of a religious cult. Thus for example in the 'Diamond Sutra' it is said that the very place on the earth in which the Word of the Buddha is proclaimed, or explained, or copied in a book form, becomes a sanctuary in which the Buddha manifests himself. In another sutra it is said that copying of the sacred Buddhist texts brings on an immeasurable (*aprameya*) religious merit (*puṇya*). Accordingly, the practice of copying texts and their veneration as sacred objects becomes more and more popular in the Buddhist world. The Word of the Buddha has been disseminated since then in a multitude of languages in innumerable manuscript and xylograph copies.

During the period of more or less five hundred years after the Buddha's nirvana, the oral tradition of the transmission of the Word of the Buddha has become strengthened and multiplied – Buddhism has evolved from the "religion of the spoken word" to the "religion of the written word".

Bibliography

Abhidharma-dīpa = *Abhidharma-dīpa with Vibhāṣā-pravṛtti*, ed. by P.S. Jaini. Patna 1977.
Abhidharma-kośa = *Abhidharmakośa-bhāṣya*
Abhidharmakośa-bhāṣya, with Yaśomitra's *Sphuṭārthā Abhidharmakośa-vyākhyā*, ed. by Swami Dwarikadas Shastri. 3rd ed. Varanasi 1987.
Abhidharma-kośa-vyākhyā = *Abhidharmakośa-bhāṣya*

---

95 *Bodhisattva-bhūmi* p. 76.22–23: *artham pratisaran bodhisattvo na vyañjanaṃ buddhānāṃ bhagavatāṃ sarva-sandhāya-vacanāny anupraviśati /*; Lamotte 1993: 20 n. 42. Cf. BHSD p. 556: *saṃdhā* 'esoteric meaning', p. 558: *sāṃdhya-bhāṣa* 'esoteric, mystical language'.

Abhidharma-samuccaya = Walpola Rahula, *Abhidharmasamuccaya. The Compendium of the Higher Teaching (Philosophy) by Asanga.* Originally translated into French and annotated by Walpola Rahula. English version from the French by Sara Boin-Webb. Asian Humanities Press, Fremont 2001.

Abhisamayālaṃkārālokā = *Aṣṭasāhasrikā-prajñāpāramitā with Haribhadra's Commentary called Āloka.* Ed. by P.L. Vaidya. Darbhanga 1960.

Artha-viniścaya-sūtra = *Arthaviniścaya-sūtra and its Commentary (Nibandhana), Written by Bhikṣu Vīryaśrīdatta of Śrī Nālandāvihāra.* Crit. ed. and annotated for the first time with Introduction and several Indices by N.H. Samtani. Patna 1971. (Tibetan Sanskrit Works Series 13).

BHSD = Franklin Edgerton, *Buddhist Hybrid Sanskrit Dictionary*, Yale University Press, New Haven 1953.

Bodhicaryāvatāra = Śāntideva, *The Bodhicaryāvatāra.* Translated with Introduction and Notes by Kate Crosby and Andrew Skilton. Oxford University Press, Oxford – New York 1996.

Bodhicaryāvatāra-pañjikā = *Bodhicaryāvatāra of Śāntideva , with the Commentary Pañjikā of Prajñākaramati.* Ed. by P.L. Vaidya. Darbhanga 1960.

Bodhisattvabhūmi = *Bodhisattvabhūmi.* Being the XVth Section of Asaṅgapāda's *Yogācārabhūmi.* Ed. by Nalinaksha Dutt. K.P. Jayaswal Research Institute, Patna 1966.

Braarvig 1993 = Jens Braarvig, *Akṣayamatinirdeśasūtra.* Vol. I: Edition of extant manuscripts with an index. Vol. II: The Tradition of Imperishability in Buddhist Thought. Solum Forlag, Oslo 1993.

Cabézon 1997 = Cabézon, José Ignacio, „Vasubandhu's *Vyākhyāyukti* on the Authenticity of the Mahāyāna *Sūtras.*" In *Texts in Context. Traditional Hermeneutics in South Asia*, Ed. by Jeffrey R. Timm. Sri Satguru Publications, Delhi, 1997, 221–243.

Jaini 2001 = Padmanabh S. Jaini, "The Vaibhāṣika Theory of Words and Meanings", in: *Collected Papers on Buddhist Studies*, Ed. by Padmanabh S. Jaini, Motilal Banarsidass, Delhi, 2001, 201–217.

Lamotte 1988 = Étienne Lamotte, *History of Indian Buddhism, from the Origins to the Śaka Era.* Translated from the French by Sara Webb-Boin under the supervision of Jean Dantinne. Louvain-La-Neuve, 1988.

Lamotte 1993 = Étienne Lamotte, "Assessment of Textual Interpretation in Buddhism", in: Lopez, 1993, 11–27.

Lopez 1993= Donald S. Lopez, Jr., (ed.) *Buddhist Hermeneutics.* Motilal Banarsidass, Delhi, 1993.

LVP, *Kośa* = Louis de La Vallée Poussin, *L'Abhidharmakośa de Vasubandhu. Traduction et annotations.* Nouvelle édition anastatique présentée par Étienne Lamotte. Institute Belge des Hautes Études Chinoises, Bruxelles 1980. Mélanges chinois et bouddhiques, volume XVI. Tome I: Introduction, Chapitres 1 et 2; Tome II: Chapitre 3; Tome III: Chapitre 4; Tome IV: Chapitres 5 et 6; Tome V: Chapitres 7, 8 et 9; Tome VI: Fragments des kārikās. Index. Additions.

Mejor 1998 = Marek Mejor, "The *Ārya-dharmadhātugarbha-vivaraṇa* ascribed to Nāgārjuna." In *Sūryacandrāya: Essays in Honour of Akira Yuyama On the Occasion of His 65th Birthday*, Eds. Paul Harrison, Gregory Schopen, *Indica et Tibetica 35*, Swisttal-Odendorf: Indica et Tibetica Verlag, 1998, 125–133.

Mvy = *Mahāvyutpatti*, ed. R. Sakaki, 2 vols. Tokyo 1962. (Suzuki Research Foundation, Reprint Series I).

Nance 2012 = Richard E. Nance, *Speaking for Buddhas. Scriptural Commentary in Indian Buddhism*. New York: Columbia University Press, 2012.

Pasadika 1994 = Bhikkhu Pāsādika, "Abhidharma-Zitate aus der *Abhidharmakośavyākhyā*, der *Abhidharmadīpa-Vibhāṣāprabhāvṛtti* und dem *Arthaviniścayasūtra-Nibandhana*", in: *Untersuchungen zur buddhistischen Literatur*, Bearb. von Frank Bandurski, Bhikkhu Pāsādika, Michael Schmidt, Bangwei Wang. Göttingen: Vandenhoeck & Ruprecht, 1994, 127–154.

Prasannapadā = *Mūlamadhyamakakārikās (Mādhyamikasūtras) de Nāgārjuna, avec la Prasannapadā commentaire de Candrakīrti*. Publie par L. de La Vallee Poussin. St. Petersbourg 1903–1913. (Bibliotheca Buddhica 4).

Pruden, *Kośa* = *Abhidharmakośabhāṣyam by Louis de La Vallée Poussin*. English translation by Leo M. Pruden. Vols. I, II, III, IV. Berkeley, California: Asian Humanities Press, 1988–1990.

Ruegg 2002 = David Seyfort Ruegg, *Two Prolegomena to Madhyamaka Philosophy. Candrakīrti's Prasannapadā Madhyamaka-vṛttiḥ on Madhyamakakārikā I.1 and Tsoṅ kha pa Blo bzaṅ grags pa / Rgyal tshab Dar ma rin chen's Dka' gnad/gnas brgyad kyi zin bris*. Annotated Translations. Studies in Indian and Tibetan Madhyamaka, Part 2. Wien: Universität Wien, 2002.

Samtani 2002 = N.H. Samtani, *Gathering the Meanings*. Dharma Publishing, Berkeley 2002. [*Arthaviniścaya-sūtra* and its *nibandhana*.]

Schayer 1931 = Stanisław Schayer, *Ausgewählte Kapitel aus der Prasannapadā (V, XII, XIII, XIV, XV, XVI). Einleitung, Übersetzung und Anmerkungen*. Prace Komisji Orientalistycznej, nr 14. Kraków: Polska Akademia Umiejętności, 1931.

Schoening 1995 = Jeffrey D. Schoening, *The Śālistamba Sūtra and its Indian Commentaries. Vol. 1. Translation with Annotation*. Wiener Studien zur Tibetologie und Buddhismuskunde, Heft 35.1. Wien: Universität Wien, 1995.

Waldschmidt 1951 = Ernst Waldschmidt, *Das Mahāparinirvāṇasūtra. Text in Sanskrit und Tibetisch, verglichen mit dem Pāli nebst einer Übersetzung der chinesischen Entsprechung im Vinaya der Mūlasarvāstivādins*. Teil II: Textbearbeitung: Vorgang 1–32; Teil III: Textbearbeitung: Vorgang 33–51. Berlin: Akademie Verlag, 1951.

Walshe 1995 = Maurice Walshe *The Long Discourses of the Buddha. A Translation of the Dīgha Nikāya*. Boston: Wisdom Publications, 1995.

Weber 1999 = Claudia Weber, *Buddhistische Sutras. Das Leben des Buddha in Quellentexten*. München: Diederichs in Hugendubel Verlag, 1999.

The Muslim Tradition of Commentary: Ibn Rushd's (Averroes's) Commentaries on the Works of Aristotle

Katarzyna Pachniak

Chair of Arabic and Islamic Studies,
University of Warsaw

The tradition of commenting works of scholarship reached Muslim culture together with the Graeco-Arabic translation movement, which reached its culmination in the early 9th century. The Graeco-Arabic translation movement itself is an extremely complex phenomenon, the causes of which are not, against all appearances, easily explainable; there was a variety of factors that determined its emergence and continuation. For it is not known exactly why the Arabs, who had arrived from the desert, and who in the course of their conquests had come across centres with thriving traditions of scholarship, assimilated that heritage, incorporating it into their own culture and religion, rather than destroy it. The fact that they had not had traditions of that kind themselves does not seem to be the sole explanation here. Dmitri Gutas, an outstanding specialist on the Graeco-Arabic translation movement, regards it as a kind of undertaking which involved many educated members of society in the early Abbasid period, i.e. after 750.[1] As a result, a significant part of the tradition of Greek scholarship, including mathematics, philosophy, optics, medicine, physics etc., was assimilated by Muslim culture.[2]

The tradition of translation as such dates back in the Middle East to the second millennium BC, and these oldest translations are of Sumerian documents into Akkadian. In the pre-Abbasid period, there had already been a translation movement from Greek into Middle Eastern languages, which, even though it cannot be directly connected with the Abbasid one, had helped pave the way for it. Of particular importance were Graeco-Syriac translations, even though it is a misconception held by some researchers that Graeco-Syriac translations were full and complete in terms of research, selection, language etc., and that all that needed to be done in the Abbasid period was to translate them from Syriac into

---

1   Dimitri Gutas, *Greek Thought, Arabic Culture* (New York: Routledge, 2005), passim; idem, *Greek Philosophers in the Arabic Tradition* (Hampshire: Aldershot 2000).
2   On traditions of Muslim scholarship, cf. Katarzyna. Pachniak, *Nauka i kultura muzułmańska i jej wpływ na średniowieczną Europę* [Muslim Scholarship and Culture and Their Impact on Mediaeval Europe] (Warszawa: Trio 2010).

Arabic.[3] For example, in the first half of the fifth century, the exegetic works by Theodore of Mopsuestia, and allegedly also Aristotle's *Categories* were translated at the School of Edessa. Another notable figure was Sergius of Resaina (Resh'ayna) (d. 536), who commented on and wrote introductions to Aristotle's works on logic, as well as on the writings of Galen. The Nestorian School of Nisibis was also an important centre of translating Aristotle's works, particularly those on logic.[4]

Immediately after the Arabs had conquered the territories of Syria and Palestine and moved on to settle these largely Greek-speaking lands, translations became a necessity in order to meet the demands of everyday life. This was the reason why in the reign of the early Umayyad rulers, numerous Greek-speaking clerks were retained and Greek became the language of administration. Nonetheless, it seems that in the Umayyad rule, i.e. before 750, no scholarly translations had been made except for occasional translations of medical texts; the focus had been, rather, on administrative and political texts, commercial documents etc. Once the great translation wave had started, translations of commentaries became a part of the 'programme' of translations of philosophical texts. It is wrong to believe that the Muslims were always perfectly well aware that the text under translation was a commentary. We touch upon a crucial problem here, namely that of finding out in how far the Muslims understood the philosophy they were assimilating and the character of the translations themselves. The translated works spanned a very long period: the Muslims acquainted themselves with Plato (for example through Galen's works, but mainly through Neoplatonic commentaries by Plotinus himself, Porphyry, and Proclus), Aristotle (whom they regarded as the most outstanding philosopher, also largely from Neoplatonic commentaries), as well as with Plotinus. Like Porphyry, Ammonius and Simplicius, they nevertheless did have a general understanding of the fundamental differences between Plato and Aristotle. In the 5th and 7th centuries, Plato and Aristotle were extensively commented upon in

---

3   This theory is propounded by P. Kunitzsch, et al., "Zur Problematik und Interpretation der arabischen Übersetzungen antiker Texte." *Oriens* 25–26 (1985): 119, 122. For an explanation of that problem, cf. D. Gutas, *Greek Thought*, 175–187.

4   Philosophical translations from Greek into Syriac are researched for example by Henri Hugonnard-Roche, *La logique d'Aristote du grec au syriaque: études sur la transmission des textes de l'Organon et leur interprétation philosophique* (Paris: Vrin 2004); idem, "Les 'Catégories' d'Aristote comme introduction à la philosophie dans un commentaire syriaque de Sergius de Resh'aynā (†536)." *Documenti e studi sulla tradizione filosofica medievale* 8 (1997): 339–363; Javier Teixidor, *Aristote en syriaque: Paul le Perse, logicien du VIᵉ siècle* (Paris: CNRS, 2003); Georg Endress, Remke Kruk, *The Ancient Tradition in Christian and Islamic Hellenism* (Leiden: Brill, 1997).

the Christian schools of Alexandria and Athens. In the Abbasid period, after the founding of Baghdad, numerous early translations are attributed to the circles connected with the first Arab philosopher, Al-Kindi (d. 863). They included a number of crucial texts in Greek cosmology, psychology, metaphysics and theology; it was also in these circles that the Fourth to Sixth of Plotinus's Enneads, called *Uthulujiyya Aristutalis*[5], as well as Proclus's *Elements of Theology*, *Kitab al-khayr al-mahd*, were translated.[6] Other translations included versions of works by Plotinus, Porphyry, Iamblichus, Themistius, Syrianus, Proclus, Pseudo-Dionysius the Areopagite, Simplicius, Philoponus and Olympiodorus; one can easily realize, therefore, that Neoplatonism had a major impact on Muslim philosophy, and that the Muslims largely got acquainted with Aristotle through Neoplatonic commentaries.[7] Thus, the Muslims were familiar with the tradition of commentary almost from the very beginning of the translation movement; moreover, with time the Muslims, rather than merely translate foreign commentaries, began to write ones of their own: both commentaries on the works of Greek philosophers and on treatises authored by Muslims; commentaries on commentaries were also penned. Most importantly, commentaries were written on the Muslims' holy Book, the Quran, but these commentaries make up a distinct category that should be considered and discussed separately.[8]

In 12th-century Muslim Al-Andalus an outstanding philosopher appeared, who considered Aristotle to be the most eminent thinker. It was Ibn Rushd, Latinised as Averroes, who decided that Aristotle had been misunderstood and misinterpreted, primarily through the contamination of his thought with Neoplatonism, by earlier Arab philosophers, such as Ibn Sina, Latinised as Avicenna.[9] This brilliant scholar (1126 – 1198) came from a prominent family of lawyers and qadis (judges) from Cordoba. Averroes himself served as a qadi

---

5   In Abdur Rahman Badawi, (ed.), *Aflutin 'inda al-'Arab* (Cairo: Dar al-kutub al-ilmiyya, 1955).

6   In A. R. Badawi, (ed.), *Aflatuniyya 'inda al-'Arab* (Cairo: Dar al-kutub al-ilmiyya, 1962).

7   Gerhard Endress, *Die wissenschaftlichte Literatur*, in Helmut Gätje et al., *Grundriss der Arabischen Philologie* (Wiesbaden: Verlag 1987) 2: 24–61.

8   An in-depth analysis of the emergence of the genre of the Quran commentary, the *tafsir*, may be found in: Walid A. Saleh, *The Formation of the Classical Tafsir Tradition: the Quran Commentary of Al-Thalabi (d. 427.1035)* (Leiden: Brill 2003); generally on commentaries, cf: Andrew Rippin, *Tafsīr*, in *Encyclopaedia of Islam* 2nd ed., CD-Version 2010.

9   General works on his philosophy include, most importantly: Oliver Leaman, *Averroes and his Philosophy* (Richmond: Curzon 1997); Dominique Urvoy, *Ibn Rushd (Averroes)* (London: Routledge 1991).

in the court of the caliph Al-Mansur of the Almohad dynasty. As Al-Andalus was troubled by political unrest at that time, and Averroes's thought was considered heretical by some of the Zahirites, or advocates of a literal interpretation of the holy Scriptures, he fell into disgrace in his mature age. However, shortly before his death he had the honours due to him restored to him. Averroes's writings are prolific, and, in addition to philosophical works, they encompass legal and medical treatises. In mediaeval tradition he was famous chiefly as the Commentator of Aristotle's works. It is difficult to say with any degree of certainty what inspired him to write his commentaries. There is a famous story that the caliph commissioned him to write commentaries on Aristotle's work so that he himself and the educated circles of Al-Andalus could better understand them. Averroes undertook to do that, treating the task as a paid commission. Whatever the case actually was, over about 26 years Averroes produced commentaries on most of the Stagirite's works. As he did not have access to Aristotle's *Politics*, he wrote commentaries on Plato's *Republic* instead.

Averroes wrote three types of commentaries on each of Aristotle's works: short, middle, and long ones. They were intended for different groups of readers, reasoning at various intellectual levels. Most probably, this division of commentaries into three kinds reflected the division of society into three categories in terms of understanding and discovering the divine truths. Averroes stated that most emphatically in his *Fasl al-maqal* (translated a. o. as *The Decisive Treatise*).[10] While stating clearly that there is only one divine truth, he discerned, however, three levels of its interpretation, designed for various groups of people, endowed with various cognitive capacities. At the bottom of the ladder, there are the masses (*amma*), which can only learn things at the lowest, simplest level, through *khitab*, or rhetoric. Theologians, to whom dialectics, or *jadal,* is available, make up the next, higher group. At the top there are philosophers who thanks to their intellectual abilities and the ability to use their reason may experience cognition at the highest level, that of logical reasoning, or *burhan*. This was the term used to denote Aristotelian syllogistic, which had been known for a long time in Muslim culture from the translations of the *Prior Analytics* and *Posterior Analytics* that had been produced at an early stage of the translation movement. By introducing such a strict division of society and placing the philosophers, making use of their reason (*aql*), at its very

---

10   Ibn Rushd, *Traktat rozstrzygający o określaniu związku między objawieniem (szari'at) a filozofią (hikma)*, (*The Decisive Treatise*), Katarzyna Pachniak, ed., transl., *Studia Antyczne i Mediewistyczne* 7/42 (2009): 37–57; on the treatise cf. K. Pachniak, "'Fasl al-makal' Ibn Ruszda." *Studia Antyczne i Mediewistyczne* 7/42 (2009): 33–37.

top, Averroes joined in the debate which had been going on from the early years of Islam, on which has primacy: reason or revelation. May one use intellectual reasoning and instruments such as logic, for example, for interpreting the religious, revealed truths at all? Those to have offered their opinions in this dispute before him included, for example, Al-Ghazali, claiming that philosophers fall into errors and heresies, and the highest form of cognition is always cognition through revelation. He discussed this issue in his treatises *Maqasid al-falasifa* (The Aims of the Philosophers) and *Tafahut al-falasifa* (The Incoherence of the Philosophers).[11] Prior to Averroes, the opposite position had been held by another philosopher from Muslim Al-Andalus, Ibn Bajjah, who also claimed that philosophers are the highest group of people, the one to whom the highest form of cognition is available. Averroes's division of the community into three groups by no means meant that there are three truths: as an orthodox Muslim, he believed that there is only one divine truth, which, however, may be interpreted at three different levels.

The task undertaken by Averroes was a difficult one, for he did not know Greek and while writing his commentaries, he worked from their translations into Arabic as well as from the existing commentaries, often ones strongly influenced by the Neoplatonic tradition. Averroes's commentaries are very important not only in terms of the perception of the Stagirite's thought; they are also crucial for the understanding of the thought of Averroes himself. Unlike Al-Farabi and Ibn Sina, who left behind treatises presenting their complete intellectual systems, in the case of Averroes we do not have a single work of that kind. His original works focus on selected issues, and his views on a number of problems may be best reconstructed precisely by studying his commentaries on Aristotle's writings. In addition to his commentaries on Aristotle, Averroes also wrote commentaries on the treatise *On the Intellect* by Alexander of Aphrodisias, the *Metaphysics* by Nicolaus of Damascus, Porphyry's *Isagoge* and Ptolemy's *Almagest*.

As has been mentioned above, the scholar wrote three types of commentaries, which corresponded to the three levels of human comprehension. The short commentaries, called *jami*, are mostly abstracts. Many of these may be considered to be quite free and pervaded by the spirit of individualism of the Cordoban philosopher. The medium commentaries, or *talkhis*, are paraphrases. The long ones are referred to as *tafsir*, i.e. by the same term that is used to denote Quranic commentaries. They comprise Aristotle's complete text with a line-by-line commentary. The spirit of individualism is very much pronounced

---

11   Al-Ghazali, *Makasid al-falasifa*, ed. Muhyi al-Din Sabri al-Kurdi, al-Qahira, 1936; idem, *Tahafut al-falasifa*, ed. Maurice Bouyges, al-Qahira, 1968.

in the commentaries, because Averroes occasionally interpreted the Stagirite's thought in a way that might have seemed alien to the commentators closer in time to the era of the Greek philosopher. On the other hand, however, even though he had worked from Arabic translations, rather than from the original Greek texts, Averroes was able to distinguish Aristotle's original views from the later additions in the form of the commentaries by Alexander of Aphrodisias or Themistius. Averroes's principal object was to reconstruct Aristotle's original view as precisely as possible.

Let us now proceed to discuss specific examples. I have selected Averroes's commentaries on Aristotle's *Metaphysics* in order to demonstrate on this example how the types of commentary differed. Moreover, Aristotle's *Metaphysics* is a work that over the centuries has accrued a continuation, mostly in the form of further commentaries, as well as shaping the metaphysical reflection in Islam. Since Averroes did not know Greek, as has been mentioned above, his commentaries were based on various translations of the *Metaphysics*, including the most extensive one, produced by a certain Ustat at the time of Al-Kindi (d. ca. 683), the 'first Arab philosopher'. Several books seem not to have been translated, and the translation itself has only survived in Averroes's *Long Commentary*. Besides, there were several other translations of longer or shorter passages.[12] The *Metaphysics* is regarded as a difficult work; that is why Muslim philosophers often preferred to use paraphrases and epitomes rather than the original text, those by Alexander of Aphrodisias and Themistius being the most popular ones. Nonetheless, Averroes's commentaries reveal a genuine and profound understanding of the Stagirite's thought and its creative interpretation. There are several terms for metaphysics in Arabic; in this commentary Averroes used the term *ma bad at-tabi'a* ('that which is outside nature'), which is a calque of the Greek term. Besides, we may find terms such as *al-falsafa al-ula*, 'the first philosophy', and *ilahiyyat*, 'that which is divine, theology'; the latter term was used by Ibn Sina (Avicenna) in his *Kitab ash-Shifa* (Book of Healing). Please note that the object of my analysis will not be the contents of Ibn Rushd's commentaries on metaphysics or the philosophical views expounded in them, but rather the characteristic features of the commentaries themselves.

---

12   An overview of these is included in a supplement to an edition of the *Long Commentary* written by Maurice Bouyges, *Notices*, Bibliotheca Arabica Scholasticorum, t. V,1, Beirut, 1952. The first edition of the Arabic text of Books A 5, 987a 5 ff., B−I and L was prepared by M. Bouyges on the basis of the manuscript MSS. Leiden or. 2074 and 2075, Bibliotheca Arabica Scholasticorum V−VII (Beirut, 1938 − 1952). A part of the Arabic version of the commentary on Book L written by Themistius was included in the edition by Abdul Rahman Badawi, *Aristu inda al-Arab* (Cairo: Dar al-kutub al-ilmiyya, 1947), 329 ff.

Short Commentary on the Metaphysics (Jawami kitab ma bad at-tabi'a).[13] This commentary is exceptional in certain respects, for generally Averroes's short commentaries follow Aristotle's original work in terms of the order in which the material is presented; in the *Jami,* however, Ibn Rushd arranged the material taken from the *Metaphysics* in a different way. Another important difference is that concerning the contents of the text. While the other short commentaries include, more or less completely, the whole text of the Stagirite's treatise being commented upon, in the *Jami* Averroes only presents passages selected by himself, arguing that he 'wants to present scholarly doctrines collected from Aristotle's treatises devoted to the science of metaphysics (*ma bad at-tabi'a)*'. Aristotle's *Metaphysics* comprises fourteen books but Ibn Rushd explains at the beginning that his treatise will present Aristotle's thought in three main parts and five chapters. He does so because he regards the *Metaphysics* as a work that may be reduced to three principal parts, devoted, in succession, to:

1. Existing sensual things and their kinds, which fall into ten categories.
2. In Part 2, he considers the principles of substances, i.e. separate things, and explains the manners of their existence, relates them to their first cause, i.e. to God, explains their attributes and acts, demonstrates relationships between God and the remaining beings, indicates that God is the ultimate perfection, the first form and the first agent (*fa'il*).
3. In Part 3, he considers subjects connected with these problems from related sciences, eliminating errors made in this area by ancient thinkers, particularly in the fields of logic, mathematics and physics.[14]

As evident from the above list, presented by Averroes himself, the author treated Aristotle's text very individually, for he looked through it and rearranged it according to his own understanding, grouping those parts which, in his opinion, were devoted to one and the same problem, for example, Sections 12 and 6 from Books VII and VIII, respectively, i.e. the unity of the defined object and the unity of the definition. Moreover, he moves to the end those problems that he believes to be arranged in a wrong order, as they require preliminary explanations, for example he moves the question of different views on substances, discussed in VII.2, to the end of his deliberations, deciding that this will make things much clearer.

The three parts mentioned above are preceded by Chapter I, in which the author included an introduction complete with an explanation of the main subject, its aim and usefulness, as well as discussing twenty eight basic terms

---

13　Rüdiger Arnzen, *On Aristotle's "Metaphysics": An Annotated Translation of the So-called "Epitome"* (Berlin – New York: Walter de Gruyter, 2010).

14　Cf. *Jawami,* ibid., 47–50.

from the area of metaphysics. The introduction includes Ibn Rushd's own considerations as well as passages from Books IV and VI. This could indicate that the Andalusian regarded these books as introductory and preliminary ones with respect to the contents of the *Metaphysics* proper, contained mainly in Books VII, VIII, IX and XII. Even these few remarks irrefutably show that this commentary may be regarded as exceptional, since, unlike the other *jami*, or short commentaries, it treats the contents very freely, thus distinctly reflecting Averroes's understanding of the text and of the philosophical notion itself.[15]

Middle Commentary on the Metaphysics (*Talkhis ma bad at-tabi'a*)[16] is, by contrast, typical of the middle commentaries written by Averroes. Each paragraph contains the first few words from the text of each original paragraph, followed by a paraphrase of the Stagirite's text. However, as pointed out by Genequard, there are certain doubts concerning the authenticity of the *Talkhis*, which had already been raised by M. Bouyges. On the other hand, other scholars, such as von Horten, consider it to be authentic. This question has not yet been well researched; Genequard emphasizes, however, that some opinions expressed in the *Talkhis* stand in absolute opposition to the views expounded in the *Tafsir*, i.e. in the *Long Commentary,* and reiterated in the *Tahafut at-tafahut* (*The Incoherence of the Incoherence*).[17] This is true, most importantly, of the Andalusian's standpoint on emanation, which he seems to present in the *Talkhis* in a way similar to that of Al-Farabi and Ibn Sina; in the *Long Commentary* and *Tahafut,* by contrast, he completely rejects it, treating it as a distortion of Aristotle's pure thought.[18] One may assume that if a scholar of Averroes's stature had dramatically changed his mind, he would probably have given his reasons for that decision. Moreover, the text of the *Talkhis* is a very precise reflection of the text of the *Tafsir*, i.e. the long commentary: it uses the same metaphors, phrasing, manner of argumentation, which, Genequard concludes, suggests that its author was strongly influenced by Ibn Rushd in intellectual terms.[19]

Long Commentary on Metaphysics (*Tafsir fi ma bad at-tabi'a*) is a very voluminous work; its Beirut edition has 1800 pages. It is, however, crucially important, both as an exposition of the views of Averroes himself on

---

15 Arnzen, *On Aristotle's "Metaphysics"*, 1–18.

16 Ibn Rushd, *Talkhis ma bad at-tabi'a*, ed. Usman Amin (Cairo, 1958).

17 Ibn Rushd, *Tahafut at-tahafut*, ed. M. Jabari (Beyruth, 1997). This treatise was written as a polemic with the views of Al-Ghazali and his attack against the philosophers presented in his *Tahafut al-falasifa*.

18 *Tahafut at-tahafut*, 184–187, and ff; *Tafsir*, 162.

19 Charles Genequand, *Ibn Rushd's Metaphysics. A Translation with Introduction of Ibn Rushd's Commentary on Aristotle's Metaphysics, Book Lam.* (Leiden: Brill, 1984), 10–11.

metaphysical problems, and because of the fact that it was through this commentary that an Arabic translation of Aristotle's *Metaphysics* had survived.

Unlike the *Short Commentary*, in the *Tafsir* Averroes tries to follow Aristotle's text faithfully, providing a line-by-line commentary, but without doing that which was characteristic of the *Jawami*: he does not reflect on the very concept of the book or on the order of the problems addressed by it, he does not paraphrase it, and his interpretation strictly relates to the contents of the original. In many places, however, he clarifies, as far as possible, whatever he considers to be unclear. It is precisely in this commentary that he determinedly tries to purify Aristotle's thought by eliminating the erroneous additions introduced by Ibn Sina. In the *Tafsir*, Averroes comments on only eleven books of the original; it does not include Books XII, XIII or XIV. Technically, the commentary follows the tradition of numerous Greek commentaries from late antiquity; namely, it is divided into *lemmata*, with the text being introduced by a phrase: *kala Aristu*, 'Aristotle said'. It is followed by a commentary, in which Averroes sometimes cites the commentaries on the *Metaphysics* written by Alexander of Aphrodisias, Themistius and Nicolaus of Damascus, known from the Arabic tradition. An in-depth analysis shows that the translation included in those *lemmata* does not come from any particular version, but rather reflects various stages in the development of the translation movement. For this reason, there are deviations from the Aristotelian order of the books. The book *Alpha Elatton* precedes *Alpha Meizon*.[20] Thus, what is characteristic of Averroes is drawing on translations; while in the *lemmata* he generally selects one, choosing e.g. exclusively that by Ustat, in the commentary he also cites a text from another translation and other commentaries. This offers researchers an exceptional opportunity to compare various translations coming from various periods.

Ibn Rushd admits that he had no access to *Book Kappa*, i.e. Book XI; nonetheless, he gives an account of its contents in the introduction to his commentary on *Book Lambda*. There had been as many as six translations of the said *Book Lambda* into Arabic, and in the *lemmata* Averroes uses two of these: the translation from Syriac by Abu Bishr Matta (d. 940), to whom was also attributed the translation of the commentary on *Book Lambda* by Alexander of Aphrodisias as well as of the paraphrase by Themistius, and later the translation

---

20 There are two known translations of Book *Alpha elatton*: the first one from 910, prepared by the famous translator Ishak Ibn Hunayn, and the second one by one obscure Ustat, who had reportedly prepared a translation of the entire *Metaphysics* for Al-Kindi. In the case of *Alpha Meizon*, on the other hand, Averroes used the 10th century translation by a certain Nazif.

by Ustat. In his own commentary, Averroes, in turn, frequently cites the commentary by Alexander of Aphrodisias, the Greek original of which has not survived until our time. He also cites other translations, namely those by Yahya ibn Adi and Ishaq ibn Hunayn.

No translation of or commentary on Books XIII and XIV has survived; however, Averroes includes their description in the introduction to Book Lambda. From the information provided by Ibn Nadim in his *Kitab Fihrist* it follows that these books had been translated into Arabic.[21] Even this sketchy presentation of Averroes's commentaries on Aristotle shows that in terms of form they drew in many respects upon the Greek tradition of commentary; in terms of contents, on the other hand, they are invaluable as an exposition of the philosophical thought of Ibn Rushd himself and as a presentation of the Muslim reception of the Stagirite's thought. Moreover, they helped transmit Aristotelian thought to Latin Europe and numerous commentaries on them were written in their turn in both Hebrew and Latin.

Bibliography

Averroès, *Tafsir mā ba'd at-tabi'at*, Texte arabe inédit, établi par Maurice Bouyges, vol. 1–3, (Bibliotheca Arabica Scholasticorum: Série arabe; t. V, 1,2. VI. VII.), Beyrouth: Imprimerie Catholique, 1938–1952.

Badawī, Abdur Rahman. *'A. Arisṭū 'inda l-'arab. Dirāsāt wa-nuṣūṣ ġayr manšūra*. Cairo: Maktabat al-nahḍa al-miṣriyya, 1947.

— *Rasā'il falsafiyya li-l-Kindī wa-l-Fārābī wa-Ibn Bājja wa-Ibn 'Adī*. Bangazi: al-Jāmi'a al-Lībiyya, 1973.

de Goeje, Michail Jan, *Catalogus Codicum Orientalium Bibliothecae Academiae Lugduno-Batavae*, vol. 5. Lugduno Batavorum, apud E. J. Brill, 1873, 324–325, no. 2821.

Genequand, Charles, *Ibn Rushd's Metaphysics: A Translation with Introduction of Ibn Rushd's Commentary on Aristotle's Metaphysics, Book Lam*. Leiden: Brill, 1984.

Ibn al-Nadīm. Kitāb al-fihrist, ed. G. Flügel et al., Leipzig, 1871–1872; ed. R. Taġaddud, Teheran: Marvi Offset Printing, 1973; ed. A. F. Sayyid, London: Al-Furqan, 2009.

Khalifat, Sahbān. *Yaḥyā ibn 'Adī*, The Philosophical Treatises: A Critical Edition with an Introduction and Study. Amman: Publications of University of Jordan, 1988.

Mishkāt, Muhammad. *Arisṭāṭālīs-i Ḥakīm*. Naḫustīn maqāla-i Mā ba'd al-ṭabī'a mawsūm bi maqālat al-Alif al-ṣuġrā tarġama-i Isḥāq b. Ḥunayn bā Yaḥyā b. 'Adī wa tafsīr-i Ibn-i Rushd. Tehran, 1967.

---

21 Ibn Nadim, *Kitab al-fihrist*, ed. A. F. Sayyid (London: Al-Furqan, 2009), chap. VII, 528–536.

Further Reading

'Afīfī Abū l-'Alā. "An Ancient Arabic Translation of the Book Lambda of Aristotle's 'Metaphysics'." Bulletin of the Faculty of Arts of the University of Egypt 5 (1937): 89–138.

Bauloye, Laurence. "La traduction arabe de la 'Métaphysique' et l'établissement du texte grec." In Aristotelica Secunda: Mélanges offerts à Christian Rutten. Liège: C.I.P.L., 1996, 281–290.

Bauloye, Laurence. "Averroès. Grand Commentaire de la 'Métaphysique' d'Aristote, Z 1 et 2. Traduction et notes." *Bulletin d'*Études Orientales 49 (1997): 53–73.

— Averroès: Grand Commentaire (Tafsîr) de la Métaphysique, livre Beta. Paris: Vrin, 2002.

Bertolacci, Amos. "On the Arabic Translations of Aristotle's 'Metaphysics'." *Arabic Sciences and Philosophy* 15 (2005): 241–275.

— *The Reception of Aristotle's Metaphysics in Avicenna's Kitāb al-Šifā': A Milestone of Western Metaphysical Thought.* Leiden: Brill. 2006.

Biesterfeldt, Hans Heinrich. "Kommunikation durch Übersetzung: Ziele und Methoden der griechisch-arabischen Übersetzungen des 9. Jahrhunderts." In *Kommunikation durch Zeichen und Wort. Stätten und Formen der Kommunikation im Altertum IV*, ed. by Gerhard Binder, Konrad Ehlich. Trier: Wissenschaftlicher Verlag, 1995, 137 – 192.

Endress, Gerhard. *The Works of Yaḥyā ibn 'Adī. An Analytical Inventory.* Wiesbaden: Reichert Verlag, 1977.

— "Die wissenschaftliche Literatur." *In Grundriss der Arabischen Philologie*, Band II: *Literatur*, ed. by von Helmut Gätje. Wiesbaden: Reichert Verlag, 1987.

— "The Circle of al-Kindī: Early Arabic Translations from the Greek and the Rise of Islamic Philosophy." In *The Ancient Tradition in Christian and Islamic Hellenism*: *Studies on the Transmission of Greek Philosophy and Sciences Dedicated to H. J. Drossaart Lulofs on His Ninetieth Birthday*, ed. by Gerhard Endress and Remke Kruk. Leiden: Brill 1997, 43–76.

Freudenthal, Jacob. *Die durch Averroes erhaltenen Fragmente Alexanders zur Metaphysik des Aristoteles.* Berlin: Verlag der Königlichen Akademie der Wissenschaften, 1885.

Geoffroy, Marc. "Remarques sur la traduction Usṭāṯ du livre 'Lambda' de la 'Métaphysique', chapitre 6," *Recherches de Théologie et Philosophie Médiévales.* 70 (2003): 417–436.

Janssens, Jules. "Avicenne et sa 'paraphrase-commentaire' du livre 'Lambda (Kitab al-insaf)'." *Recherches de Théologie et Philosophie Médiévales.* 70 (2003): 401–416.

Madkour, Ibrahim. "La 'Métaphysique' en terre d'Islam." *Mélanges de l'Institut Dominicain d'Etudes Orientales.* 7 (1962 – 1963): 21–34.

Martin, Aubert. "La 'Métaphysique': Tradition syriaque et arabe." In *Dictionnaire des Philosophes Antiques*, ed. by Richard Goulet. Paris: Ed. du CNRS, 1989, 528–534.

Martini Bonadeo, Cecilia. "La 'Métaphysique': Tradition syriaque et arabe: Mise à jour bibliographique." In *Dictionnaire des Philosophes Antiques: Supplément*, ed. by Richard Goulet. Paris: CNRS, 2003, 259–264.

— "La tradizione araba dei primi due libri della 'Metafisica' di Aristotele: Libri a-A." In *Aristotele e Alessandro di Afrodisia nella tradizione araba*, ed. by Cristina D'Ancona, Giuseppe Serra. Padova: Il Poligrafo, 2002, 75–112.

— "Un commento ad 'Alpha Elatton sicut litterae sonant' nella Baġdād del X sec." *Medioevo* 28 (2003): 69–96.

— "*ΩΣ ΕΡΩΜΕΝΟΝ*: alcune interpretazioni di *Metaph.* Λ 7." In. *Aristotele e i suoi esegeti neoplatonici: Logica ed ontologia nelle interpretazioni greche e arabe*: *Atti del convegno internazionale Roma, 19–20 ottobre 2001.*, ed. by Vincenza Celluprica, Cristina D'Ancona. Roma Bibliopolis, 2004, 209–243.

— "The Arabic Aristotle in the 10th Century Baġdād. The Case of Yahya ibn 'Adi's Commentary on *Metaph. Alpha Elatton*." *Veritas* 52 (2007): 3, 7–20.

— "The Arabic version of book 'Alpha Meizon' of Aristotle's 'Metaphysics' and the testimony of MS. 'Bibl. Apostolica Vaticana, Ott. Lat. 2048'." In *Les traducteurs au travail: Leurs manuscrits et leurs methods*: *Actes du Colloque international organisé par le "Ettore Majorana Centre for Scientific Culture" (Erice, 30 septembre – 6 octobre 1999)*, ed. by Jacqueline Hamesse. Turnhout: Brepols 2001, 173–206.

Mattock, John N. "The Early Translations from Greek into Arabic: an Experiment in Comparative Assessment." In *Symposium Graeco-Arabicum: Akten des Zweiten Symposium Graeco-Arabicum, Ruhr-Universität Bochum, 3–5 März* 1987, ed. by Gerhard Endress. (Archivum Graeco-Arabicum, 1). Amsterdam: 1989, 73–102.

Neuwirth, Angelika. "Neue Materialien zur arabischen Tradition der beiden ersten Metaphysik-Bücher." *Die Welt des Islams* 18 (1977–1978): 1–2, 84–100.

Ramón Guerrero, Rafael. "Nota sobre la presencia del libro 'Lambda' de la 'Metafísica' de Aristóteles en el mundo árabe." *La Ciudad de Dios* 198 (1985): 117–121.

Prose Criticism in the Bush Warbler's Hideout: *Mumyōzōshi* as the Earliest Literary Critical Commentary on *Genji monogatari*

Adam Bednarczyk

Japanese Language and Culture Center,
Nicolaus Copernicus University, Toruń

Exactly thirty years have passed since the publication of the first translation of *Mumyōzōshi* 無名草子 (*The Untitled Book*) by Michele Marra.[1] For many decades of the twentieth century, when various works of Japanese literature were being consecutively translated into foreign languages, no translation of *Mumyōzōshi* appeared, even as an excerpt. Based on Marra's M.A. thesis, the English translation with an accompanying introduction to the work is an important accomplishment, which provides a deep insight into the perception of the court literature.

The *Mumyōzōshi* is an early Kamakura (1195–1333) semi-fictional work written in *kana* and generally recognized as the earliest text in Japanese literature devoted primarily to prose criticism. The greater part of the *Mumyōzōshi* is focused on the analysis of works in the *monogatari* 物語 ('narrative', 'tale') genre and of other writings. However, the author displays a particular interest in one of them, namely *Genji monogatari* 源氏物語 (*The Tale of Genji* by Murasaki Shikibu). Initially, the tale was probably simply a *monogatari* enjoyed above all by women, but it became one of the most influential classical Japanese works, one which has been interpreted, analyzed, and evoked over centuries. The discussion of *Genji monogatari* is the most detailed part of *Mumyōzōshi*, and about one-third of the comments on *monogatari* are devoted to the greatest masterpiece of Japanese literature from the beginning of the 11th century.[2] Although in the early Kamakura period existed already two philological commentaries that represent a transition in the reception of Murasaki's work – *Genjishaku* 源氏釈 (*Interpretations of the Tale*

---

1   Michele Marra, "Mumyōzōshi: Introduction and Translation," *Monumenta Nipponica* 39 (1984):115–145, 281–305, 409–434.

2   Thomas H. Rohlich, "In Search of Critical space: The Path to Monogatari Criticism in the Mumyozoshi," *Harvard Journal of Asiatic Studies* 57 (1997):180.

of Genji, 12th c.) by Fujiwara no Koreyuki 藤原伊行 (1139?–1175?)[3], which begins the long line of scholarly commentaries that are still being written today[4], and *Okuiri* 奥入 by Fujiwara no Sadaie (Teika) 藤原定家 (1162–1241), written some three decades after *Mumyōzōshi*[5] – only *The Untitled Book* provides a rare glimpse into the literary discourse of individual works in a systematic and critical manner.[6] As I will attempt to show below, the method of interpretation

---

3 Known also as Sesonji Koreyuki 世尊寺伊行, he was a court official and a calligrapher of the late Heian period and the author of an important calligraphy treatise *Yakaku teikinshō* 夜鶴庭訓抄 [*Secret Teachings of the Sesōnji School of Calligraphy*, ca. 1170).

4 In the pre-modern period, until the Tokugawa shogunate was officially established in Edo in 1603, over thirty commentaries on *Genji monogatari* were been composed. Apart from *Okuiri* by Fujiwara no Sadaie (Teika) from the beginning of the thirteenth century, two important commentaries from the late thirteenth century should be mentioned, which were provided by Kawachi family who competed with Teika and his heirs to establish an authoritative recension of *The Tale of Genji*. Minamoto no Chikayuki 源親行 produced *Suigenshō* 水原抄 [*Water Spring Notes*], a compendium of Kawachi school teachings, and Priest Sojaku 素寂 *Shimeishō* 紫明抄 [*Notes on Explicating Murasaki*]. The *Suigenshō* differs from previous commentaries in explaining the historical context of the social background of the court life depicted in *The Tale of Genji*. Haruo Shirane, *Envisioning the Tale of Genji: Media, Gender, and Cultural Production* (New York: Columbia University Press, 2013), 24. The first major commentary written in the Muromachi period (1333 – 1568) was Yotsutsuji Yoshinari's 四辻善成 *Kakaishō* 河海抄 [*Book of Seas and Rivers*, 1387 – ca.1394], which is notable for references to previous annotations. In the same time there appeared another work by Yotsutsuji – *Sangohishō* 珊瑚秘抄 [*A Secret Treatise of Coral*, 1397), *Sengenshō* 仙源抄 [*Notes of the Immortals' Origins'*, 1381] written by the emperor Chōkei 長慶, and *Chidorishō* 千鳥抄 [*Notes of a Thousand Birds* or *Notes of a Plover*, 1419] by Hirai Sōsuke 平井相助. Late Muromachi commentators concentrated on narratological interpretations, and an example focusing on these issues is provided by *Amayo danshō* 雨夜談抄 [*Notes on the Rainy Night Discussion*, 1485] by Japanese poet, Sōgi 宗祇. Ibid., 25.

5 Ishida Yoshisada 石田吉貞, "Mumyōzōshi sakusha kō 無名草子作者考," *Kokugo to kokubungaku* 国語と国文学 21 (1944): 15–28; Higuchi Yoshimaro 樋口芳麻呂, "Mumyōzōshi no hottan 無名草子の発端," *Kokugo to kokubungaku*, 55, no. 10 (1978): 7; Suzuki Hiromichi 鈴木弘道, *Mumyōzōshi* (Chikuma Shobō, 1970); Kuwabara Hiroshi 桑原博史, *Mumyōzōshi*, vol. 7 of *Shinchō Nihon koten shūsei* (Shinchō, 1976), 133–153, cited in Marra, "Mumyōzōshi", 116.

6 Some studies discussing late Heian fiction written under an obvious influence of *Genji monogatari* suggest that also *Sagoromo monogatari* 狭衣物語 (ca. 1075, by Rokujō no Saiin Senji 六条斎院宣旨, who served the Kamo Priestess Princess Baishi 禖子内親王) and *Hamamatsu Chūnagon monogatari* 浜松中納言物語 (ca. 1060, attributed to the author of *Sarashina nikki* 更級日記) provide examples of how earlier readers could interpret various aspect of the tale, can therefore be regarded as a kind of commentary. According to Tyler, „The *Sagoromo* and *Hamamatsu* authors did not identify themselves

and commenting on *Genji monogatari* in *Mumyōzōshi* – in contrast with *Genjishaku*'s textual glosses – is unlike such annotations.

Alleged author and date of *Mumyōzōshi*

The authorship of *Mumyōzōshi* has for a long time been discussed, but numerous evidence suggest that a woman of service at court wrote the book. Although it has been suspected at first that Fujiwara no Shunzei 藤原俊成 (1114 – 1204), a noted Japanese poet, or Jōkaku 上覚 (1147 – 1226), the author of *Waka Irohashū* 和歌色葉集 (*Primer of Japanese Poetry or Coloured Leaves of Japanese Poetry*, ca. 1198), may have written the text, this possibility has been rejected.[7] A detailed study of the text showed that *Mumyōzōshi*'s author was in fact a woman well known to Fujiwara no Teika and his half-brother, Fujiwara no Takanobu 藤原隆信 (1142 – 1205). In scholars' opinion, the woman was a person known as Shunzeikyō no musume 俊成卿女, 'Daughter of Lord Shunzei'[8], and a poet ranked with princess Shikishi 式子 (1149 – 1201)[9].

---

as commentators on *Genji monogatari*, nor have they been recognized as such. However, their work contains passages and motifs that illuminate *Genji* reception in a time before formal *Genji* commentary began – a time when *Genji* was still a *monogatari* among others and not yet a recognized cultural monument." He also distinguishes three main issues discussed in both works: (1) the meaning of the *Genji* chapter title "Yume no ukihashi," (2) the question of what happens to Ukifune between "Ukifune" and "Tenarai," and (3) the significance of Genji's affair with Fujitsubo. Royall Tyler, "'Sagoromo' and 'Hamamatsu' on 'Genji': Eleventh-Century Tales as Commentary on 'Genji monogatari'," *Japan Review* 18 (2006): 3–28.

7 In the early Kamakura period *monogatari* were considered to be marginal writings, falling mainly within the purview of women's literary output, and often disregarded by men. For that reason such hypotheses were doubtful, just as "the imitation theory", suggesting that Shunzei may have written the *Mumyōzōshi* from the point of view of a woman, as *Tosa nikki* 土佐日記 [*Tosa Diary*, 935] has been composed by famous Heian poet, Ki no Tsurayuki 紀貫之. Marra, "Mumyōzōshi", 115. On Tsurayuki's falsification of the authorship of *Tosa nikki,* cf. Donald Keene, *Seeds in the Heart. Japanese Literature from Earliest Times to the Late Sixteenth Century* (New York: Columbia University Press, 1999), 363.

8 Also Fujiwara no Toshinari no musume (1171 – 1252); cf. Ryan C. Davis, "The Fate of Being a Woman," in *Feminist Writings from Ancient Times to the Modern World: A Global Sourcebook and History,* ed. by Tiffany K. Wayne (Santa Barbara – Oxford: Greenwood, 2011): 55–57.

9 Princess Shikishi (Shikishi naishinnō) was the third daughter of the emperor Go-Shirakawa (1127 – 1192, r. 1155 – 1158); after some years of service at the Kamo Shrine in Kyoto, she became a Buddhist nun; she was the author of 49 poems included in the *Shinkokin(waka)shū* 新古今和歌集 [*New Collection of Poems Ancient and Modern*, 1205].

Fujiwara no Toshinari (Shunzei)'s 藤原俊成 (1114 – 1204)[10], eldest daughter Hachijōin Sanjō 八条院三条 was her mother, which means she was actually his granddaughter. Presumably, the fact that the author belonged to Shunzei's household, or Mikohidarike 御子左家 ('the family of Prince of the Left') was particularly significant while she was writing *Mumyōzōshi*. Some quotes in the book may be based on the *Genji* studies, which were considered the specialty and monopoly of Shunzei's family.[11]

Apart from the *Mumyōzōshi*'s close connection with two of Shunzei's family members – Teika and Takanobu – mentioned by name in the text, the authorship of a female author can be also recognized in another way. As Rohlich writes, "the author reveals intimate knowledge of the preferences of the female writers and readers of the age. Without more convincing proof to the contrary it is reasonable to assume that the author was a woman."[12]

Shunzeikyō no musume, born probably in 1171, was very active in literary circles for the most of her life. Two years after her marriage with Minamoto no Michitomo 源通具 (1171 – 1227) in 1200 she went into service of the retired Emperor Go-Toba 後鳥羽, and in 1213, at the age of forty-three, she received the tonsure. She lived into the 1250s, past the age of eighty.[13] As a person knowledgeable in the narratives and poetic anthologies of her day, she had participated for many years in contests of poetry (*utaawase*). A considerable amount of evidence points to the period from 1198 to 1202 as the most probable date of the composition of *Mumyōzōshi*. Firstly, a direct reference to Minor Captain Teika (Teika no shōshō 定家の少将), and avoidance of honorific terms when mentioning him, implying close relations, explicitly show that the author wrote *Mumyōzōshi* in Teika's lifetime. Secondly, the text provides a reference to one of the early Kamakura poetry contests, *Sendō Jūnin Utaawase* 仙洞十人歌合, from 1200, although it makes no mention of the anthology *Shinkokinshū*, commissioned by Go-Toba in the eleventh month of 1201. As

---

10 A Japanese poet and critic, an innovator of *waka* (classical Japanese poems) and a compiler of the *Senzai(waka)shū* 千載和歌集 [*Collection of a Thousand Years*, 1187], the seventh imperial anthology of classical Japanese poetry, and an author of a critical work *Korai fūteishō* 古来風体抄 [*Notes on Poetic Style Through the Ages*, 1197]; he emphasized the ideal of *yūgen*, the subtle communication of romantic beauty with the complex overtones of memory and, often, melancholy; he was considered to be the first critic to have recognized the importance of the *Tale of Genji*.

11 Rohlich, „In Search of Critical Space", 182.

12 Ibid., 183.

13 For more details of the author's life cf. H. Richard Okada, "Fujiwara Shunzei's Daughter," *Japanese Women Writers: A Bio-critical Sourcebook*, ed. By Chieko I. Mulhern (Westport, Conn.: Greenwood Press, 1994), 69–73.

Marra noted, "it is unlikely that the author would have passed over the *Shinkokinshū* in silence"; *Mumyōzōshi* must therefore have been written before the compilation of the eighth imperial anthology was begun.[14]

The most difficult thing to give up in this world

The opening section of the *Mumyōzōshi* is highly allusive, and gives us a hint about the real subject of the lengthy dialogue[15] between eighty-three-years-old nun and three or four younger ladies – the *monogatari* world. The mentioning of the nun's age evokes a number that has a literary significance. The author's reference to Chinese poetry by the favorite Tang poet of Heian courtiers, Bai Juyi 白居易 (772 – 786), and to various Heian writings – including *Sanbō ekotoba* 三宝絵詞 [*Illustrated Tales of The Three Treasures*, 984], *Eiga monogatari* 栄花物語 [*A Tale of Flowering Fortunes*, 1092], and *Ōkagami* 大鏡 [*The Great Mirror*, 1120] – through the "eighty-three years" works as an implicit reflection on the use of profane literature for religious salvation. This literary trope alludes to "an apologia for literature as an expedient means to understand deeper truths", and refers to the problem of relationship between literature and religion.[16] Exactly the same matter is discussed for the first time in "Hotaru" 蛍 ["Fireflies"] chapter of *Genjim*.[17] While the initial fragment of the *Mumyōzōshi* is only an intricate allusion to the topic of discussion focused on narratives, an explicitly expressed interest in *monogatari* appears after a long dialogue inspired by the elderly nun-narrator.

The setting of *Mumyōzōshi* is an abandoned residence in a deserted place in Higashiyama area of Kyoto, where the aged woman is wandering. The time of year is the middle of the fifth month, which is a rainy season of early summer. The nun, who has formerly served at court as an attendant of the retired Empress

---

14   Yamagishi Tokuhei 山岸徳平, "Genji Monogatari Kenkyū no Shoki 源氏物語研究の初期," *Kokugo to kokubungaku* 2, no. 10 (1925): 275–352, cited in Marra, "Mumyōzōshi", 118.

15   The dialogue form used in *Mumyōzōshi* appears in various medieval epic works. Most of the thirteenth-century historical works known as *kagami*, or mirrors, have a similar construction. Thus, the central figure is sometimes called the *shite* after the protagonist of the classical Japanese musical drama *nō*. Earl R. Miner, Robert E. Morrell and Hiroko Odagiri, *The Princeton Companion to Classical Japanese Literature*, (Princeton: Princeton University Press, 1988), 41.

16   Rohlich, „In Search of Critical Space", 186.

17   Mikołaj Melanowicz, *Od VI do połowy XIX wieku*, vol. 1 of *Literatura japońska* (Warszawa: Wydawnictwo Naukowe PWN, 1994), 178–185; Kikuta Shigeo 菊田茂男, "'Genji monogatari' Hotaru no maki no monogatariron 「源氏物語」蛍の巻の物語論" *Bunka* 文化 30, no. 2 (1966): 96–136.

Seishi and later as a servant of the Emperors Rokujō 六条[18] and Takakura 高倉[19], unexpectedly meets a group of three or four highly educated ladies. They start to talk on many diverse topics – from the moon to letters, from tears to dreams. The nun tells the ladies about her own life and her devoting of her time to the recitation of the Lotus Sutra (Jap. 妙法蓮華経 *Myōhōrengekyō*). She also explains why she finds it the most beautiful and splendid:

又、「功徳の中に何事かをろかなると申す中に、思へど／＼めでたく覚えさせ給ふは、法花経こそおはしませ。いかにおもしろくめでたくき絵物語といへど、二三遍も見つればうるさきものなるを、これは千部を千部ながら聞くたびにめづらしく、文字ごとに初めて聞きつけたらん事のやうに覚ゆるこそ、浅ましくめでたけれ。「無二亦無三」と仰せられたるのみならず、「法花最第一」とこそあめれば、事あたらしくかやうに申すべきにはあらねど、さこそは昔より言ひ伝へたる事も、必ずさしも覚えぬ事も侍を、これはたま／＼生まれ合ひたる思ひ出、たゞこの経に逢ひ奉りたるばかりとこそ思ふに、など源氏とてさばかりめでたきものに、この経の文字の一偈一句おはせざるらむ。何事か作りの残し、書き漏らしたる事一言も侍。これのみなん第一の難と覚ゆる」と言ふなれば（後略）[20]

'When I consider the relative merits of virtuous things, I realize that the Lotus Sutra is the most wonderful of all. However interesting the illustrated romances may be, I become bored after looking at them two or three times. But each time I listen to the words of the Lotus Sutra is a new experience for me and I feel as if I am hearing them for the first time. It is such amazingly wonderful experience. According to the Lotus Sutra, "There are not two nor are there yet three," and "The Dharma Blossoms is foremost." Of course, I am not telling you anything new. Even if things such as the Lotus Sutra have been transmitted from ancient times, we don't necessarily have to think of them as splendid. But when I consider that Buddha has granted us the Lotus Sutra to call to mind our good fortune to have been born as human beings, I wonder why there does not appear a word of this sutra in such an excellent work as *Genji monogatari*? Perhaps something has been accidentally deleted from the text? No, surely everything is there. I think that this is the only weak point in *Genji monogatari*.'[21]

The discussion on magnificence of the scripture focuses finally on *monogatari*, which appears to be the nun's favorite subject:

---

18 Emperor Rokujō (1164 – 1176, r. 1165 – 1168) was the 79th emperor of Japan and a son of the emperor Nijō.

19 Emperor Takakura (1161 – 1181, r. 1168 – 1180) was the 80th emperor of Japan and the fourth son of the emperor Go-Shirakawa.

20 *Mumyōzōshi* in *Kodai chūsei geijutsuron* 古代中世芸論 [*Theories of Ancient and Medieval Art*], ed. Hayashi Tatsusaburō, vol. 23 of *Nihon shisō taikei* 日本思想体系 (Tokyo: Iwanami shoten, 1973), 354–355.

21 Marra, "Mumyōzōshi", 136–137.

「さてもこの源氏作り出でたる事こそ、思へど／＼この世一つならずめづ
らかに覚ゆれ。まことに仏に申請ひたりける験にやとこそ覚ゆれ。それよ
り後の物語は、思へばいと易かりぬべきものなり。かれを才覚にて作らむ
に、源氏にまさりたらむ事を作り出す人ありなん。わづかに宇津保・竹取
・住吉などばかりを物語とて見けん心地に、さばかりに作り出でけん、凡
夫のしわざとも覚えぬことなり」など言へば、またありつる若き声にて、
「未だ見侍らぬこそ口惜しけれ。それを語らせ給へかし。聞き侍らむ」と
言へば、「さばかり多かるものを、諳にはいかゞ語り聞えん。本を見てこ
そ言ひ聞かせ奉らめ」²²

'I can't help being surprised when I think about the appearance of *Genji monogatari*.
However much I think about it, its origin is surely not of this world. Didn't is spring
from the fervent worship of the Buddha? I believe that all subsequent novels must
have been produced with ease. Perhaps in the future someone will be able to write a
novel superior to *Genji monogatari* in the light of his knowledge of that work. But
Murasaki knew only *Utsuho monogatari*, *Taketori monogatari*, and *Sumiyoshi
monogatari*, and so to have written such a masterpiece under such conditions cannot
be the work of an ordinary being.'

To this, the lady who had spoken just before remarked, 'It is regrettable that I
haven't yet been able to have a look at *Genji monogatari*. Please talk about the novel
and I will listen.' 'How could I recite such a work by heart? Let me look at the text
while I recite it.'²³

Genji monogatari, the most important court tale that "cannot be considered the
work of an ordinary being", from now on is discussed extensively, part by part,
detail by detail.²⁴

---

22 *Mumyōzōshi*, 354–355.

23 Marra, "Mumyōzōshi", 137.

24 Besides *Genji monogatari* and other extant narratives discussed or mentioned in
Mumyōzōshi, there also appear names of nineteen scattered or completely lost
monogatari: *Tamamo ni asobu* 玉藻に遊ぶ [*Playing Among Jewel-like Seaweeds*],
Kakure mino 隠れ蓑 [*The Invisible Straw Cloak*], *Kokoro takaki tōgū no senji*
心高き春宮の宣旨 [*Generous Messenger of the Crown Prince*], *Asakura* 朝倉, *Tsuyu
no yadori* 露の宿り [*A Lodge of Dew*], *Iwa utsu nami* 岩うつ浪 [*Waves Beating Against
the Rocks*], *Kawagiri* 河霧 [*River Mist*], *Ama no karu mo* 海人の刈藻 [*A Diver's
Harvest of Seaweed*], *Sueba no Tsuyu* 末葉の露, [*Sueba no Tsuyu*] *Mikawa ni sakeru*
みかはにさける [*Bloomed Near the Garden Stream*], *Uji no kawa nami* 宇治の河浪
[*Waves of the Uji River*], *Koma mukae* 駒迎へ [*Meetings with a Colt*], *Odae no numa*
緒絶への沼 [*A Thong-breaking Swamp*], *Ukinami* うきなみ [*The Floating Waves*],
Hatsuyuki 初雪 [*First Snow*], *Namiji no himegimi* 浪路の姫君 [*A Sea Route Princess*],
Yumegatari 夢語り [*Dream Telling*], *Asajigawara no naishi no kami*
浅茅原の内侍のかみ [*The Principal Handmaid of Asajigawara*; unless the same as
Asaji ga Tsuyu), *Yotsugi* 世継 [*Yotsugi*].

Magic of a rainy night[25]

Dialogue used in *Mumyōzōshi* for judging court narratives must have been regarded as a convenient and effective means of exchanging opinions between disputants. As it is suggested, the Daughter of Shunzei chose this form of works presentation not incidentally. The author probably knew some earlier texts, like for instance *Ōkagami*, in which a discussion constitutes the main element of narration. An interesting model of an evaluative dialogue is described in "Hahakigi" 帚木 ("The Broom Tree"), the second chapter of *Genji monogatari*. In contrast to the female discussion in *Mumyōzōshi*, the "Hahakigi" scene is a noblemen's talk devoted to the varieties of women, who "with no merits are as rare as women with no faults"[26]. Moreover, the role of Genji and the nun during the discussion is noteworthy. Analogically to Murasaki's work, where Genji initiates the conversation, in *Mumyōzōshi* the wise old nun of long experience and comprehensive knowledge gives the young court ladies an incentive to exchange reflections and opinions on many subject matters. They both become also heedful listeners, who yield to other characters.[27] In *Genji monogatari* "two young courtiers, a guard officer and a functionary in the ministry of rites, …both were devotees of the way of love and both were good talkers", so "the discussion progressed, and included a number of rather unconvincing points"[28]. Genji leaning against an armrest was silent, even having a nap, which contrasted with the young officer's slightly comical manner "as if he were a sage expostulating upon the deepest truths of the universe"[29]. The scene seems to be echoed in *Mumyōzōshi*:

---

25 The term 'rainy night(s)' (*amayo* 雨夜) refers to the rainy season in the early summer (so called *samidare* 五月雨, or 'rain(s) of the fifth month (of the lunar Calendar)' or drizzling in late autumn and early winter. Then the autumn shower is called *shigure* 時雨. In the Heian period, rainy nights have been considered as a particular season, closely connected with the rituals of courtly love. Lovers forced to spend the rainy days separately tried to forget about the beloved person and escape from idleness. They indulged then in a variety of entertainments such as court plays and games, competitions, conversations, reading of tales and other narratives etc. The famous discussion on women at Genji's residence, quoted and discussed in *Mumyōzōshi* as well, is one of the most representative illustrations of the cultural meaning of *amayo*. For more details cf. Iwona Kordzińska-Nawrocka, *Japońska miłość dworska* (Warszawa: Wydawnictwo Trio, 2005), 144–151.

26 Murasaki Shikibu, *The Tale of Genji*, transl. Edward G. Seidensticker, (Tokyo: Tuttle Company, 1987), 1: 22

27 Rohlich, „In Search of Critical Space", 195.

28 Murasaki Shikibu, *The Tale of Genji*, 23.

29 Ibid., 27.

「今は休み誇り、花・紅葉・月・雪につけても心々とり／.＼に言ひ合へる
もいとをかしければ、つく／.＼と聞き臥したるに、三四人はなをゐつゝ、
「さても／＼何事かこの世にとりて第一に捨て難きふしある。各心に思され
む事を宣へ」と言ふ人あるに[30]

'Let us have a rest,' I suggested. But although I lay down, the ladies kept up a
desultory conversation, praising and criticizing the good and bad points of the
scripture. It was most interesting to listen to them expressing their different opinions
also about flowers, *momiji* [Japanese maples], the moon, and snow, and while I was
lying there listening intently, three or four ladies sitting close to me continued
talking quietly.[31]

Although the discussion's participants are represented by two socially
differentiated groups – male courtiers and women[32] – the convergence of the
encounter's time[33], the form of the meeting, as well as the manner of discourse
discernible in both cases, show a scene of *shinasadame* 品定め ('evaluation',
'criticism', 'discussion on the merits'). The famous episode is widely known as
amayo no shinasadame 雨夜の品定め ('judgments of a rainy night'). It is
suggested that not only the second chapter of *Genji monogatari* should be
perceived as rating women. Some scholars also believe that the real motive of
Murasaki's work is exactly to criticize and comment on women, or that it is a
discussion about *fujinron* 婦人論 ('views on women').[34]

---

30 *Mumyōzōshi*, 351.

31 Marra, "Mumyōzōshi", 133.

32 For a more detailed analysis of the gender and social roles of men and women in the
times of Murasaki Shikibu cf. Iwona Kordzińska-Nawrocka, "Wieczorna rozmowa
bohaterów 'Genji monogatari' a kulturowy wzorzec kobiecości w społeczeństwie
dworskim," in *W kręgu tradycji dworu Heian*, ed. by Iwona Kordzińska-Nawrocka
(Warszawa: Wydawnictwo Trio, Warszawa 2008), 15–31.

33 "The summer rains came, the court was in retreat… It has been raining all day… Back in
his own palace quarters, also unusually quiet, Genji pulled a lamp near and sought to
while away the time with his books." *The Tale of Genji*, 20–21; "it was sometime after
the Fifth Month. The early summer rain had been falling for several days…"; Marra,
"Mumyōzōshi", 130.

34 Fujioka Sakutarō 藤岡作太郎, *Kokubungaku zenshi* 国文学全史, vol. 2 (Tōkyō:
Iwanami shoten, 1963); Abe Akio 阿部秋生, *Genji monogatari kenkyū josetsu*
源氏物語研究序説 (Tōkyō: Tōkyō Daigaku shuppan kaikan, 1959), cited in Takehara
Hiroshi 武原 弘, "Genji monogatari shudairon yobi kōsetsu: Hahakigi maki 'amayo no
sadame' joseiron no shudaisei ni tsuite 『源氏物語』主題論予備考説：帚木巻「雨
夜の品定め」女性論の主題性について," *Nihon bungaku kenkyū* 日本文 学研究 34
(1999): 3.

The way of judging

Mumyōzōshi touches upon many different topics that can be found in *Genji monogatari*. The technique of judgment relies on categorization of diverse matters described *inter alia* in court narratives. As they discuss feelings and situations of *monogatari* characters, the ladies use numerous of attributive expressions such as 'beautiful', 'fascinating', 'impressive' etc. These evaluative categories refer not only to positive elements of personalities and attitudes of the narrative's characters, but also become a means of analysis of the weakest points of a particular tale (*ketten* 欠点).

The way of judgment in *Mumyōzōshi* was considerably influenced by poetic theory and its critical terms. Marra mentions some outstanding critical works on poetry and the concepts of the early thirteenth century discussed by the Daughter of Shunzei.[35] Because she was aware of the poetry views of her famous family members, Shunzei and Teika, she could apply many of the poetry principles to the art of fiction. She attached a special importance to the three fundamental elements of the *monogatari*'s composition – diction, inspiration, form – that are expressed as descriptive words and phrases. [36] When the author refers to the atmosphere and inspiration (*kokoro*), she uses such phrases as *aware ni kanashi* あはれに悲し ('intimately sad'), *aware ni imiji* あはれにいみじ ('overflowing with emotion'), *aware ni itooshi* あはれにいとほし ('intimately pitiful'), *kokoro aru mono nari* 心あるものなり ('deep in inspiration'). A good diction (*kotobazukai*) is often assessed as *aware* あはれ ('moving'), *en* 艶 ('charming'), *imiji* いみじ ('impressive'), *furumekashiku* 古めかし ('old-fashioned'), *imamekashiku* 今めかし ('up-to-date'), *tezutsuge* 手づつげ ('clumsy'), whereas the expression *chiru kokoro mo naku* ちる心もなく ('not losing track of the story') appears during the discussion of the form (*sugata*).[37]

Mumyōzōshi on *Genji*'s chapters

The first part of the discussion on *Genji monogatari* concentrates on the general characteristic of the most famous and significant chapters of the tale. A laconic

---

35 Ibid., 124.

36 "She appreciated the long debates on the elements of a good poem that occupied the minds of generations of poets starting from Ki no Tsurayuki, 884–946. She notes that a poem should be refined, with inspiration (*kokoro* 心), diction (*kotoba* 言葉), and form (*sugata* 姿), as in the case of the poems in *Kingyokushū* 金玉集 [*Collection of Jewels*]." Ibid., 125.

37 Ibid.

and terse form of evaluation only preludes a more elaborate and deepened exchange of views:

「巻々の中にいづれがすぐれて心にしみてめでたく覚ゆる。」と言へば、「『桐壺』に過ぎたる巻やは侍べき。「いづれの御時にか」とうち始めたるより、源氏初元結の程まで、言葉続き有様を始め、**あはれに悲しき**事この巻にこもりて侍ぞかし。『帚木』の雨夜の品定め、いと**見どころ多く**侍めり。『夕顔』は一筋にあはれに心苦しき巻にて侍るめり。『紅葉の賀』『花の宴』、とり／＼**艶におもしろく**、えも言はぬ巻々に侍べし。『葵』、い**とあはれにおもしろき**巻なり。『賢木』、伊勢の御出で立ちの程も**艶にいみじ**。院隠れさせ給ひて後、藤壺の宮様変へ給ふ程など**あわれなり**。『須磨』、**あはれにいみじき**巻なり。京を出で給ふ程の事ども、旅の御住居の程などいとあはれにこそ侍れ（後略）[38]

'Which of the chapters do you think is the best and the most moving?'

'How could there be a chapter superior to "Kiritsubo"? From its opening words, "In a certain reign…", down to Genji's coming-of-age ceremony, an **intimately sad mood** permeates this chapter as regards tone and content.'

'It seems to me that **there are many good points** in the Rainy Night Judgment in "Hahakigi".'

'"Yūgao" is a **most touching** chapter that **arouses our sympathy**.'

'"Momiji no Ga" and "Hana no En" are both **deeply interesting**; the beauty of these two chapters is too sublime for words.'

'"Aoi" is a **very moving and interesting** chapter. The passage about the departure for Ise in "Sakaki" is **fascinating and elegant**. Fujitsubo's becoming a nun after the emperor's death in **most moving**.'

'"Suma" **overflows with emotion**. The passages about Genji's leaving the capital and the places where he stayed during his journey are **really touching**'…[39]

In most cases the evaluative expression judging the respective chapter is *aware* あはれ, a term basically indicating the good and bad in Japanese poetry (*uta no zen'aku* 歌の善悪). This word ought to be noted due to its critical meaning and its application to rating of narratives. Meli remarks that "here [in *Mumyōzōshi*] is not only the question of which chapters are described, but also the more general fact that "being *aware*-like" or "being filled with *aware*" has become a criterion for positively judging the worth of literary work".[40]

---

38 *Mumyōzōshi*, 355–356.

39 Marra, "Mumyōzōshi", 137–138. All bold-faced phrases in the article are the author's emphasis.

40 Mark Meli, "'Aware' as a Critical Term in Classical Japanese Poetics," *Japan Review* 13 (2001): 74.

Fascinating, pleasant, and pitiful women

After general discussion on *Genji*'s chapters the ladies pass on to talk about various female characters. All women are mentioned not as a result of fortuitous selection, but they are classified into three categories: fascinating (*medetaki onna* めでたき女, *imijiki onna* いみじき女), pleasant (*konomoshiki hito* 好もしき人), and pitiful persons (*itooshiki hito* いとほしき人). At the very beginning the debaters enumerate the most "refined and wonderful" women.

> この若き人、「めでたき女は誰々か侍」と言へば、「桐壺の更衣、藤壺の宮、葵の上の我から心用ひ。紫の上さらなり。明石も心にくくいみじと言ふなり。又、いみじき女朧月夜の内侍のかみ。源氏流され給ふもこの人のゆゑと思へばいみじきなり。（中略）「宇治の姉宮こそ返す／＼いみじけれ。又、六条の御息所の中将こそ宮仕人の中にいみじけれ。[41]

(...) a young lady asked, 'Who are the beautiful women in Genji Monogatari?'

'The attendant Kiritsubo, the princess Fujitsubo, Aoi, who is certainly an introverted character, and of course Murasaki. Lady Akashi, too, is a **refined and wonderful** lady.'

A lady continued, 'Oborozukiyo, the Head of the Attendants, is a **warm-hearted** woman. She is a **fascinating** character when we consider that Genji was exiled on her account. ...The elder daughter of Uji is **fascinating** indeed. Among the maids, Chūjo, Lady Rokujō's attendant, is **most beautiful**.[42]

In comparison with the concise appraisal of selected chapters, the discussion becomes more precise and meaningful when the tale's characters are judged. It is not merely a simple opinion on whether something is "deeply interesting" or "most touching" but the judgement is supplemented with a more or less percipient explanation which validates mentioning of each "refined and wonderful" woman. The manner of description and evaluation of characters is even more obvious in the passage concerning "pleasant women". An example of such commentary can be provided by a presentation of Suetsumuhana, the impoverished daughter of the Prince Hitachi, who is judged from the perspective of the episode in which she waited for Genji to return from exile.

> 又、「末摘花好もしと言ふ」とて、にくみ合せ給へど、大弐の誘ふにも心強く靡かで、死にかへり、昔ながらの住居改めず、つひに待ちつけて、「深き蓬のもとの心を」とて分け入り給ふ見る程は、誰よりもめでたくぞ覚ゆる。みめより始めて、何事もなのめならむ人の為には、さばかりの事のいみじかるべきにも侍らず。その人柄には仏にならむよりも有難き宿世には侍らずや。[43]

---

41 *Mumyōzōshi*, 357.

42 Marra, "Mumyōzōshi", 140.

43 *Mumyōzōshi*, 357–358.

I know that you will all disagree with me when I say that Suetsumuhana was a **pleasant** woman. I mean, she resolutely declined Daini's invitation and, resigned to her fate, she continued waiting for Genji to the very end without moving from her old dwelling. I think that the incident of Genji's clearing a way through the wormwood, reciting, "On the deep wormwood where nobody walks…" is most impressive. Such an attitude wouldn't have been correct for a common lady, particularly with her appearance. Wasn't Suetsumuhana's destiny rarer than that of becoming a Buddha?[44]

The same way of commenting is used when the ladies criticize "pitiful women". By quoting fragments of poems or referring to specific scenes, the debaters use diverse arguments to support all their views. Moreover, they attempt to consider the appearance, attitudes and life's situation of each woman. An interesting illustration of such presentation is the discussion on Onnasannomiya:

女三の宮こそいとほしき人とも言ひつべけれど、（中略）かやうの人は、
一筋に子めかしくおほどきたればこそらうたけれ。浅ましき文、大殿に見
ゆる事も、その御心のしわざぞかし。さる事ありと思さむには、とゞまらむ
をだに強ひてそそのかし出だしてむとぞ思さるべきを、さかしらに心苦しげ
なる事ども言ひ、とゞめて（後略）[45]

'Onnasannomiya is **truly a pitiful** lady. …She does not talk like a person of her age, and I don't like the tense atmosphere of the amorous scenes.

　　'People like Onnasannomiya are **attractive** precisely because of their childish behavior. The embarrassing letter seen by the Minister Genji is the work of her heart. If she had realized the consequences of her actions, she should have broken with Genji even if he was still visiting her. Instead her coquettish behavior entranced him and kept him tied to her.[46]

As contrasted with lapidary opinions on *Genji*'s chapters, the discussion concerning various types of female characters is based on women's experiences and their relationships with men. The word "pitiful [person/lady/woman/girl]" – but also "fascinating" or "pleasant" – acts as a generally classifying phrase, whereas additional attributive expressions describing female personality, attitudes, or behaviors act as specifying phrases. The opinion on Onnasannomiya expressed in the above-quoted excerpt, which also brings out some traits of her character by asserting that people like her are sometimes "attractive precisely because of their childish behavior" or "coquettish behavior", should be regarded as of particularizing character. It lets us distinguish and familiarize with individual personalities called with one word "pitiful" as well.

44　Marra, "Mumyōzōshi", 140.

45　*Mumyōzōshi*, 359.

46　Marra, "Mumyōzōshi", 141–142.

Essay on men and *Genji*'s miscellanea

In addition to the discussion of *fujinron* ('views on women'), the *Mumyōzōshi* features a *shinasadame* of male characters. The response to the question of one of the ladies: "Among the men, who is the most wonderful?" was as difficult as in the case of women. The discussion's participants appreciated around ten most excellent noblemen. They were judged through the prism of various scenes that display and accentuate personality traits of the men. Among "the most wonderful" noblemen, Hotaru ('The Fireflies Prince', or Sochi no Miya 'The Viceroy Prince') is mentioned, who was Genji's half-brother and who performed the function of Hyōbukyō no Miya 兵部卿の宮 ('His Highness of War')

> 兵部卿の宮、さしてその、事のよしあしなどは覚えぬ人の、源氏の大臣の御兄弟いと多かる中に、とりわき御仲よくて、何事もまづ聞え合はせ給ふ、いと心にくきなり。玉鬘の御事えしえ給はぬむげに心後れたる。[47]

> 'I believe that the Minister of War has no particular merits or demerits; among Genji's many half-brothers, he enjoyed the best relationship with him. The fact that Genji always sought his advice first in every matter shows that he was a refined gentleman. His failure in his affair with Tamakazura indicates that he was a shy man.[48]

The evaluative expressions used while discussing the male characters do not differ considerably from those used while judging the female characters. The debaters refer to the dedication of the Palace Minister, Tō no Chūjo, "who was close to Genji from his youth and never parted him", to the tactfulness of Captain of the Right Guards, Kashiwagi, who was "a good man from the beginning", to Kaoru, who was "the true, ideal gentleman" and "it is rare to find a man like him, either in fiction or in reality, in the past or in the present".[49] Also Hotaru is appreciated as "a refined gentleman", but of "no particular merits or demerits".

Moreover, the male characters are portrayed in the context of male-female relationships. Like many ladies such as Oborozukiyo, Tamakazura, Asagao, Hanachirusato etc., whose fortunes and, as a result, attitudes and behaviors often relied on relations with men, also the aristocrats are being judged by the old nun's companions as characters involved in complicated relationships with women. As the ladies emphasize, the Fireflies Prince's "failure in his affair with Tamakazura indicates that he was a shy man". On the other hand, "the most tactful" Kashiwagi "becomes blameworthy when he is involved in the Onnasannomiya's affair, even at the risk of his life"[50]. In case of Yūgiri, "he wasn't fickle regarding the many marriage proposals he received. He spent his

---

47 *Mumyōzōshi*, 360–361.
48 Marra, "Mumyōzōshi", 143.
49 Ibid., 142–145.
50 Ibid., 144.

life, as he has hoped, with Kumoinokari, but then in his last years he courted the less attractive Ochiba. And so he ruined his reputation as a faithful husband (...)".[51] Commenting on all those men, the participants of the discussion make allusions and references, presumably to "female" episodes, which enable to highlight the most characteristic features of the noblemen's personalities.

The ladies not only express their subjective opinions on the *Genji*'s noblemen but also refer to someone else's criticism. For instance, an opinion on Kaoru 薫, the fruit of an adulterous union between Kashiwagi and Onnasannomiya, may serve as an illustration of such way of judging:

> 又、人、「さはあれど、気近くまめ／＼しげなる方は後れたる人にや。浮舟
> の君、巣守の中の君などの、兵部卿の宮には思ひ貶し侍るこそ口惜しけれ。
> 」と言ふなれば、[52]

> A lady interrupted her, 'You are quite right, but as far as personal relations go, is he not less friendly than Niou? It's a pity that Ukifune, Sumori no Naka no Kimi, and others consider Kaoru weaker than the Minister of War.'[53]

Kaoru's weakness is not a personality trait subjectively attributed by a participant of the dialogue. The opinion on his weakness is a result of the women's point of view that has explicitly been expressed in *Genji monogatari*, and repeated again in *Mumyōzōshi*.

It should also be mentioned that the female debaters of *amayo no shinasadame* discuss and comment on miscellaneous subject matters concerning Murasaki Shikibu's work. Issues such as moving, pitiful, inspiring jealousy, and amazing things are brought up. For instance, the emperor's sorrow at the death of Kiritsubo, Genji's mother, the scene of Yūgao's death, and "the Minister's tears on seeing Genji's writing" are judged as the most moving passages.[54] In comparison with the commentaries on specific chapters and characters in *Genji monogatari*, the discussion on miscellaneous things is supplemented with many *waka* poems. The verses are compositions of *Genji*'s characters and are used as arguments supporting judgments.

Conclusion

According to the author of *Mumyōzōshi*, literature ought to be discussed in terms of literary fiction. It should be perceived as a form of communication, entertainment, encouragement, and permanent immortalization of diverse

---

51 Ibid.
52 *Mumyōzōshi*, 362.
53 Marra, "Mumyōzōshi", 145.
54 Ibid., 281–282.

matters for the next ages. On the one hand, literature should be based on reality, and on the other hand, the text cannot be denuded of the author's imagination. Unlike poetry, narratives are not so geared towards abstract scenes. Hence, poetry is not meant as a way of meditation and religious experience.[55]

The commentaries on *Genji monogatari* in *Mumyōzōshi* have a distinctly different character than those written in other well-known treatises and studies, in which interpretations, explanations, opinions, and reflections from many centuries have been included. Due to the dialogue-form and the exchange of opinions and reflections concerning *Genji monogatari*, the comments on the tale's characters, episodes, and other texts do not constitute a sequence of subjective remarks uttered by one person and one author, but they are being co-evaluated. Therefore, literary comments on Murasaki's work, but also on other texts from the Heian period mentioned and discussed in *Mumyōzōshi*, hold a particular value. In fact, it is no exaggeration to say that they have a unique character in the early medieval period.

The work by Shunzeikyō no musume also provides an interesting insight into the perception and criticism of literary fiction by educated Japanese people of that time. *Mumyōzōshi* shows that the old court narratives, with *Genji monogatari* at the top, aroused emotions, compelled the readers to reflect on frequently intricate situations. In this respect, it is difficult to find a critical work similar to *Mumyōzōshi* among the scholarly commentaries on *Genji* from the early medieval period. In addition to extensive quotations from Murasaki Shikibu's work, philological commentaries include also their authors' annotations, but generally do not include their subjective remarks. The common reader appreciates *Mumyōzōshi* for its noteworthy way of commenting on scenes and characters of *Genji monogatari*. As a result of the use of a dialogue as a means of *shinasadame*, 'evaluation', and of the interpretation of the Murasaki's masterpiece, *Mumyōzōshi* cannot be acknowledged as a philological or (quasi-)scholarly work, but rather as the earliest literary critical commentary on *Genji monogatari*.

Bibliography

Davis, Ryan C. "The Fate of Being a Woman." In *Feminist Writings from Ancient Times to the Modern World: A Global Sourcebook and History*, ed. by Tiffany K. Wayne. Santa Barbara – Oxford: Greenwood, 2011.
Keene, Donald. *Seeds in the Heart. Japanese Literature from Earliest Times to the Late Sixteenth Century*. New York: Columbia Univiversity Press, 1999.

---

55   Ibid., 128.

Kikuta, Shigeo 菊田茂男. "«Genji monogatari» Hotaru no maki no monogatariron 「源氏物語」 蛍の巻の物語論." *Bunka* 文化 30, no. 2 (1966): 96–136.

Kordzińska-Nawrocka, Iwona. *Japońska miłość dworska* [Japanese Court Love]. Warszawa: Wydawnictwo Trio, 2005.

Kordzińska-Nawrocka, Iwona. "Wieczorna rozmowa bohaterów 'Genji monogatari' a kulturowy wzorzec kobiecości w społeczeństwie dworskim." In *W kręgu tradycji dworu Heian* [In the Circle of Heian Court Tradition], ed. Iwona Kordzińska-Nawrocka. Warszawa: Wydawnictwo Trio, Warszawa 2008.

Marra, Michele. "Mumyōzōshi: Introduction and Translation." *Monumenta Nipponica* 39 (1984): 115–145, 281–305, 409–434.

Melanowicz, Mikołaj. *Od VI do połowy XIX wieku*. Vol. 1 of *Literatura japońska* [Japanese Literature, from the 6th to the Middle of the 19th Century]. Warszawa: Wydawnictwo Naukowe PWN, 1994.

Miner, Earl R., Morrell, Robert E., and Odagiri, Hiroko. *The Princeton Companion to Classical Japanese Literature*. Princeton: Princeton University Press, 1988.

Mumyōzōshi. In *Kodai chūsei geijutsuron* 古代中世芸論 [Theories of Ancient and Medieval Art]), ed. by Hayashi Tatsusaburō, vol. 23 of *Nihon shisō taikei* 日本思想体系. Tōkyō: Iwanami shoten, 1973.

Murasaki, Shikibu. *The Tale of Genji*, vol. 1, trans. Edward G. Seidensticker. Tokyo: Tuttle Company, 1987.

Okada, H. Richard. "Fujiwara Shunzei's Daughter." In *Japanese Women Writers: A Bio-critical Sourcebook*, ed. by Chieko I. Mulhern. Westport Conn.: Greenwood Press, 1994.

Rohlich, Thomas H. "In Search of Critical Space: The Path to Monogatari Criticism in the Mumyozoshi." *Harvard Journal of Asiatic Studies* 57 (1997): 179–204.

Shirane, Haruo. *Envisioning the Tale of Genji: Media, Gender, and Cultural Production*. New York: Columbia University Press, 2013.

Takehara, Hiroshi 武原 弘. "Genji monogatari shudairon yobi kōsetsu: Hahakigi maki 'amayo no sadame' joseiron no shudaisei ni tsuite 『源氏物語』 主題論予備考説: 帚木巻 「雨夜の品定め」 女性論の主題性について." *Nihon bungaku kenkyū* 日本文学研究 34 (1999): 1–12.

Tyler, Royall. "'Sagoromo' and 'Hamamatsu' on 'Genji': Eleventh-Century Tales as Commentary on 'Genji monogatari'." *Japan Review* 18 (2006): 3–28.

Andrew of Caesarea's Commentary on the Book of Revelation and Its Role in Medieval Orthodox Slavonic Literature

Paweł Dziadul

Institute of Slavonic Philology,
Adam Mickiewicz University, Poznań

Every culture seems to be a hierarchically organized system composed of "layers". Texts (in their semiotic meaning) which enjoy the greatest respect are usually situated at the top of that system. The Bible became the most respected text in Christianity, determining the homogeneity and cultural universality of Christian medieval Europe. It was believed that the divine act of creation presented in the Holy Scripture has a continuous character, therefore biblical books, their symbols, ideas, imagery, etc. were constantly actualized and updated in the Middle Ages. In the medieval, universal model of the world, every historical event was thought to be a reflection of "holy events". That is why human history was considered a planned (and encoded in biblical prophecies) "history of salvation" from the Creation until the Second Coming of Christ. It was necessary to understand its sense by decoding biblical books; Christian exegesis became a universal device for this.

There is no need to discuss the specific background of the process of developing the Christian exegetical tradition in the Christian East (where the Greek philosophical heritage played a crucial role), owing to the specificity of the Orthodox Slavonic theological and ecclesiastic milieu. Despite the fact that the South and East Slavs adopted cultural patterns from Byzantium, knowledge of Greek philosophy was rather minimal; in consequence, many Greek exegetical works, even in Slavonic translations, were incomprehensible. Exegetical texts, especially commentaries on the *Book of Daniel* and the *Book of Revelation*, were not very popular among the Orthodox Slavs in the Middle Ages. Commentaries on the *Book of Daniel* and the *Book of Revelation* were especially important in the Byzantine culture because they influenced the creation of the specific politico-theological program of the East Roman Empire, based on the idea of a universal empire and on the theory of the succession of world monarchies, which were later reinterpreted by the Slavs according to their needs and circumstances. As for commentaries on the *Book of Daniel*, only

Hippolytus' third-century work was known[1] (some passages of the *Izbornik of 1073* and the *Primary Chronicle* were influenced by it). Moreover, there was a Slavonic translation of Hippolytus' work *On Christ and the Antichrist*[2] (the oldest Slavonic copy dates from the twelfth century[3]). Despite the fact that it is a rather dogmatic work, it has an exegetical character to a great extent, as Hippolytus tried to explain and interpret many fragments of the *Revelation* enriching the text with anti-Roman undertones.[4] As for exegetical literature on the *Revelation*, Andrew of Caesarea's (Archbishop of Caesarea in Cappadocia) commentary from the late sixth or the early seventh century was translated into Old Church Slavonic and its oldest copy in a condensed or abbreviated form (some sections and patristic quotations were removed)[5] comes from the mid-thirteenth century. Andrew's commentary is to be found in the so-called Nikol'skij Apocalypse Codex[6] (originally from Novgorod), the oldest existing Slavonic manuscript containing the text, now in the Library of the Russian Academy of Sciences in St Petersburg (the "Nikol'skij's collection", MS. 1). However, there are evident signs of the existence of Andrew's commentary on the Orthodox Slavonic territory much earlier. The Slavonic translation may have come into being as far back as the ninth or tenth century. Archaic linguistic features indicate that it was originally written in Glagolitic letters. It is possible that a commentary on the *Apocalypse* appeared in the Moravian milieu or in the

---

1 Gerhard Podskalsky, *Byzantinische Reichseschatologie: Die Periodisierung der Weltgeschichte in den vier Grossreichen (Daniel 2 und 7) und dem tausendjährigen Friedensreiche (Apok. 20): Eine motivgeschichtliche Untersuchung* (München: Wilhelm Fink, 1972), 66.

2 Измаил И. Срезневский, *Сказания об антихристе в славянских переводах с замечанями о славянских переводах творений св. Ипполита* (Санкт-Петербург: Типография императорской академии наук, 1874), 1 –30.

3 MS. 12 the collection of Chudovsky monastery, the State Historical Museum in Moscow (the manuscript contains also the Old Slavonic translation of Hippolytus' commentary on the *Book of Daniel*).

4 It is possible that Hippolytus wrote a separate commentary on the *Book of Revelation*. See: Dominika Budzanowska and Waldemar Linke, eds., *Pierwsze łacińskie komentarze do Apokalipsy: Hipolit, Wiktoryn, Hieronim, Tykoniusz* (Warszawa: Wydawnictwo Uniwersytetu Kardynała Stefana Wyszyńskiego, 2011), 30–32.

5 Eugenia Scarvells Constantinou, ed. and transl., *Andrew of Caesarea: Commentary on the Apocalypse* (Washington: the Catholic University of America Press, 2011), 40.

6 See: Thomas Hilary Oller, *The Nikol'skij Apocalypse Codex and Its Place in the Textual History of Medieval Slavic Apocalypse Manuscripts* (Providence: Brown University Press, 1993).

Russian lands[7], but it was probably translated in the South Slavonic area, as unquestionable evidence of its existence comes from the eleventh-century Bulgaria.

As opposed to the *Book of Daniel*, the canonical status and credibility of the *Apocalypse* attributed to Saint John was undermined in the Christian East. There are two major consequences of the early doubts. Firstly, the *Revelation* played no direct role in the Orthodox liturgy; it has no place in the lectionary cycle. Secondly, Greek commentaries on the *Book* did not appear before the sixth century, as opposed to the Christian West, where exegetes began to comment on it in the fourth century or even earlier (Victorinus of Pettau, Caesarius of Arles, Cassiodorus, Ticonius and others). The *Revelation* raised doubts in the Christian East owing to the fact that the text was often used by various sects and heretical movements. Despite the fact that the *Revelation* was finally acknowledged as a canonical book (it was the last book to be accepted as a part of the Christian biblical canon), it has always enjoyed greater respect in the Latin West, which accepted it at the council of Carthage in 397 (or later a council in 419), while the Christian East at the council in Trullo in 692. It is worth mentioning that the *Revelation* is generally considered as a book not used in the liturgical practice of the Orthodox Church. However, there are some interesting exceptions. For instance, there is a reading from the *Apocalypse* (Rev. 12:7–12) in the Pskov Parimeinik from 1271 designed for an evening service during the feast of Saint Michael the Archangel. It is possible to find the *Revelation* in some copies of the Jerusalem Typicon (instructions referring to readings for an all-night vigil after the blessing of breads). Furthermore, the *Book* is read in the Greek Church on the eighth (twenty-first) of May during the Feast of John the Theologian.

There are only two basic Greek commentaries on the *Apocalypse,* written by Oecumenius and Andrew of Caesarea[8], with the exception of Arethas of Caesarea (the ninth/tenth century), who was rather a compiler, and later post-Byzantine commentaries from the Ottoman period. Oecumenius was a direct predecessor of Andrew, whose commentary is sometimes regarded as a kind of response to the former's exegetical work. Andrew's commentary is the most important interpretation of the *Revelation*; he formed the ecclesiastical tradition of the *Revelation* exegesis by creating an Orthodox and Chalcedonian commentary, designed to calm apocalyptic fears.[9] Andrew's commentary reveals the attitude to

---

7   Анатолий А. Алексеев, Ольга П. Лихачёва, "К текстологической истории древнеславянского Апокалипсиса," in М. В. Кукушкина, ed. *Материалы и сообщения по фондам Отдела рукописной книги* (Ленинград: Академия наук СССР, 1987), 8–22.

8   His commentary on the *Apocalypse* was published in: *Patrologia Graeca*, vol. 106, cols. 215–457.

9   Eugenia Scarvells Constantinou, ed. and transl., *Andrew of Caesarea*, 10–11.

eschatology typical of the Eastern Christianity: paschal, pastoral, and liturgical elements prevail over the pessimistic, gloomy, and apocalyptic ones.

The popularity of Andrew's commentary contributed to the manuscript transmission of the *Apocalypse*. The existence of the commentary increased the number of the *Apocalypse* copies and resulted in a unique text type known as the Andreas text type in the Byzantine and Orthodox Slavonic manuscript tradition. Generally, Andrew's work functioned in three main variants: complete, condensed, and "intermediate".[10] The *Revelation* was copied either separately or together with Andrew's commentary (in this case, each verse of the *Book* was followed by explanatory comments). The latter form was typical especially of the East Slavonic manuscript tradition. A commented type of the *Apocalypse* (*Апокалипсис толковый*), i.e. with Andrew's commentary, existed in diverse codices and differed in contents. For example, there were codices with patristic and monastic contents (the *Apocalypse* with the commentary can be found among the works of John of Damascus, Gregory of Nazianzus, Philip Monotropos and others, for example, in MS. 122 from the fifteenth century from the collection of the Trinity Lavra, the Russian State Library in Moscow), codices with apocalyptic contents (the *Apocalypse* with the commentary is to be found among such works as: the *Apocalypse of Pseudo-Methodius*, the *Life of Andrew the Fool*, the *Life of Basil the New* and others, for example, in MS. BOZ 92 from the fifteenth-sixteenth century, the National Library of Poland in Warsaw), codices with hymnography (MS. 120 from the end of the fourteenth century from the collection of the Trinity Lavra, the Russian State Library in Moscow). The *Apocalypse* with the commentary was also incorporated into Macarius' *Great Menaion Reader* (*Великие Четьи-минеи*), containing hagiographies.[11] These codices provide only few examples of the use of the commentary; the list is intended as and outline for further consideration rather than a comprehensive treatment of the subject.

It is possible to find evidence of early existence of Andrew's commentary on the Orthodox Slavonic territory in an Old Bulgarian apocryphal work created during the eleventh-century Byzantine domination. There is one interesting passage in the apocalyptic work known as the *Interpretation of Daniel*, directly influenced by Andrew's commentary and his interpretation of the theory of the succession of world monarchies[12], which served as a model for periodization of

---

10 Ibid., 41–42.

11 *Великия Минеи Четии, собранныя всероссийском митрополитом Макарием. Сентябрь* (Санкт-Петербург:Типография императорской академии наук, 1883), 1696–1795.

12 Gerhard Podskalsky, *Byzantinische Reichseschatologie*, 86–88.

time. Like Andrew of Caesarea, the anonymous Bulgarian author reinterpreted the theory of succession which usually embraced a model of four monarchies by substituting them with seven kingdoms, in keeping with chapter seventeen of the *Revelation* in which the image of a beast with seven heads and ten horns, symbolizing seven kings (kingdoms), appears: "they are seven kings, of whom five have fallen, one is living, and the other has not yet come; and when he comes, he must remain for only a little while. As for the beast that was and is not, it is an eighth but it belongs to the seven, and it goes to destruction" (Rev. 17:9–11). The Archbishop of Caesarea provided his own interpretation that identified the "kings" with successive monarchies, comprehended as seven places in which at particular times the ruling kingdoms of the world were established ("the seven famous kingdoms are the famous ones from the beginning until now, of which five already have fallen and the sixth, during which the Revelation was seen, was the one during the old Rome, and the seventh has not yet come, i.e. the one in the New [Rome]"[13]): Assyria, Media, Babylonia, Persia, Macedonia, the pagan Rome (Old Rome) and the Christian New Rome (Byzantium). This corresponded to another periodization model typical of the Christian East. It was believed that the world history was divided into "seven ages" ("seven thousands") which reflected the week of creation from the *Book of Genesis* (each thousand years comprised a "day") and the *Second Epistle of Peter*: "one day is like a thousand years, and a thousand years are like one day" (2 Pet. 3:8, cf. Ps. 90:4). Andrew claimed that "after the passage of the six ages during the days of the seventh age, meaning the time of the seventh trumpet, the things said by the holy prophets to happen before the end of time will receive their end. The good news is the fulfillment of these things by the preparation of the repose of the saints".[14] The seventh age, symbolized by the seventh trumpet of the *Revelation* (10:7), was identified by Andrew with the messianic period foretold by the Old Testament prophets (the messianic promises such as: a return of theocracy, a new holy alliance, restoration of the house of David and Israel; see: Isa. 55: 3–5; Jer. 31:31; Ezek. 37:26) and by Saint John in the vision of the thousand-year kingdom (Rev. 20:5–6) – the repose of the saints, "eschatological Saturday" before "Sunday", the resurrection comprehended as the eternal "eighth age" in the Heavenly Kingdom. Andrew referred to earlier chronological theories of Hippolytus or Irenaeus, who

---

13 Eugenia Scarvells Constantinou, ed. and transl., *Andrew of Caesarea*, 187. Cf. Андрей Кесарийский, *Толкование на Апокалипсис святого Иоанна Богослова* (Минск: Белорусский Дом печати, 2009), 157.

14 Eugenia Scarvells Constantinou, ed. and transl., *Andrew of Caesarea*, 129. Cf. Андрей Кесарийский, *Толкование на Апокалипсис*, 89.

believed in the end of time after 6000 years "from the creation of the world", although the Archbishop of Caesarea tried to allay apocalyptic or even chiliastic expectations, being rather uncertain about the length of time.

Andrew listed seven kings associated with the seven kingdoms ("Nino of the Assyrians, Arbaces of the Medians, Nebuchadnezzar of the Babylonians, Cyrus of the Persians, Alexander of the Macedonians, Romulus of the ancient Rome, and Constantine of the New Rome"[15]), but the author of the Old Bulgarian *Interpretation of Daniel* modified it a little: "first was Senil among the Assyrians; second – Avarak in Rome, third Nebuchadnezzar in Babylon; fourth – Cyrus among the Persians; fifth Alexander among the Greeks; sixth Romulus in Rome; seventh Constantine in Constantinople".[16] But the most important and crucial innovation in the theory of succession occurs in the passage where the author of the apocryphal work describes the "beginning of the sorrows" before the coming of the Antichrist, Parousia, and the end of the world: "And when the beginning of the sorrows of the whole world comes, Michael Kagan will arise among the Bulgarians. And the Bulgarians were not given a kingdom but they took it by force".[17] The character of Michael with a proto-Bulgarian title "kagan" probably refers to Prince Boris-Michael, who is connected here with the theory of succession and presented as "the last emperor", a specific *topos* of Byzantine-Slavonic apocalyptic literature (it originally appeared in the *Apocalypse of Pseudo-Methodius of Patara*).[18] According to Andrew, the last world monarchy seemed to be Byzantium (New Rome), although the Bulgarian author set "the last ruler" – Michael – between Byzantium and the Antichrist's reign. He tried to show the specific position of Bulgaria, the history of which was happening before the "end of time". Bulgaria is conceived as the last kingdom in human history, existing after the downfall of the seventh empire, Byzantium. Moreover, Bulgaria is presented here as if it existed besides the seven world kingdoms. Generally speaking, the theory of succession of world kingdoms gained popularity in Bulgarian apocalyptic literature in the eleventh century and flourished during Byzantine domination, when we observe a sudden

---

15   Eugenia Scarvells Constantinou, ed. and transl., *Andrew of Caesarea*, 186. Cf. Андрей Кесарийский, *Толкование на Апокалипсис*, 157.

16   VasilkaTapkova-Zaimova and Anisava Miltenova, *Historical and Apocalyptic Literature in Byzantium and Medieval Bulgaria*, transl. M. Paneva, M. Lilova (Sofia: Изток–Запад, 2011), 181.

17   Ibid., 181.

18   Paul Alexander, *The Byzantine Apocalyptic Tradition* (Berkeley: University of California Press, 1982), 151-184. András Kraft, "The Last Roman Emperor Topos in the Byzantine Apocalyptic Tradition," *Byzantion* 82 (2012): 213–257.

outbreak of eschatological and messianic moods[19], a fact which resulted from the coincidence of several factors such as destabilization caused by Byzantine domination, the Crusades, and the passage of thousand years from Christ in the half of the seventh millennium (=6500 "from Adam").[20] Another outbreak of eschatological moods in the Bulgarian lands appeared in the first half of the thirteenth century – this time it was linked to the Fourth Crusade, the fall of Constantinople (1204), and then the council of Lyon (1274). The Bulgarian empire started functioning as an heir to Byzantium and a guardian of orthodoxy, a fact which was reflected in the new cycle of apocalyptic works. It is possible to find the influence of Andrew's commentary in one of them – the *Vision of Prophet Isaiah of the last times*.[21] First of all, this Bulgarian apocalyptic apocryphal text demonstrates similar lexis to the first Slavonic translation of Andrew's work.[22] References to Andrew's commentary in Old Bulgarian apocalyptic apocryphal literature demonstrate that the line between "official" and "unofficial" literature was unusually changeable, flexible and unstable, a fact which facilitated the exchange of ideas, symbols and imagery, especially in the field of apocalyptic literature.

Andrew's commentary was reinterpreted by Slavonic authors to prove the legitimacy of eschatological ideas flourishing in the context of apocalyptic moods or fears. Moreover, Andrew's commentary, his theories, and imagery became an immanent part of the normative system inherited by the Orthodox Slavs from Byzantine culture. It is a well-known fact that when studying the Orthodox Slavonic literature of the Middle Ages, one notices unchanging compositional and stylistic elements, rhetorical devices, and typical methods of interpreting historical events, which resulted from the religious conception of literature. Medieval authors tried to highlight the continuity of salvation, and therefore they followed and imitated patterns in literature; such strategy is known as "literary etiquette", and it connects the contents of a literary text with

---

19   VasilkaTapkova-Zaimova and Anisava Miltenova, *Historical and Apocalyptic Literature*, 27-57. Иван Билярски, *Сказание на Исайя пророка и формирането на политическата идеология на ранносредновековна България* (София: ПАМ Пъблишинг Къмпани ООД, 2011), 55–70.

20   Depending on chronological calculations, there were different dates of the supposed end of the world in Old Bulgarian prophecies, for instance: 992 AD, 1025 AD, 1042 AD.

21   VasilkaTapkova-Zaimova and Anisava Miltenova, *Historical and Apocalyptic Literature*, 338–345.

22   Ангел Николов, „Някои проблеми на държавно-политическата и етническата терминология в два средновековни славянски превода на тълковния апокалипсис," *Кирило-Методиевски студии* 17 (2007): 506.

its form.[23] This influenced the rhetorical framework of medieval Orthodox literature. A medieval author had to find an analogy from the "holy history" to maintain the "rational" order of Christian history. Those analogies could be derived from texts perceived as "sacred", inspired by God, usually biblical or patristic, but due to the blurred line between the "official" and "unofficial" literature, they could be of apocryphal origin as well (of course, apocryphal from the modern point of view).

One passage from the *Galician-Volhynian Chronicle* (the oldest copy in the *Hypatian Codex*), covering the period from 1201 to 1292, provides an example of such specific medieval analogies. We find the influence of Andrew's commentary in the presentation of events taking place in the year 1205. The author of the *Chronicle* tried to describe the situation in Halych, where the Hungarian palatine, Benedict, arrived with soldiers sent by King Andrew II of Hungary, who wanted to take advantage of the chaos and anarchy in the city.[24] Benedict's arrival and visit in the city are presented in an extremely negative way. The character and the context of his activities are interpreted by Timothy, the Galician writer originally from Kiev, through the prism of Andrew of Caesarea's theories on the Antichrist, which referred to chapter 13 of the *Revelation*: "This calls for wisdom: let anyone with understanding calculate the number of the beast, for it is the number of a person. Its number is six hundred and sixty-six" (13:18). Timothy was called a "very wise man of letters" (*премудръ книжникъ*), a term which had a specific meaning in Old Russian and generally Old Church Slavonic literature; it designated a person who was able to explain enigmatic and mysterious passages of the Holy Scripture, as in the case of the passage about the number associated with the beast. Timothy, then, was presented as a gifted exegete, despite the fact that he only connected Andrew's conceptions with a concrete situation. Owing to his disgraceful activities, Benedict was associated with the Antichrist, who would take on three names in the "last times".[25] Referring to former works by Hippolytus (*On Christ and the Antichrist*) and Irenaeus (*Adversus Haereses*)[26], Andrew of Caesarea claimed that there were many names contained in the apocalyptic number six hundred and sixty-six (a specific system of numerology assigning a numerical

---

23 Dmitrij Lichaczow, *Poetyka literatury staroruskiej*, transl. A. Prus-Bogusławski (Warszawa: PWN, 1981), 88–112.

24 *Библиотека литературы древней Руси* (Санкт-Петербург: Наука, 2005), 5:188.

25 Ibid., 188.

26 Hippolytus and Irenaeus mentioned three names which contained the required apocalyptic beast's number six hundred sixty-six: Evanthas, Teitan and Lateinos. According to both authors, the name – Lateinos was the most crucial, because it referred to the "last kingdom" (of the four seen by Daniel) indicating the Roman Empire.

value to a word, *gematria*, was employed) such as Lampetis, Teitan, Lateinos, or Benedict, interpreted as "one who is blessed or blessed perhaps in imitation of the truly blessed one, Christ our God".[27]

As noted previously, Andrew's commentary became especially popular among the Orthodox Slavs in periods of vivid eschatological moods, usually triggered by destabilizing factors such as wars, catastrophes, epidemics, significant symbolic dates, and Catholic proclivities toward union with the Orthodox Church. Those proclivities often caused strong anti-Latin and anti-Catholic attitudes, which began to flourish in Muscovite Rus' from the second half of the fifteenth to the first half of the sixteenth century. They resulted, *inter alia*, as a response to the council of Florence (1439) and to the expansion of Polish-Lithuanian Catholic culture. It was believed that the Greeks betrayed the orthodoxy during the council and that the fall of Constantinople in 1453 was a "logical" result of that. In general, all Orthodox lands had been conquered by the Ishmaelites (the Ottoman Turks), therefore Muscovy became the sole guardian of the Orthodox Church and was burdened with a particular mission; this view is reflected, for example, in Philotheus of Pskov's polemical letter to Misuria Munekhin (the *Letters Against Astrologers*; 1523/1524), which was created to counter Nicolas Bulev's pro-Catholic and pro-union theories. This is the first formulation of the idea of the "third Rome" identified not with the city, Moscow, but rather with the country, Muscovy. According to the Pskovian monk, all the Christian tsardoms came to an end and were gathered in one tsardom – the Roman tsardom identified with the "third Rome", Muscovy[28]; because two Romes have fallen, the third stands, and the fourth will not be. The old (first) Rome fell into the Apollinarian heresy (the usage of unleavened bread in the church service), the second Rome (Byzantium) fell due to the betrayal of orthodoxy at the council of Florence. In general, Philotheus referred to the theory of the succession of world monarchies in a manner characteristic of the Byzantine exegetical tradition, in which a particular, providential Roman mission was propagated (Rome initiated by the Messiah). Rome was interpreted as the universal kingdom of Christ, which was transferred to Muscovy[29] after the fall of the first and the second Rome, a fact which was understood not in political, but rather ecclesiastical and confessional terms.

---

27 Eugenia Scarvells Constantinou, ed. and transl., *Andrew of Caesarea*, 154. Cf. Андрей Кесарийский, *Толкование на Апокалипсис*, 120.

28 Pierangelo Catalano and Vladimir Pašuto, eds., *Идея Рима в Москве XV – XVI века: Источники по истории русской общественной мысли: L'idea di Roma a Mosca secoli XV – XVI: Fonti per la storia del pensiero sociale russo.* (Roma: Herder Editrice e Libreria, 1989), 145.

29 Ibid., 145.

In reference to one passage in the *Revelation*, the Pskovian monk claimed that the Church – "a woman clothed with the sun" (Rev. 12:1) – was saved in the "third Rome" from the dragon and the infidels, who had captured other Orthodox lands. Therefore, the Church found, according to him, its pure place – the "wilderness", where it should exist until the end of time (because the fourth Rome "will not be"; „четвертому не быти"[30]). The theory of the "third Rome" was developed in other works such as the *Letter About the Sign of the Cross* (about 1524 – 1526) and the *Work About the Offences* (the 1530s or 1540s). In the latter work, the anonymous author changed the original sense of the idea of the "third Rome", which was transformed from an optimistic prophecy of the future to an apocalyptic warning. Referring to the twelfth chapter of the *Revelation* in the interpretation of Andrew of Caesarea[31], the author speaks directly about transfer of the Church, which stands for "pure faith" (the orthodoxy) from the first Rome to the second one, and later to the "third Rome" („иже есть в новую Великую Русию"[32]), identified with the "wilderness" from the *Revelation* (12:6). However, it was not an idyllic place, but rather one of insufficient faith.[33] The author highlighted the sins of the "third Rome" and interpreted them as signs of the "end of times". Nevertheless, the "third Rome", Muscovy, still seemed to be the only truthful mainstay of the orthodoxy and faith, guarded and saved by a Muscovite sovereign.[34] The author wanted to issue a warning against the greatest danger, namely an infringement of the "sacred tradition" or an abandonment of the "third Rome's" mission.

The new identity of Muscovy and its specific ideological program, which was eschatological in nature, crystalized after the expiry of the apocalyptic atmosphere at the end of the fifteenth and the beginning of the sixteenth century. Andrew's commentary could play a crucial role in "eschatological polemics" because it offered traditional Eastern patristic exegesis of the subject of the "last times". This is why his theories were used to counterbalance strictly apocalyptic conceptions connected usually with pessimistic fears and imagery, and awaiting of the Parousia and the Last Judgment. The Archbishop of Caesarea rejected a literal exegesis of the *Revelation* in favour of a spiritual one, claiming that Christians should not speculate about when the end of the world will arrive. Moreover, he did not apply the symbols of the *Revelation* to specific events or

---

30 Ibid., 147.

31 Eugenia Scarvells Constantinou, ed. and transl., *Andrew of Caesarea*, 141. Cf. Андрей Кесарийский, *Толкование на Апокалипсис*, 105.

32 Pierangelo Catalano and Vladimir Pašuto, eds., *Идея Рима в Москве*, 171.

33 Александр Л. Гольдберг, "Три послания Филофея: Опыт текстологического анализа." *Труды отдела древнерусской литературы* 29 (1974): 90–91.

34 Pierangelo Catalano and Vladimir Pašuto, eds., *Идея Рима в Москве*, 171.

dates, despite the fact that he believed that he was living in the seventh and final age, in the era of the final kingdom.[35] He concluded that the end of the world was not near, offering a typical Orthodox and traditional interpretation, since the Orthodox Church, as opposed to common worshippers, whose imagination was often inspired by apocalyptic apocryphal literature, has never specified a concrete date of the Second Coming of Christ based on the Bible and patristic writings. The *Book of Revelation* has been treated suspiciously in the Christian East for a long time, but Andrew of Caesarea helped to resolve doubts. Still, Saint John's work has always enjoyed greater popularity in the Latin West, both on the literary and iconographic levels.

Bibliography

Alexander, Paul. *The Byzantine Apocalyptic Tradition*. Berkeley: University of California Press, 1982.

Budzanowska, Dominika and Waldemar Linke, eds. *Pierwsze łacińskie komentarze do Apokalipsy: Hipolit, Wiktoryn, Hieronim, Tykoniusz* [First Latin Commentaries on Apocalypse...]. Warszawa: Wydawnictwo Uniwersytetu Kardynała Stefana Wyszyńskiego, 2011.

Catalano, Pierangelo and Vladimir Pašuto, eds. Идея Рима в Москве XV – XVI века: Источники по истории русской общественной мысли: L'idea di Roma a Mosca secoli XV – XVI: Fonti per la storia del pensiero sociale russo. Roma: Herder Editrice e Libreria, 1989.

Kraft András. "The Last Roman Emperor Topos in the Byzantine Apocalyptic Tradition." *Byzantion* 82 (2012): 213–257.

Lichaczow, Dmitrij. *Poetyka literatury staroruskiej* [Poetics of Old Russian Literature], trans. A. Prus-Bogusławski. Warszawa: PWN, 1981.

Oller, Thomas. The Nikol'skij Apocalypse Codex and Its Place in the Textual History of Medieval Slavic Apocalypse Manuscripts. Providence: Brown University Press, 1993.

Podskalsky, Gerhard. Byzantinische Reichseschatologie: Die Periodisierung der Weltgeschichte in den vier Grossreichen (Daniel 2 und 7) und dem tausendjährigen Friedensreiche (Apok. 20): Eine motivgeschichtliche Untersuchung. München: Wilhelm Fink, 1972.

Scarvells Constantinou, Eugenia, ed. and trans. *Andrew of Caesarea: Commentary on the Apocalypse*. Washington: the Catholic University of America Press, 2011.

Tapkova-Zaimova, Vasilka and Anisava Miltenova. *Historical and Apocalyptic Literature in Byzantium and Medieval Bulgaria*, trans. M. Paneva, M. Lilova. Sofia: Изток-Запад, 2011.

---

35 Eugenia Scarvells Constantinou, ed. and transl., *Andrew of Caesarea*, 38.

Алексеев, Анатолий А. and Ольга П. Лихачева. "К текстологической истории древнеславянского Апокалипсиса." In *Материалы и сообщения по фондам Отдела рукописной книги*, ed. М. В. Кукушкина. Ленинград: Академия наук СССР, 1987, 8–22.

Библиотека литературы древней Руси. Vol. 5. Санкт-Петербург: Наука, 2005.

Билярски, Иван. Сказание на Исайя пророка и формирането на политическата идеология на ранносредновековна България. София: ПАМ Пъблишинг Къмпани ООД, 2011.

Великия Минеи Четии, собранныя всероссийском митрополитом Макарием. Сентябрь (Санкт-Петербург:Типография императорской академии наук, 1883).

Гольдберг, Александр Л. "Три послания Филофея (опыт текстологического анализа)." *Труды отдела древнерусской литературы* 29 (1974): 68–97.

Кесарийский, Андрей. *Толкование на Апокалипсис святого Иоанна Богослова*. Минск: Белорусский Дом печати, 2009.

Николов, Ангел. "Някои проблеми на държавно-политическата и етническата терминология в два средновековни славянски превода на тълковния апокалипсис." *Кирило-Методиевски студии* 17 (2007): 505–512.

Срезневский, Измаил И. Сказания об антихристе в славянских переводах с замечанями о славянских переводах творений св. Ипполита. Санкт-Петербург: Типография императорской академии наук, 1874.

Hieronymus' Revision of Victorinus' Commentary and Augustine's Summary of Tyconius' *Rules*

Dominika Budzanowska

Institute of Classical Philology and Culture Studies,
Cardinal Stefan Wyszyński University in Warsaw

Hieronymus of Stridon (Saint Jerome), who produced many commentaries on Scriptures, did not write one on the *Apocalypse*. Yet, he composed the *Recensio*, a revision of an earlier Latin commentary on the Apocalypse by Victorinus of Poetovio, who was a chiliastic exegete. Augustine of Hippo (Saint Augustine), on the other hand, summarized and discussed a work of Tyconius, titled *Book of Rules* (*Liber regularum*), in his *On Christian Doctrine* (*De doctrina Christiana*; abbreviated *DC*). Tyconius, a Donatist exegete, wanted to give rules – „the keys" – for understanding of the Bible. The both texts provide examples of how the great Doctors of the Church of Rome summarized and commented on works written by theologians representing a contested interpretation of the Christian faith. Hieronymus appreciated Victorinus' *Commentary on the Apocalypse* and Augustine read with respect Tyconius' *Book of Rules*, though both felt obliged to exercise caution and correct non-Catholic interpretations in several points.

I. Victorinus and Hieronymus

Victorinus of Poetovio lived in the second half of the third century and was martyred during the Great Persecution of Diocletian in 304. He was probably Greek, as Hieronymus says in *On Illustrious Men* (*De viris illustribus*).[1] Victorinus was a bishop of the city of Poetovio (Poetovium or Poetavium; modern Ptuj, Slovenia).[2] As the first Latin-writing exegete of the Bible, he commented on some books of the Old Testament (*Genesis, Exodus, Leviticus, Isaiah, Ezekiel, Habakkuk, Ecclesiastes, Song of Songs*), but only fragments of few of these commentaries are extant (for instance, a fragment of *On the Creation of the World* (*De fabrica mundi*), a commentary on *Genesis* 1[3]). His

---

1   Cf. Hieronymus, *De viris illustribus* 74; ed. E. Richardson, Leipzig, 1896.

2   Cf. ibid.

3   Text[s], ed. by M. Dulaey, in: Sources Chrétiennes (SCh) 423, Paris, Éd. du Cerf (1997); *De fabrica mundi* ed. by J. Haussleiter, Corpus Scriptorum Ecclesiasticorum Latinorum (CSEL), vol. 49 [Vindobonae – Lipsiae], 1916), 1–9.

only commentary that survived almost complete is dedicated to the last book of the New Testament; it was written in 260 and is an exception among his exegetical writings.

As a Holy Martyr, Victorinus joined the chorus of Saints of the Catholic Church, despite his chiliastic belief that the Earthly Kingdom is coming. The Millennialism (or the Chiliasm), from Latin *mille* and Greek *chilios* ('thousand'), was a doctrine that understood the thousand years of Christ literally; the main inspiration for this belief was Apocalypse 20–21. The Chiliasts believed that before the end of the world there will be a thousand-year reign of Christ and His saints (who will emerge from dead), during which Christ will finally overcome Satan and enter His eternal glory.[4] The idea of Messiah's kingdom was rooted in Jewish tradition.[5] Among Christian proponents of the Millennialism were Papias, Justin, Irenaeus, Tertullian, Hippolytus of Rome, Methodius of Olympus, and, in the 12th century, Joachim of Fiore; the doctrine's opponents were Clement of Rome, Hermas, Dionysius of Alexandria, Cyprian, Origen, and Ephrem. Early Christian writers (known as Patristic Writers or Church Fathers) interpreted the *Revelation* in various ways – literally, symbolically, or allegorically, which led them to divergent conclusions and gave birth to theological mistakes. The Catholic Church regards the Millennialism as *doctrina erronea* (but not as a heresy).[6]

Victorinus' work was the first Latin commentary on the *Apocalypse* in the West. It is a concise commentary, at times of a summarizing character, but comprehensive – it discusses the whole of the *Apocalypse*. Although Hieronymus appreciated Victorinus' achievement, he decided to write a revision of his *Commentary on the Apocalypse*; his *Recensio* is dated to 398. Consequently, we have two versions of Victorinus' commentary: his original text (edited in 1916[7]) and the Hieronymian edition.

In the prologue, which has the form of a letter, Hieronymus states that he rejects some of Victorinus' explanations as being *secundum litteram* (literal), in particular passages concerning the chiliastic thousand-year kingdom (*quod in eorum commentariis de mille annis regnorum repperi*). Hieronymus explains the thousand years of Apocalypse 20:6 as the time between the Incarnation and the end of the world, and the first resurrection as a resurrection of souls through

---

4   Cf. G. O'Collins, E. G. Farrugia, *Zwięzły słownik teologiczny*, Kraków 1993, pp. 46 and 141.

5   Cf. A. Jankowski, commentary, in: *Apokalipsa świętego Jana*, Poznań 1959, 265.

6   Cf. J. Sily, *El Milenarismo*, in: *Estudios*, vol. 65, (Buenos Aires) 1941, 115–134: "Aunque el milenarismo no haya sido censurado como herejía, sin embargo el sentimiento común de los teólogos de todas las escuelas ve en él una doctrina errónea".

7   Ed. J. Haussleiter, CSEL 49 (see above, n. 210), 11–154

faith (*per fidem*). He argues that the reign of Christ should not be interpreted as an earthly kingdom. The Holy Jerusalem signifies for him a gathering of saints, the precious stones symbolize the men who are *fortes in persecutione*, etc.[8]

Hieronymus dedicated his revision to Anatolius. In the prologue, he writes about various sea dangers: a violent storm of winds (*turbo ventorum vehementior*) and a moderate air (*moderatior aura*). The first danger causes terror (*formido*), the second is associated with a fear of traps (*pertimescunt insidias*). The dangers represent Hieronymus' problems with Victorinus' chiliastic work. According to Hieronymus, Victorinus was an eminent man (*egregius vir*), but the study of his text is dangerous (*est periculosum*) and gives the opponents an opportunity to "bark" (*obtrectatorum latratibus patens*), just as works of Papias, a bishop of Hierapolis, and Nepos, a bishop in Egypt, who shared Victorinus' views on the thousand-year kingdom (*mille annorum regnum*), did.

What is the structure of Hieronymus' revision of Victorinus' *Commentary*? He incorporated much of Victorinus' commentary into his *Recensio* without substantial changes. In numerous passages, he made either no modifications at all or only minor ones, which did not affect the meaning (some minor differences may be a result of scribal errors), e.g.:

Victorinus' *Commentary* (III 1)	Hieronymus' *Recensio* (III 1)
Quinta classis, electio **aut** *conversatio sanctorum declarat homines neglegentes, aliud quam quod oportet in saeculo agentes...*	*Quinta classis,* **id est conlectio vel** *conversatio sanctorum, declarat homines neglegentes* **et** *aliud quam quod oportet in saeculo agentes...*

Significant differences between Hieronymus' revision and Victorinus' commentary are found in chapter IV 4, in which the symbols of a lion, a man, a bull, and an eagle and their relation to the four evangelists are discussed:
- Victorinus: **John** – lion, Matthew – man, Luke – bull, **Mark** – flying eagle (cf. Iren. *Adv. haer.* 3, 11, 8);
- Hieronymus: **Mark** – lion, Matthew – man, Luke – bull, **John** – flying eagle (cf. Hier. *Comm. in Matth.*, praef.).

Hieronymus also expanded chapter XIII 3, where he added an extensive explanation of the symbolic meaning of the number 666:

---

8   Cf. M. Simonetti, *Lettera e/o allegoria. Un contributo alla storia dell'esegesi patristica,* Roma, 1985, (Studia ephemeridis *Augustinianum* 23), p. 297.

His number is the name of a man and his number is Six hundred and sixty and six[9] –
it means: (according to codex Y) it concerns Greek letters, which are numbers too:
[*A*. I. *N*. L. *T*. CCC. *E*. V. *M*. XL. *O*. LXX. *C*. CC : ANTEMOC. Γ. III. *E*. V. *N*. L.
C. CC. *H*. VIII. *P*. C. *I*. X. *K*. XX. *O*. LXX. *C*. CC: ΓENCHPIKOC.] (according to
codex Φ :) [*This number is number of man*, it is enumerated according to Greek
letters – (...) Teitan, named by pagans Sol or Phoebus, is translated and enumerated:
tau – CCC, epsilon – V, iota – X, tau – CCC, alpha – I, nu – L, it is number
DCLXVI. A Latin version of this name is Diclux: *D* – five hundred, *I* – one, *C* – one
hundred, *L* – fifty, *V* – five, *X* – ten, it is number DCLXVI. Greek name Teitan is
equivalent to the Latin name Diclux and it is a name of Antichrist. Though he is
stripped of the light of Heaven and is thrown [into the bottomless pit], *he himself is
transformed into an angel of light*[10], and dares to name himself the *light* (*lux*).]

The last differences between Hieronymus and Victorinus are found at the end of
their works, especially in passages concerning the thousand-year kingdom and
the new Jerusalem (cf. *Apocalypse* 20–21).

**Differences between Hieronymus and Victorinus in their commentaries on
the Apocalypse 20**[11]

a. **Victorinus** wrote:
– *the scarlet devil is imprisoned* and all his fugitive angels *in the
Tartarus of Gehenna* at the coming of the Lord; no one is ignorant of this;
after the thousand years he is released because of the nations which will
have served Antichrist: so that they alone might perish, as they deserved;
– then there is the general judgment and *the first resurrection: the dead*
who were written in the book of life came alive *and they reigned with
Christ a thousand years. (...) Blessed and holy is he who has a part
in the first resurrection: toward this one the second death has no
power. In this time of the first resurrection 144 thousands will be
standing* with Christ (*the Lamb*), namely those of the Jews in the last time
who will have become believers through the preaching of Elijah, those who,
the Spirit bears witness, are virgins not only in body, but also in language
(cf. Apocalypse 20:4);

---

9   Cf. Apocalypse 13:18.
10   Cf. 2 Corinthians 11:14.
11   Based on transl. by: R.E. Wallis. *From Ante-Nicene Fathers*, vol. 7. Edited by A. Roberts,
J. Donaldson, and A. C. Coxe. (Buffalo, NY: Christian Literature Publishing Co., 1886.)
Revised and edited for New Advent by K. Knight (http://www.newadvent.org/fathers/
0712.htm) and K.P. Edgecomb (http://www.bombaxo.com/victapoc.html).

– then comes the second resurrection (there are two resurrections): the dead will be raised immortal for bearing punishments, but it is shown that we are to be changed and to be covered in glory; however many were not previously to rise in the *first resurrection* and *to reign with Christ* over the world, over all nations, will rise at the last trumpet, after the thousand years, that is, in the last *resurrection*, among the impious and sinners and perpetrators of various kinds: *Blessed and holy is he who has a part in the first anastasis: toward this one the second death has no power*[12] (for the second death is being thrown into hell).

b. **Hieronymus** explained:
– thousand years wherein Satan is bound are in the first advent of Christ, even to the end of the age: they are called thousand according to that mode of speaking, wherein a part is signified by the whole (*pars significatur a toto*) – just as is that passage: *the word which He commanded for a thousand generations* (cf. Psalm 104:8), although they are not a thousand;
– there are two resurrections, but the first resurrection is now of the souls that are by the faith (*per fidem*), which does not permit men to pass over to the second death;
– *he says, and he casts him into the abyss* – he says so because the Satan, excluded from the hearts of believers, began to take possession of the wicked, in whose hearts, blinded day by day, he is shut up as if in a profound abyss;

He shut the door upon the Satan, it is said, that is, he forbade and restrained his seducing those who belong to Christ; He put a seal upon him, because it is hidden who belong to the side of the devil, and who to that of Christ; then the devil must be loosed for a short season, that is, for three years and six months, when with all his power he will avenge himself under Antichrist against the Church.

Then Hieronymus put the cross sign: †. Before this sign, he corrected scribal errors; after it, he added a comment about the thousand-year kingdom. According to him, the reign of Christ should not be interpreted as an earthly kingdom (*regnum terrenum*): „but if it is thus to be thought of, they cease to reign when the thousand years are finished". Then Hieronymus argues that the number 'ten' signifies the Decalogue, and 'one hundred' symbolizes the crown of virginity: "he who shall have kept the undertaking of virginity completely, and shall have faithfully fulfilled the precepts of the Decalogue, and shall have destroyed the untrained nature or impure thoughts within the retirement of the heart, that they may not rule over him, this is the priest of Christ, and

---

12   Cf. Apocalypse 20:6.

accomplishing the millenary number thoroughly, is thought to reign with Christ; and truly in his case the devil is bound. But one who is entangled in the errors and the dogmas of heretics, the devil is loosed in him and he shall be overthrown, and shall enter the lake along with the devil."

Finally Hieronymus reminds the reader that after a little time the earth shall return the bodies of the saints, who "shall enter an eternal kingdom with an immortal King, as they who are not only virgins in body, but, moreover, with equal inviolability have protected themselves, both in tongue and thought, from wickedness"; and they, it shows, shall dwell in eternal joy with the Christ.

Differences between Hieronymus and Victorinus in their commentaries on the Apocalypse 21: the Holy Jerusalem – *civitas sancta*.

a. **Victorinus** wrote:
- *the holy city* appears in the kingdom and in the first resurrection; this city is *descending from heaven, foursquare*, walled around with *stones* of various kinds, and precious and coloured *like fine gold*, that is, bright;
- the gifts of the kings-servants of regions and nations are brought there;
- the city is spoken of as all those provinces of the Eastern region promised to the Patriarch Abraham in Genesis 13;14ff and it is located in Syria: all these provinces are to be levelled and cleansed at the coming of the Lord;
- in the kingdom of the Lord (*Dei regnum*) people are serving a perfect faith, that is, established firmly upon their baptism and having their confession in their mouth they are rejoicing there;
- in this kingdom, those who have been killed or defrauded of their goods because of the name of the Lord, *they will receive their consolation*, that is, heavenly crowns and riches; whole creation will be saved and, by the command of God, will give forth the good things hidden in it; then the saints will receive *bronze, gold, and iron, silver* and precious stones; *the priests of the Lord will be called the servants of God*, just as they have been called sacrilegious; in this kingdom *they will drink wine and be anointed with ointments* and they will be given to rejoicing;
- there are different stones in the city: it stands for the most precious variety of the faith of each man; the *gates of pearls* show the Apostles; these gates *will not be closed*, as grace is given through them;
- in this place *they will see face to face*, and *one will not request of another*; and *the names* of the Fathers and the Apostles are to be *both on the foundations and over the gates*: they and men who are to rule in this kingdom, *they will judge the world*.

b. **Hieronymus** explained:

– *the square city* (*civitas quadrata*) shows the gathering of the multitude of the saints, among whom now nothing can make faith waver, as was commanded to Noah, that he would make the ark out of squared wood, so that it would be able to bear the force of the flood; *precious stones* (*pretiosi lapides*) are men standing strong during persecution, who are neither moved by the storm of the persecutors nor the forces of their floods are able to loosen them from the true faith; they are associated with *pure gold*, which the Great King decorates the city with, and their hearts are shown as *the road* (*platea*) where the Lord walks; the *river of life* (*flumen vitae*) means grace to flow in spiritual birth; *the tree of life of either bank* symbolizes the coming of Christ according to the flesh; the diverse graces of the Twelve Apostles are shown as *twelve fruits through each of the months*: these graces receive from one wood of the Cross, satiating peoples consumed by hunger with the preaching of the Word of God;

– *in the city the sun will not be necessary*, it plainly shows the immaculate Creator of lights to shine in its midst; *from the four sides will be three gates*: these are the four virtues (*virtutes*: wisdom, courage, justice, temperance), which relate each one to another, and when mixed together they complete the number twelve; *the twelve gates* mean the number of the Apostles, who are showing the way to the saints by the four virtues as precious shining pearls, by the light of their doctrines, for making entrance to the city of the saints, so that the chorus of angels might praise their way of life.

At the end Hieronymus speaks against the Millennialism, which – according to him – is a heresy. The phrase *the gates may not be closed* clearly shows that the doctrine of the Apostles will not be overcome by any storms (*fluctus*) of criticism, even if the waves of the nations and the insane superstition (*insana superstitio*) of heretics rage against the true faith; their foam (*spumae*) will be dissolved (*superatae*) because Christ is a rock (*petra*), by whom and through whom the Church was founded, who will not be overcome by any waves of insane men (*insanientes homines*). Therefore, one should not listen to those who affirm that the kingdom of the thousand years is to be earthly, which they believe following the millenialist heretic Cerinthus.

Hieronymus was an antagonist of the Millennialism and he corrected a chiliastic commentary. Though he appreciated Victorinus and his work, he argued against his millennialist beliefs and literal interpretation of the Revelation which he considered dangerous. According to him, the thousand-year kingdom of Christ is the reign of the Lord in the hearts of His saints.

II Tyconius and Augustine

Tyconius Afer or Tychonius the African (around 330–390 AD), the great
Berber theologian and the greatest Donatist exegete, lived in the Roman North
Africa: „He was an African by nationality and an African by religion".[13] In the
latter half of the fourth century the African Church was struggling with many
problems such as persecutions, heresies, etc. After the great Diocletian
Persecution, the Donatist community separated itself from the Church on
account of differing from it on the question of the Lapsed (the *traditores*, who
had surrendered the sacred books to the persecutors): „In Africa the Donatists
formed a strong party and kept up their organization for a couple of centuries,
holding Catholic doctrine, but refusing communion both with the lapsed and
those who had received the lapsed. They were thus an isolated body of Latin-
speaking Christians".[14] Probably in 311 Caecilian, a new bishop of Carthage,
was consecrated by some *traditor* and a rigorist party set up a rival bishop, who
was succeeded in 313 by Donatus the Great, after whom the schism was named:

> Under his energetic leadership the movement spread through all of North Africa.
> The Donatists held that the Sacraments administered by one deserving
> excommunication were invalid, that the Catholic Church, failing to excommunicate
> such, had ceased to be the true church, that even its baptism was invalid, and that
> they alone, because of their strict discipline and the absolute purity of their members
> and clergy, were the true bride of Christ (...). When ecclesiastical commissioners
> and a synod decided against the Donatists, they were subjected to persecution, their
> churches closed, and their bishops exiled. Since persecution was regarded as a mark
> of the true Church, their fanaticism only increased, and death met at the hands of the
> military sent to suppress the revolt to which the *Circumcelliones*, fanatical ascetics
> allied with the Donatists, had incited the peasants, was regarded as martyrdom.[15]

Augustine of Hippo did not agree with the Donatists and their struggle against
the Church, but he protested against harsh treatment and persecutions of them:

> The concern of those who preserve the public security issued an indictment and
> brought certain Circumcelliones and Donatist clerics before the courts of law. When
> these were tried by the most illustrious and admirable tribune and chancellor, your
> brother and my son, Marcellinus, after they were coerced, not by the torments of
> iron claws and of flames, but of rods, they confessed to terrible crimes that they

---

13 F.C. Burkitt, *Introduction*, in: *The Book of Rules by Tyconius*, ed. F.C. Burkitt,
    Cambridge 1894, p. XI.
14 Ibid.
15 L. Fuerbringer, *The Concordia Cyclopedia The Handbook of Religious Information with
    Special Reference to the History Doctrine Work and Usages of the Lutheran Church*
    (http://tera-3.ul.cs.cmu.edu/cgi-bin/getImage.pl?target=/data/www/NASD/4a7f1db4-5792-
    415c-be79-266f41eef20a/009/499/PTIFF/00000227.tif&rs=1).

committed against my brothers and fellow priests, namely, that they slew one of them who was taken by ambush and mutilated another who was taken from his home, by tearing out an eye and cutting off a finger. When I discovered that they had confessed to these crimes and, for this reason, had no doubt that they would come under the jurisdiction of your authority, I rushed this letter to Your Excellency. In it I beg and plead by the mercy of Christ that we may rejoice over your greater and more certain good fortune without their receiving comparable punishments in return. And yet the laws cannot, in imposing punishment, cut off a finger with blows of a stone or gouge out an eye, as these men were able to do in their savagery. Hence, I am confident concerning these men, who confessed that they did this, that they will not received the same punishment in turn. But I fear that either these men or those others whose act of murder has been revealed may be condemned to death by the sentence of your authority and, in order that this may not happen, I as a Christian beg the judge and as a bishop warn a Christian (Epistula 134.2).[16]

Tyconius was learned in theology, sufficiently instructed in history, and not ignorant of secular knowledge, as Gennadius says.[17] His theological thought focused on christology and ecclesiology, the two fields being at the core of the doctrinal conflict between the Donatists and the Church of Rome. He wrote about the generality of Church. He knew that the concept of the Church has different meanings depending on context. According to him, there is a community of perfect Christians and a community of sinners who can be converted. In this point he rejected Donatists' simple dualism which distinguished sharply between the True (i.e. Donatist) Church and the community of heretics associated with the Church of Rome. Tyconius was condemned by his own church, but he never joined the Church of Rome.

Tyconius wrote Donatist apologies, *De bello intestino* (*On Civil War*) and *Expositiones diversarum causarum* (*Explanations of Diverse Causes*), „in which, to defend his side, he quotes ancient synods; from which he is seen to have been of the Donatist party", and he „also explained the whole Apocalypse of John, understanding all of it in a spiritual sense, nothing carnally" [18]. But Tyconius' best known work is the *Book of Rules*, highly valued by both his contemporaries (e.g. Augustine of Hippo, who also composed *Contra epistulam Parmeniani libri tres* as an answer to Parmenianus, a successor of Donatus in

---

16   Augustine, *Letters 100–155*, vol. II/2. Transl. and notes by Roland Teske; ed. by Boniface Ramsey. Hyde Park, New York: New City Press, 2003, pp. 205–206 (http://books.google.pl/books?id=jg7ZOUWnHeMC&printsec=frontcover&hl=pl&sourc e=gbs_ge_summary_r&cad=0#v=onepage&q&f=false).

17   Cf. Hieronymus und Gennadius, *De viris illustribus*, ed. C. Bernoulli, Freiburg a. Br.-Leipzig, 1895, pp. 68–69.

18   Ibid.

the primatial see of Carthage and an author of a letter against Tyconius) and later authors (e.g. Isidore of Seville and Bede). Tyconius composed seven rules for discovering the meaning of the Scriptures.

In his theological interpretations Tyconius focused on Christ and His Church understood as the Christ's body. In his handbook for interpreting the Scriptures, he dedicated three rules to the issue of mystery of this body: I. *The Lord and His Body*, II. *The Lord's Bipartite Body* and VII. *The Devil and His Body*. These rules emphasize ambiguity of particular figures and images in the Bible. The other rules (III. *The Promises and the Law*, IV. *The Particular and the General*, V. *Times*, VI. *Recapitulation*) explore ambiguity of scriptural things, numbers, and narratives[19]; they help to interpret the text of Scripture.

Tyconius' seven rules for interpretation of the Bible, arranged by him in one book, are quoted and explained by Augustine, who explicitly referred to the *Book of Rules* in his own work on exegesis, *De doctrina Christiana* (3.30–37). Augustine wrote critically about Tyconius' rules:

these rules, as expounded by their author, do indeed, when carefully considered, afford considerable assistance in penetrating the secrets of the sacred writings; but still they do not explain all the difficult passages for there are several other methods required which are so far from being embraced in this number of seven, that the author himself explains many obscure passages without using any of his rules; finding, indeed, that there was no need for them, as there was no difficulty in the passage of the kind to which his rules apply (*DC* 3.30).[20]

Nevertheless, we can see the influence of Tyconius' exegetic method in Augustine's *De doctrina Christiana*.

The second and the seventh rules.

In the first group of rules Tyconius explained that Christ and the Church are one body and that Jesus is the head and the most important part of this body. Tyconius wrote: *Et apostolus Paulus, corpus Christi Christum apellat (…) id est Christi corpus, quod est Ecclesia* (Tyconius, *Lib. reg.* I: „And the apostle Paul calls the body of Christ 'Christ' (...) the body of Christ which is the Church"[21]).

a. In the second rule **Tyconius**, supporting his argument with many biblical passages, argued that:

---

19   Cf. http://www.britannica.com/EBchecked/topic/1082779/Tyconius.

20   Transl. from: http://www.ccel.org/ccel/augustine/doctrine.pdf.

21   Transl. by W.S. Babcock (*Tyconius: The Book of Rules*, transl., with introduction and notes by W.S. Babcock, Atlanta 1989).

- the one body is both good and evil (...) Thus, in all the Scriptures, the Lord gives testimony that the one body of Abraham's line, in every case, both grows and flourishes and goes to ruin (*unum corpus et bonum esse et malum (...) Ita Deus in omnibus Scripturis unum corpus seminis Abrahae in omnibus crescere et florere atque perire testatur*).

Augustine abridged the second rule and explained it in the following way:
- the twofold division of the body of the Lord is not a suitable name, for that is really no part of the body of Christ which will not be with Him in eternity and because, not to speak of eternity, hypocrites cannot even now be said to be in Him, although they seem to be in His Church (and Augustine offered the name of this rule: *About the true and the mixed body of the Lord,* or *the true and the counterfeit,* or *Concerning the mixed Church*);
- this rule requires the reader to be on his guard (and Augustine cites a few fragments of the Bible; cf. *DC* 3.32).

But in building the unity of the Church (which was divided by sin) the Berber theologian went further than the Great Doctor of the Western Church, Augustine, who argued that the Christ's body is perfect.[22]

b. Tyconius admonished in the seventh rule that:
- the relation of the devil and his body can be conceived in short order, if we keep in mind, here also, what we have said about the Lord and his body; the transition from head to body is recognized by the same kind of reasoning;
- the devil is not separate from the person who belongs to him; the devil is in such a man; so also the Lord cannot be called a man without being in a man, nor a man can be called God without being in Christ;
- when a man sins, he is cast down from the mountain of God (*mons Dei*)[23]; and *there will be nothing left to catch fire* once the Spirit has been lost, and he is burned *to ash.*

Augustine wrote about the last rule:
- the devil is the head of the wicked, who are his body in a sense, and destined to go with him into the punishment of everlasting fire, just as Christ is the head of the Church, which is His body, destined to be with Him in His eternal kingdom and glory;

---

22 Cf. W. Linke, *Tykoniusz i jego komentarz do Apokalipsy,* in: *Pierwsze łacińskie komentarze do Apokalipsy: Hipolit, Wiktoryn, Hieronim, Tykoniusz,* ed. D. Budzanowska, W. Linke, Warszawa 2011, pp. 174–175.

23 The mountain is made up of holy men, cf. *Rule* VII.

–   but when the Scripture speaks of one and the same person, this rule leads us
    to take pains to understand which part of the statement applies to the head
    and which to the body; so this rule shows us that statements are sometimes
    made about the devil, whose truth is not so evident in regard to himself as in
    regard to his body; and his body is made up not only of those who are
    manifestly out of the way, but of those also who, though they really belong
    to him, are for a time mixed up with the Church, until they depart from this
    life (Augustine added here a passage of Isaiah with an interpretation as an
    example; cf. *DC* 3.37).

Augustine ended his quotation:

> all these rules, except the one about the promises and the law, make one meaning to
> be understood where another is expressed, which is the peculiarity of figurative
> diction; and this kind of diction, it seems to me, is too widely spread to be
> comprehended in its full extent by anyone. For, wherever one thing is said with the
> intention that another should be understood, we have a figurative expression, even
> though the name of the trope is not to be found in the art of rhetoric. And when
> expression of this sort occurs where it is customary to find it, there is no trouble in
> understanding it; when it occurs, however, where it is not customary, it costs labour
> to understand it (…) students of these venerable documents ought (…) to pray that
> they may understand them (*DC* 3.37).

Although Augustine critically described Tyconius' rules, he did not accuse
Tyconius of dogmatic errors: according to the bishop of Hippo, in the area of
ecclesiology and the doctrine of grace the Berber Donatist theologian was an
orthodox thinker.[24]

---

24   Cf. B. Czyżewski, „Ocena *Liber regularum* Tykoniusza przez św. Augustyna", *Studia
     Bydgoskie* 3 (2009), p. 246; C. Kannengiesser, *A Conflict of Christian Hermeneutics in
     Roman Africa: Tyconius and Augustine*, Center for Hermeneutical Studies, Berkeley
     1989, passim. Augustine „applied Tyconius's techniques to derive nonapocalyptic
     meanings for phrases and figures in the Gospel According to Matthew and the Book of
     Revelation. Drawing on Tyconius's principle that the quotidian church must consist of
     both the righteous and the reprobate, Augustine developed a powerful critique of and
     polemic against Donatist perfectionist ecclesiology. Finally, and most significantly,
     Augustine encountered Tyconius's reading of Paul and his scriptural meditation on
     divine grace and human freedom in a period when Augustine himself was struggling with
     his own understanding of the apostle. Although he came to reject Tyconius's particular
     interpretation of the relation between divine foreknowledge and salvation, Augustine
     adopted Tyconius's insight that salvation history (the course of events from the Creation
     to the Last Judgment) is both linear (the narrative of Scripture) and interior (the spiritual
     development of the individual)" (http://www.britannica.com/EBchecked/topic/1082779/
     Tyconius).

Byzantine Theory of Paraphrase in Rhetorical Treatises and Commentaries and the Original Version of Theon's *Progymnasmata*[1]

Angelika Modlińska-Piekarz

Library of The John Paul II Catholic University of Lublin

Intentional and deliberate imitation of an existing text which retains its general sense while changing the form – later called paraphrasing or paraphrase – was practiced as a rhetorical exercise by Greek speakers already in the fifth century BC. One of the oldest and most significant references to paraphrasing comes from Isocrates, who in his Πανηγυρικός justified the value of repeating the same thing in various ways (*Panegyricus* 7–9). Also Plutarch provides testimony of the practice of paraphrase when he relates that Demosthenes was famous on account of his ability to talk about the same topic in many different ways, and that he had a habit of paraphrasing his own orations as well as speeches of others (*Demosthenes* 8.2).[2] As a rhetorical exercise, paraphrase was also used by Roman orators, which is confirmed by Cicero (*De oratore* 1.154).

However, none of Greek or Roman rhetors discussed paraphrase as fully and comprehensively as Theon did. Theon treats paraphrase in the introductory chapter to his Προγυμνάσματα (*Progymnasmata*), preserved in the Greek original (*Prog.* 62.10–24 Spengel)[3], where he defines it as an expression of the

---

1   This paper is a part of a larger study on theory of paraphrase up to the seventeenth century. However, in this thematic approach it should be treated as a modest gloss to Michael Roberts's excellent and unsurpassed study on theory and practice of paraphrase from the oldest ancient texts to the late Middle Ages, which was my main source of references to paraphrase in ancient and medieval texts (though it has to be added that since the publication of Robert's book in 1985, many valuable and important scholarly publications appeared – studies as well as editions and translations of sources – which shed new light on some Roberts' considerations). See Michael Roberts, *Biblical Epic and Rhetorical Paraphrase in Late Antiquity* (Liverpool, 1985), 5–60.

2   Ibidem, 7.

3   See: "ἡ δὲ παράφρασις οὐχ ὥς τισιν εἴρηται ἢ ἔδοξεν, ἄχρηστός ἐστι· τὸ γὰρ καλῶς εἰπεῖν, φασίν, ἅπαξ περιγίνεται, δὶς δὲ οὐκ ἐνδέχεται· οὗτοι δὲ σφόδρα τοῦ ὀρθοῦ διημαρτήκασι. τῆς γὰρ διανοίας ὑφ᾿ ἑνὶ πράγματι μὴ καθ᾿ ἕνα τρόπον κινουμένης, ὥστε τὴν προσπεσοῦσαν αὐτῇ φαντασίαν ὁμοίως προενέγκασθαι, ἀλλὰ κατὰ πλείους, καὶ ποτὲ μὲν ἀποφαινομένων ἡμῶν, ποτὲ δὲ ἐρωτώντων, ποτὲ δὲ πυνθανομένων, ποτὲ δὲ εὐχομένων, ποτὲ δὲ

same thought in different words and in a different way. He justifies this practice arguing that the same thing can be presented well not once but many times and by different means: as an assumption, a question, a request, and a wish. Theon emphasizes usefulness of paraphrase as an exercise in word usage and naming things properly, and he defends it against those who believe that one idea can be expressed well and properly only in one way. To support his argument, he says that both poets and historians used paraphrase and rephrased both their own texts and texts of others.[4]

In another passage of the extant version of the *Progymnasmata* (*Prog.* 69.23–28 Spengel)[5] Theon claims that ancient authors did not follow direct instructions for paraphrasing because they regarded it not only as an exercise, but also as an emulation. Unfortunately, the entire chapter devoted to paraphrase, which was a part of the original version of Theon's *Progymnasmata*, is no longer extant, but is known to us only from an Armenian translation, made probably in the sixth century and preserved in manuscripts from the thirteenth and seventeenth century. The Armenian text was first published in 1938[6], but it was unavailable and completely unknown to the majority of European and American researchers who did not know the Armenian language until 1997, when Michel Patillon in collaboration with Giancarlo Bolognesi translated it into French and edited along with the Armenian text.[7] Before Patillon's edition, scholarship relied for the most part on the Greek version of Theon's text, in which there is a discrepancy between rhetorical exercises announced by the author and rhetorical exercises discussed in the text. As can be judged from the introduction, the original version of the treatise, besides the rhetorical exercises known from our Greek version (fable (μῦθος), chreia (χρεία), narration (διήγημα), refutation (ἀνασκευή) and confirmation (κατασκευή), common-

---

κατ' ἄλλον τινὰ τρόπον τὸ νοηθὲν ἐκφερόντων, οὐδὲν κωλύει κατὰ πάντας τοὺς τρόπους τὸ φαντασθὲν ἐπίσης καλῶς ἐξενεγκεῖν. μαρτύρια δὲ τούτου καὶ παρὰ ποιηταῖς καὶ ἱστορικοῖς, καὶ ἁπλῶς πάντες οἱ παλαιοὶ φαίνονται τῇ παραφράσει ἄριστα κεχρημένοι, οὐ μόνον τὰ ἑαυτῶν ἀλλὰ καὶ τὰ ἀλλήλων μεταπλάσσοντες" in Leonard Spengel, ed., *Theonis Progymnasmata*, in *Rhetores Graeci* vol. 2. (Lipsiae: Teubner, 1854), 62.10–24.

4   For examples, see G.A. Kennedy, transl., *Progymnasmata: Greek Textbooks of Prose Composition and Rhetoric* (Atlanta: Society of Biblical Literature, 2012), 6–8.

5   Leonard Spengel, ed., *Theonis Progymnasmata*, 69.

6   The text was published in 1938 in Armenian language: Hacob Manandyan, ed., *T'éovnay Yaiagas čartasanakan krt'ut'eanc'* (Yerevan, 1938).

7   Michel Patillon ed., transl., *Aelius Théon Progymnasmata*, texte établi et traduit par… avec l'assistance, pour l'arménien, de G. Bolognesi (Paris: Les Belles Lettres, 1997). About the Armenian text, see CXXXVI–CLII; about the paraphrase, XXVIII and CVI–CVII; for the Armenian text with French translation, 107–110.

place (τόπος), encomion (ἐγκώμιον), invective (ψόγος), comparison (σύγκρισις), personification (προσωποποιία), ecphrasis (ἔκφρασις), proposition (θέσις) and law (νόμος), contained also five additional exercises, namely reading aloud (ἀνάγνωσις), listening to a work read aloud (ἀκρόασις), paraphrase (παράφρασις), elaboration (ἐξεργασία), and contradiction (ἀντίρρησις). The Armenian translation has retained the contents of these five chapters, which are missing from the Greek text, and therefore is of the main importance for my discussion of paraphrase.

In the chapter on paraphrase Theon gives its definition and discusses types and examples of paraphrastical exercises suitable for students of rhetorical schools (*Prog.* 107–110 Patillon).[8] According to him, paraphrase (also called metaphrase) consists of changing the form of an expression with simultaneous keeping of its original meaning. We can distinguish four types of paraphrase, which correspond to four ways of modifying the paraphrased text: 1) syntactical paraphrase, which rearranges parts of a statement, but keeps the same words (*Prog.* 108 Patillon), 2) paraphrase by addition, in which the original expression is developed (*Prog.* 108 Patillon), 3) paraphrase by subtraction, in which some elements of the original statement are removed, but the general sense is preserved (*Prog.* 108 Patillon), 4) paraphrase by substitution, which is based on replacing some words with other words of the same meaning, for example by using synonyms, by substituting metaphors for common words, or by replacing several words with one word and inversely, one word with several words (*Prog.* 108 Patillon). In addition, Theon allows combinations of these four methods. He also believes that there are other ways of modifying a text according to the rules described in the chapter on narration, for example rewriting an assertion as a question, a question as a sentence expressing possibility, or similar (*Prog.* 109 Patillon)[9] – this type of modification may be interpreted as using different figures of thought. At the end, Theon presents two paraphrastical exercises. In the first one, the student is to reflect on the contents of a speech and then to reproduce it using the same or similar words and maintaining the composition's order. The second exercise consists of changing the style of a speech, for example a speech of Lysias is to be recomposed in the style of Demosthenes and vice versa, a speech of Demosthenes – in the style of Lysias. Theon observes that the same can be done with texts of other orators and historians (*Prog.* 109

---

8   This summary of Theon's chapter on paraphrase is based on Michel Patillon, ed., transl., *Aelius Théon Progymnasmata*, 107–110 and George A. Kennedy, transl., *Progymnasmata*, 70–71.

9   Theon probably used here the phrase "κατὰ πολλοὺς καὶ ποικίλους τρόπους", like in the chapter on narration (*Prog.* 86.1 Spengel).

Patillon). The aim of the first exercise is to repeat the text and learn it by heart, and its result depends on the student's ability to memorize and understand it. The second exercise is a stylistic paraphrase, in which the style of expression is changed; the student must use here the mode of substitution – the words and the style of the first author must be replaced with equivalent words and style of the second author. Theon warns, however, that not every text is suitable for paraphrase, but only one that can be replaced by other good texts (*Prog.* 109 Patillon). He recommends to begin with paraphrasing simple, short texts, for instance parts of speeches (such as an argumentation, introduction, or narration). Only then, after gradually having mastered the skill, a young man will acquire the ability to paraphrase the whole speech, and as a result he will obtain the ability of an excellent orator (*Prog.* 110 Patillon).

The previously missing part of the Theon's treatise, to which we now have access, convinces us that the rhetorician of Alexandria developed a coherent definition of paraphrase and distinguished its different forms, depending on the way in which the original text has been modified. Certain elements of his definition appear in later rhetorical treatises; in some cases, they might have been drawn directly from the original text, in others, from indirect sources (i.e. from commentaries and summaries) whose authors had access to Theon's chapter on paraphrase. Unfortunately, because Theon's work was intended for teachers of rhetoric, and therefore for an educated audience, it was soon overshadowed by simpler handbooks of preliminary exercises by Pseudo-Hermogenes and Aphthonius, which did not include sections devoted to paraphrase. This is probably the reason why the extant version of Theon's treatise does not contain exercises which could not be found in Pseudo-Hermogenes and Aphthonius's *Progymnasmata*.[10]

Because of the loss of the original version of his text, Theon's essential role in the creation of foundations of the theory of paraphrase was not recognized by subsequent centuries; the honor was handed over to Quintilian, who probably lived about the same time as the rhetorician of Alexandria.[11] All later theories of

---

10　Much valuable information about Theon's *Progymnasmata* and their reception can be found in the vast, extremely erudite work of B. Awianowicz, *Progymnasmata w teorii i praktyce szkoły humanistycznej od końca XV do połowy XVIII wieku.* (Toruń: Wydawnictwo Naukowe UMK, 2008), 35–38.

11　Quintilian lived between ca. 35 and 96 AD; as for Theon, there are three possibilities: he might have lived during the reign of the Emperor Hadrian (117–138); he might have been active in the first half of the first century AD (in this case, his treatise would be earlier than the *Institutio oratoria*); finally, he might have lived in the fourth century. See B. Awianowicz, *Progymnasmata,* 35–36 for a discussion of the dating of Theon's treatise; for the third possibility, see Malcolm Heath, "Theon and the History of the

paraphrase are secondary to Theon's ideas, which were transferred to the rhetorical and literary tradition of the Western Europe by various authors (among others Quintilian) who had been familiar with *Progymnasmata* of Theon. It is no wonder, because up to the sixth century there certainly existed copies of the original version of the treatise. This is confirmed by discoveries made in the twentieth century, such as a Greek papyrus from the fourth or fifth century with a fragment of the lost version of Theon's treatise and a fragment of its Latin translation from the third century.[12]

In the Greek rhetorical tradition, theoretical reflection on paraphrase was continued by an author of the treatise Περὶ μεθόδου δεινότητος (*De methodo vehementiae*), who for centuries was identified with Hermogenes and today is referred to as Pseudo-Hermogenes. Chapter 24 of this work, entitled Περὶ τοῦ λεληθότως τὰ αὐτὰ λέγειν ἢ ἑαυτῷ ἢ ἄλλοις (*De meth.* 440.6–441.14 Rabe)[13], turned out to be extremely important for the theory of paraphrase. Pseudo-Hermogenes describes here three methods – shortening, extension, and

---

Progymnasmata." *Greek, Roman and Byzantine Studies* 43 (2002/2003), 129–160. Today, when the contents of the original version of Theon's *Progymnasmata* is known, the assumption that Quintilian knew his work and was inspired by it seems even more likely (he twice refers to Theon the Stoic: *Inst.* 3.6.48 and 9.3.76). In Quintilian's Institutio oratoria, there are two passages discussing paraphrase (Inst. or. 1.9.2 and 10. 5.4–11). About Quintilian's theory of paraphrase, see Michael Roberts, Biblical Epic..., 14–18. Angelika Modlińska-Piekarz, Votum Davidicum. Poetyckie parafrazy psalmów w języku łacińskim w XVI–XVII wieku. (Lublin, 2009), 38–41; Angelika Modlińska-Piekarz, "Retoryczna teoria parafrazy w starożytności i w epoce renesansu." In Studia rhetorica. Materiały z konferencji naukowej „Retoryka dawna". Kraków, 16–17 marca 2009 roku, ed. by Michał Choptiany, Wojciech Ryczek. (Kraków: Księgarnia Akademicka, 2011), 145–162. Besides Quintilian, paraphrase, understood as a preliminary exercise consisting of changing the form of a text, is also recommended by Pliny the Younger in a letter to Fuscus Salinator (*Ep.* 7.9).

12 See B. Awianowicz, *Progymnasmata...*, 35–38.

13 Τοῦ ταὐτὰ λέγοντα ἢ ἑαυτῷ ἢ ἄλλῳ τινὶ μὴ δοκεῖν τὰ αὐτὰ λέγειν διπλῆ μέθοδος· τάξεως μεταβολή, καὶ μήκη καὶ βραχύτητες. ἡ δὲ αὐτὴ καὶ τοῦ παραφράζειν μέθοδος· ἢ γὰρ τὴν τάξιν μεταβάλλεις, ἥπερ ἐκεῖνος ἐχρήσατο, ἢ τὸ μέτρον· εἴπερ γὰρ διὰ μακρῶν ἐκεῖνος, ταῦτα ἐν βραχέσι συνελὼν λέγεις, ἢ τὸ ἐναντίον. Τίς δὲ ἑκατέρου τούτων ὁ καιρός; ἡ μὲν συμβουλευτικὴ μήκη καὶ βραχύτητας ἐπιδέχεται. τῆς γὰρ τάξεως μεταβολὴν οὐ δύναται ἔχειν, ὅτι ἐν συμβουλῇ πάντως πρῶτον τὸ κατεπεῖγον εἶναι δεῖ παρὰ παντὶ συμβουλεύοντι. ἐν δὲ τῇ πανηγυρικῇ νόμος ἐστὶ τῶν κεφαλαίων τῆς τάξεως ἀμετάβλητος ἡ φύσις τῶν πραγμάτων (*De meth.* 440.6–19 Rabe), in Hugo Rabe, ed., *Hermogenis* Περὶ μεθόδου δεινότητος, in: *Hermogenis Opera, Rhetores Graeci*, vol. 6. (Lipsiae: Teubner, 1913), 440–441 (entire chapter 24). Polish translation: Henryk Podbielski, transl., *Hermogenes: Sztuka retoryczna*. (Lublin, 2012), 599–600.

change of order – which can be used when one wants to repeat a text (either his own or somebody else's) but in such a way that the repetition is concealed (*De meth.* 440.6–19 Rabe); he also compares this procedure to paraphrase. We can see here clearly the influence of Theon's treatise and there are numerous references to Theon's chapter on paraphrase (*Prog.* 107–110 Patillon). The three methods mentioned by Pseudo-Hermogenes were previously described by Theon – Pseudo-Hermogenes omits only the paraphrase by substitution and the paraphrase by changing the manner of expression (that is by using different figures of thought). He observes, moreover, that in advisory speeches the composition is very important, and therefore the change of the order of arguments is usually not advisable in them. Pseudo-Hermogenes elaborates the issue of appropriateness of these modifications in different kinds of texts, supporting his excursus with examples from Demosthenes, yet referring not only to speech-writing but to prose in general, including also philosophical dialogues (Plato) and historical works (Thucydides). It should be emphasized at this point that although Pseudo-Hermogenes compares the discussed modifications to paraphrase, he does not completely identify them with it, indicating that while the three techniques of transforming the contents are appropriate also for paraphrase, they are used here for a different purpose (namely to conceal the repetition). The ability to conceal that something has been said before was very important and useful in rhetorical practice; by expressing the same idea in other words, orators were able to avoid monotony and unnecessary repetitions. There is a distinction made, then, between, on one hand, modification practiced as an exercise or for display (which Theon called paraphrase) and, on the other, modification (not named by Pseudo-Hermogenes) the aim of which is to hide the repetition. The author of the treatise Περὶ μεθόδου δεινότητος had to know the original version of Theon's *Progymnasmata*: the influence can be most clearly seen in his distinction of the three techniques of paraphrasing (development, shortening, and change of order), known to us from the chapter on paraphrase included in the original version of Theon's work.

Some important theoretical reflections on paraphrase come from texts from the Byzantine period: the treatise Περὶ τρόπων ποιητικῶν by Georgius Choeroboscus, three commentaries on Aphthonius's *Progymnasmata* (by John of Sardis, John Doxopatres, and an anonymous author of *scholia*), and two commentaries on chapter 24 of the treatise Περὶ μεθόδου δεινότητος, which were written by John the Deacon and Gregory of Corinth.

Choeroboscus, a Byzantine grammarian and teacher, who lived in the eighth and ninth century[14], undoubtedly knew Theon's text on paraphrase very well. He was the first author who established a distinction between metaphrase and paraphrase (III 251.13–14 and 17–24 Spengel)[15], which for Theon had the same meaning (*Prog.* 107 Patillon). For Choeroboscus, the two differ in modes and purposes of modification: metaphrase is a quantitative change of style (that is expanding or shortening), whereas paraphrase consists of a substitutive change of style (i.e. replacing words with others of a similar meaning). Conceived as an extension or a shortening of the original text, Choeroboscus' metaphrase is equivalent to Theon's two types of paraphrase. According to Choeroboscus, the aim of metaphrase is to embellish the original – so, it is an emulatory practice. In his definition, we can see a reference to chapter 24 of Περὶ μεθόδου δεινότητος of Pseudo-Hermogenes, who considered extension and shortening as belonging to the same category of changes (while changing the order of a text was considered a distinct category). As an example of metaphrase, Choeroboscus presents a rewriting by some unknown metaphrast – the same author, who will be later quoted by Doxopatres, John the Deacon, and Gregory of Corinth (the last two call him Sopater).[16] Choeroboscus does not clearly define paraphrase, but presents one example of it, in which a metrical and poetic form of a text is replaced with prose, sublime and full of pathos vocabulary is replaced with common words, and a noble style is replaced with a simple, ordinary one. Choeroboscus does not mention the purpose of this conversion but we can suppose that its aim is to explain the poetic text by using different, prosaic words; therefore, there is no emulation here.

---

14 Eleanor Dickey, *Ancient Greek Scholarship: a Guide to Finding, Reading, and Understanding Scholia, Commentaries, Lexica, and Grammatical Treatises, from Their Beginnings to the Byzantine Period* (Oxford, 2007), 80–81.

15 See: "διαφέρει δὲ φράσις, περίφρασις, μετάφρασις, ἔκφρασις, ἀντίφρασις καὶ σύμφρασις [...] μετάφρασις δὲ ἡ ἐναλλαγὴ τῶν λέξεων κατὰ τὸ ποσὸν ἢ πλειόνων ἢ ἐλαττόνων μετὰ ῥητορικοῦ κάλλους γινομένη, ὡς ὁ Μεταφραστὴς ἡμῖν δείκνυσιν ἐν ταῖς μεταφράσεσι· παράφρασις δὲ ἡ ἐναλλαγὴ τῶν λέξεων κατὰ τὸ ποσὸν τῶν αὐτῶν, ὡς τὸ μῆνιν ἄειδε θεά, παραφράζων εἶπε, τὴν ὀργὴν εἰπὲ ὦ Μοῦσα" (Περὶ τρόπ. III 251.13–14 and 17–24 Spengel). Leonard Spengel, ed., *Georgii Choerobosci* Περὶ τρόπων ποιητικῶν, in *Rhetores Graeci*, vol. 3. (Lipsiae: Teubner, 1856), 244–256.

16 The author of Μεταποιήσεις is Sopater, a fourth-century rhetorician, who restated a passage of *Iliad* (17.629–642) in seventy-two different ways and a passage of Demosthenes's Περὶ τοῦ στεφάνου (18.60) in seventy-four different ways. See Stephan Glöckner, „ Aus Sopatros Μεταποιήσεις." *Rheinisches Museum für Philologie* 65 (1910): 504–514; Michael Roberts, *Biblical Epic...*, 12–13.

John of Sardes, a Byzantine scholar, who lived in the ninth century, in his commentary on *gnome* (which is listed among preliminary exercises in Aphthonius's *Progymnasmata*), repeats Theon's definition of paraphrase almost word for word. According to him, in paraphrase the style is changed, while the thought of a statement remains unaltered. For him, as for Theon, paraphrase and metaphrase mean the same (*Comm. in Aph. Prog.* 64.23–65.5 Rabe).[17]

John Doxopatres, who lived in the ninth century, in his commentary on *chreia* in Aphthonius's *Progymnasmata* (II 269.20-270.5 Walz) also refers to Theon's theory of paraphrase[18], but he interprets it in an original way. Paraphrasing is for him, as for the rhetorician of Alexandria, a conversion of a statement in which the style is changed, while the original meaning is retained. Similarly as Choeroboscus and contrary to Theon, Doxopatres distinguishes between paraphrase and metaphrase. Metaphrase is a qualitative change of style and can be of two types: a stylistic conversion of a text from a valuable one to a poor one, or from a poor one to a valuable one. Paraphrase is not a qualitative change as it keeps the same style, valuable or simple, but changes the vocabulary of the original statement. He explains that the expression "in a paraphrasing manner" refers to one idea or one action; when one uses the term

---

17 See: "Παράφρασις δέ ἐστιν ἑρμηνείας ἀλλοίωσις τὴν αὐτὴν διάνοιαν φυλάττουσα. τὸ αὐτὸ δὲ καὶ μετάφρασις προσαγορεύεται· δεῖ γὰρ ἡμᾶς οὕτω ταύτην προφέρειν, οὔτε τοῦ λεχθέντος ἢ πραχθέντος ἀφισταμένους, οὔτε ἐπ' αὐτῶν ἀκριβῶς τῶν λέξεων μένοντας" (*Comm. in Aph.* 64, 23–65, 5 Rabe) in: Hugo Rabe, ed., *Joannis Sardiani Commentarium in Aphthonii Progymnasmata*, in *Rhetores Graeci*, vol. 15. (Lipsiae: Teubner, 1928), 64–65.

18 See: "Παραφραστικῷ. Τὸ παραφραστικὸν ἀναλογεῖν λέγεται τῇ διηγήσει, παρόσον ἐν αὐτῷ ἀφηγούμεθα τὸ πεπραγμένον ἢ λελεγμένον. Δέον οὖν ἐστιν εἰπεῖν, τί διαφέρει παράφρασις, μετάφρασις, ἔκφρασις, ἀντίφρασις καὶ περίφρασις [...] ἡ δὲ μετάφρασις διττή ἐστιν, ἢ γὰρ τὰ ὑψηλὰ καὶ ἀνηγμένα μεταβάλλει εἰς [τὰ εὐτελῆ καὶ ταπεινά, ὡς ἡ τῶν τοῦ Ὁμήρου Ἰλιάδων μετάφρασις, ἢ τοὐναντίον εὐτελῆ μεταβάλλει εἰς] ὑψηλότερα, ὡς αἱ τοῦ Λογοθέτου ἔχουσι μεταφράσεις [...] παράφρασις δέ ἐστι τὰ εἰρημένα μεταβάλλειν εἰς ἕτερα μήτε εὐτελέστερα, μήτε ὑψηλότερα, ἀλλ' ἴσα, καὶ τὰς μὲν λέξεις μόνας ἐξαλλάττειν, καὶ ἀντ' αὐτῶν ἑτέρας ὁμοίας τιθέναι, τὸν δὲ νοῦν τὸν αὐτὸν φυλάττειν. παραφραστικὸν δὲ καὶ οὐ παράφρασιν τὸ παρὸν ὀνομάζει κεφάλαιον, διότι λόγον ἕνα μόνον, ἢ μίαν πρᾶξιν ἐν αὐτῷ μεταποιοῦμεν, τὴν δὲ παράφρασιν εἶναι βούλονται ἑρμηνείας ἀλλοίωσιν" (Ῥητ. II 269, 20–24, 26–29, 31–34 and 270,1–5 Walz), in Christian Walz, ed., *Doxopatris Ῥητορικαὶ ὁμιλίαι εἰς τὰ τοῦ Ἀφθονίου Προγυμνάσματα*, in *Rhetores Graeci*, vol. 7. (Stuttgart: Cotta, 1835), 269–270; Ronald F. Hock, transl., *The Chreia and Ancient Rhetoric. Commentaries on Aphthonius's Progymnasmata* (Atlanta: Society of Biblical Literature, 2012), 222–223.

"paraphrase", on the other hand, one means changing the whole statement and reworking it in a comprehensive manner.

A very important comment on paraphrase was made by an anonymous scholar who, like Theon, considered paraphrase as a preliminary exercise and understood it as change of style with keeping the thought (II 590.29–34 Walz).[19]

John the Deacon is the author of the earliest of remaining comments on Περὶ μεθόδου δεινότητος of Pseudo-Hermogenes (141.9–143.4 Rabe).[20] In the commentary on chapter 24 of this text, he follows Pseudo-Hermogenes and discusses three ways of hiding the fact that something has been said before; then he compares them to paraphrase, yet, like Pseudo-Hermogenes, does not identify the two procedures. For him, they both are modifications of one's own or someone else's oration and may be of two types: they may consist of change of order (τὴν τάξιν μεταβαλεῖς) or of quantitative change, i.e. lengthening or shortening of a text (εἴπερ ἐκεῖνος διὰ μακρῶν, ταῦτα ἐν βραχέσι λέγεις συνελὲν, ἢ τὸ ἐναντίον). Paraphrase, however, is reconceptualization of ideas in a different manner and its aim is to clarify intricate, difficult content. As an example John brings forth the paraphrases of Themistius, who in an accessible way restated the content of works of Aristotle – John explicitly refers to Themistius' paraphrases of the *Physics, On the Soul,* and *On Sophistical Refutations.* According to John, Themistius modified Aristotle's texts either by

---

19 See: "Ἡ παράφρασις γυμνάζει εἰς τὸ τὰ αὐτὰ διαφόρως δύνασθαι ἀπαγγέλλειν τῇ ἑρμηνείᾳ· τοιαύτη δέ τις ὀφείλει εἶναι, οἷον μήτε ἀφισταμένη τοῦ προκειμένου, μήτε ἐπ' αὐτῶν τῶν λέξεων ἀκριβῶς μένουσα" (II 590.29–33 Walz) in: Christian Walz, ed., Ῥητορικαὶ ὁμιλίαι εἰς τὰ τοῦ Ἀφθονίου Προγυμνάσματα, in *Rhetores Graeci*, vol. 2. (Stuttgart: Cotta, 1835), 590.

20 See: "ἡ δὲ αὐτὴ καὶ τοῦ παραφράζειν μέθοδος· ἢ γὰρ τὴν τάξιν μεταβαλεῖς, ἧπερ ἐκεῖνος ἐχρήσατο, ἢ τὸ μέτρον. εἴπερ ἐκεῖνος διὰ μακρῶν, ταῦτα ἐν βραχέσι λέγεις συνελὲν, ἢ τὸ ἐναντίον. ὥσπερ ἐν μελέταις ἢ ἐν ἄλλῃ λογογραφίᾳ ἔστι σοι τὰ αὐτὰ μὲν λέγειν, λανθάνειν δὲ ὑπαλλάττοντα τὴν τάξιν, ἢ τὰ συνεσταλμένα ἐκτείνοντα, καὶ τὰ ἐκτεταμένα συστέλλοντα, οὕτω καὶ ὅταν παραφράζῃς τινὰ νοῦν ἀλλότριον ἤγουν μεταβάλλῃς ἀπὸ τοῦ ἀσαφεστέρου ἐπὶ τὸ σαφέστερον, ὥσπερ ὁ Θεμίστιος τῶν τοῦ Ἀριστοτέλους πολλά, τὰ Φυσικά, τὴν Περὶ ψυχῆς πραγματείαν, τὴν Ἀποδεικτικήν, ἔνθα πῆ μὲν τὴν τάξιν ὑπαλλάσσει ἢ τὰ συνεστραμμένα ἀναπτύσσει. τοῦτο ποιεῖ καὶ Σώπατρος ἐν ταῖς Μεταβολαῖς αὐτοῦ καὶ μεταποιήσεσι τῶν Δημοσθενικῶν χωρίων [...] Καὶ τοσαῦτα μὲν περὶ τοῦ παραφράζειν διεξιόντες ἠγάγομεν παραδείγματα ἐκ Σωπάτρου τῆς τε τῶν σχημάτων μεταβολῆς καὶ τοῦ τὰ συνεσταλμένα ἐκτείνειν καὶ τὸ ἐναντίον. περὶ δὲ τάξεως ἀρκέσει ἐν ἡμῖν ἐκ Προκοπίου τοῦ Γάζης παράδειγμα" (141.9–13 and 142.36–143.4) in Hugo Rabe, "Aus Rhetoren-Handschriften.5. Des Diakonen und Logotheten Johannes Kommentar zu Περὶ μεθόδου δεινότητος" *Rheinisches Museum für Philologie* 63 (1908): 127–151.

making changes in the order of composition or by rendering the philosopher's ideas in a more understandable manner. We can see, then, how the commentator understands the difference between paraphrase and the transformations of a text described by Pseudo-Hermogenes (who does not define the difference): their methods are the same, but purposes of both procedures are different: the aim of paraphrase it to explain the original text, created earlier by someone else, and the aim of modifications described by Pseudo-Hermogenes – to hide the fact of repetition, whether during rhetorical exercises or during the process of when one is creating a speech on the same topic. It should be mentioned that the idea that the purpose of modification is to explain the original text is John's own – it does not appear in the commented text. As prosaic paraphrases of poetical texts and paraphrases of philosophical works were very often practiced, we can suspect that this idea was a result of John's familiarity with these types of compositions. But John is also probably developing Theon's concept of paraphrase by substitution, which consists of replacing difficult phrases and sentences with other, simpler ones. After all, one of the paraphrastical exercises listed by Theon is restatement of a work in student's own words, according to his understanding of the text – therefore, it is, in a way, an act of explanation. Next, John the Deacon cites the example of Sopater, who in his Μεταποιήσεις rewrote the same passage of Demosthenes' *On the Crown* (Περὶ τοῦ στεφάνου) (Dem. 18.60) in several different ways.[21] To make things clear, he cites various ways (different figures of thought) of rewriting the same passage by Sopater: upliftingly, loftily, censoriously, separately, wishfully. He believes that all Sopater's modifications are based either on changing the manner of expression (i.e. by using different figures of thought, which were named in Theon's work κατὰ πολλοὺς καὶ ποικίλους τρόπους and in John's treatise are named τῶν σχημάτων μεταβολή) or on appropriate developing / shortening of its elements. As an example of changes introduced in composition he mentions Procopius of Gaza, a rhetorician who lived at the turn of the fifth and sixth century and was an author of Homeric paraphrases.[22] The rhetorical performances of Sopater or Procopius of Gaza, cited here as examples of paraphrasing, indicate that, besides hiding the repetition and explaining complicated contents, there are also other purposes of modifications, namely to diversify the character of a speech or demonstrate one's rhetorical skills in emulation. The text of John the Deacon is not quoted in full by Hugo Rabe, who

---

21 Stephan Glöckner, "Aus Sopatros Μεταποιήσεις.", 504–515.
22 Alexander Brinkmann, "Die Homer-Metaphrasen des Prokopios von Gaza." *Rheinisches Museum für Philologie* 63 (1908): 618–623; on paraphrastical techniques of Procopius of Gaza, see: Michael Roberts, *Biblical Epic...*, 45–46.

compared only its relationship to an earlier published commentary of Gregory of Corinth, which in fact was produced later[23] than the text of John the Deacon, and might have even been directly based on it.

Gregory, a bishop of Corinth around years 1092–1156[24], wrote numerous rhetorical and religious works. He is the author of a commentary, published by Christian Walz, which is very similar to the commentary of John the Deacon (1292.2–1295.20 Walz).[25] Besides the three modes of changing a text listed by Pseudo-Hemogenes (development, shortening, and change in order), Gregory also mentions the possibility of changing the manner of expression. As an example of hiding the text which is being restated, he discusses a transformation

---

23 Hugo Rabe, *Joannis Diaconi Kommentar...*, 127–131; Michel Roberts, *Biblical Epic...*, 25–26; Eleanor Dickey, *Ancient Greek Scholarship...*, 82–83.

24 Michel Roberts, *Biblical Epic...*, 25–26; Eleanor Dickey, *Ancient Greek Scholarship...*, 82–83.

25 See: "μέθοδον ἡμῖν διπλῆν παραδίδωσιν, ἐξ ἧς ὁρμώμενοι δόξομεν οὔτε ἡμεῖς ταυτολογεῖν ἑαυτοῖς κἂν τὰ μάλιστα τὰ αὐτὰ λέγωμεν, οὔτε ἑτέροις, ἂν τὰ ἐκείνων ὑφαιρώμεθα καὶ σφετεριζώμεθα· ἤγουν τὴν τάξιν μεταβαλεῖς, φησί, καὶ ἃ εἴτε παρὰ σοῦ ἐτέθησαν, εἴτε παρ᾽ ἄλλου, πρῶτα, ὕστερα θήσεις, εἴτε τὰ ὕστερα πρῶτα, ἢ τὰ ἐκτεταμένα συνεσταλμένα ἐρεῖς, ἢ τὸ ἐναντίον. καὶ ταυτὶ μὲν ὁ τεχνικός. ἔστι δὲ εἰπεῖν, ὅτι καὶ διὰ τῆς τῶν σχημάτων μεταβολῆς τοῦτο γίνεται· ὥσπερ ὁ θεολόγος ἐν τῷ εἰς τοὺς Μακκαβαίους λόγῳ Ὁμηρικόν τι παραλαβὼν ἔλαθε τοὺς πολλούς, σχημάτων ὑπαλλαγῇ χρησάμενος. ὁ γὰρ Διομήδης πρὸς τὸν Γλαῦκόν φησιν· [...] τοῦτο καὶ ὁ θεολόγος εἰσήγαγε τοὺς Μακκαβαίους λέγοντας. Τί γάρ, κἂν μὴ νῦν ἀποθάνωμεν, οὐ τεθνηξόμεθα πάντως; [...] ὁ μὲν οὖν ποιητὴς τῷ ἀντιθέτῳ ἐχρήσατο σχήματι, ὁ δὲ θεολόγος τῷ κατ᾽ ἐρώτησιν. Ἡ δὲ αὐτὴ καὶ τοῦ παραφράζειν μέθοδος. ὥσπερ ἐν μελέταις ἢ ἐν ἀλληλογραφίαις, ἔστι σοι τὰ αὐτὰ μὲν λέγειν, λανθάνειν δὲ ὑπαλλάττοντι τὴν λέξιν, ἢ τὰ συνεσταλμένα ἐκτείνοντι, καὶ τὰ ἐκτεταμένα συστέλλοντι, οὕτω καὶ ὅταν παραφράζῃς τινὰ νοῦν ἀλλότριον ἤγουν, ὅταν μεταβάλλῃς ἀπὸ τοῦ ἀσαφεστέρου ἐπὶ τὸ σαφέστερον. ὥσπερ ὁ Θεμίστιος πολλὰ τῶν τοῦ Ἀριστοτέλους, ἔνθα καί πη μὲν τὴν τάξιν ὑπαλλάσσει, ἢ τὰ συνεσταλμένα ἀναπτύσσει. τοῦτο ποιεῖ καὶ Σώπατρος ἐν ταῖς μεταβολαῖς αὐτοῦ καὶ μεταποιήσεσι τῶν Δημοσθενικῶν χωρίων· ὡς μεταποιῶν γὰρ τὸ πλεονέκτημα (Demosthenes 18.60) [...] τοῦτο δὲ τὸ χωρίον μεταποιεῖ καὶ κατὰ τὰ σχήματα. ἐξάγει γὰρ εὐκτικῶς, παθητικῶς, ἐπιτιμητικῶς καὶ ἀσυνδέτως, εὐκτικῶς [...] Καὶ τοσαῦτα μὲν περὶ τοῦ παραφράζειν διεξιόντες ἠγάγομεν παραδείγματα ἐκ Σωπάτρου. Τίς δὲ ἑκατέρου τούτων ὁ καιρός; πρῶτον ἡμῖν παρέδωκε μέθοδον, πῶς ἄν τις ταυτολογῶν ἢ ἑαυτῷ ἢ ἄλλοις λάθοι. νῦν δὲ καὶ τὴν χρῆσιν τοῦ μεθόδου παραδίδωσι, καὶ διδάσκει τὸν καιρὸν τῆς τε συστολῆς καὶ τῆς ἐκτάσεως καὶ τοῦ ἀμείβειν τὴν τάξιν" (1292.1–1295.10 Walz) in: Christian Walz, ed., *Gregorii Corinthi* Εἰς τὸ Περὶ μεθόδου δεινότητος, in *Rhetores Graeci*, vol. 7. (Stuttgart: Cotta, 1834), 1292–1295 (chapter 24:1292–1298, the whole treatise: 1090–1352).

of Homeric phrases in Gregory of Nazianzus' speech in honor of the Maccabees (Gregory of Nazianzus, PG 35.924B). At first, he quotes a passage of the *Iliad* (12.322–328) and then explains alterations which were made by the great Christian theologian: "*The same thought was used by the theologian in the way that here it is expressed by the Maccabees*". To clarify the change of narration, he adds: "*The poet used here an antithetical method, and the theologian used the questioning method*".

Characteristic for Gregory's commentary is that, besides citing and discussing Pseudo-Hermogenes, he also often supplies additional information and extensively interprets the commented text using his rhetorical knowledge in an attempt to clarify thoughts and frequently general statements of the ancient author. For example, this is how he defines change of order: "This, what for you or for someone else was presented as being the first, you put as a second, and what was the second, you put as first". It is also noteworthy how precisely the Metropolitan of Corinth outlines the objectives of the author of the commented work, which are, according to him, indication of the method of operation, of practical application, and of appropriateness of discussed techniques. Gregory, like Pseudo-Hermogenes and John the Deacon, states that paraphrase uses the same methods as modification which aims to hide the repetition. He also points out the explanatory function of paraphrase and cites as an example the paraphrases of Themistius, which, however, he quotes without providing the titles (which were specified by John the Deacon). He also refers to Sopater's modifications as examples of paraphrase. After a long quotation from Μεταποιήσεις, he adds by means of summary: "*The same passage [Sopater] modifies in different ways: he restates the same subject in an uplifting, noble, lofty, censorious, separative, or wishful way*". Both John the Deacon and Gregory of Corinth, then, include modification of a text by changing its expression in different ways (διὰ τῆς τῶν σχημάτων μεταβολῆς τοῦτο γίνεται), which they explicitly call paraphrase – this sort of modification is absent from Pseudo-Hermogenes' work and must have been taken from Theon's treatise (*Prog.* Patillon 109), though not necessarily from the chapter on paraphrase, but also possibly from the original introduction. The question which version of the treatise – the original one or the later version, which did not contain the chapter on paraphrase – the two Byzantine commentators were using remains open. However, their clear descriptions of all known methods of transforming statements may indicate that they knew the original text of Theon's preliminary exercises. Oscar Hoppichler suspected that Gregory of Corinth knew the original version of Theon's *Progymnasmata*, which included five additional exercises among which, besides paraphrase, there was also contradiction (ἀντίρρησις).[26] Following this path, Lydia Zimmermann compared Gregory's discussion of contradiction with chapter on contradiction in the Armenian translation of Theon's treatise and noticed numerous similar sentences and phrases, which suggests that Gregory might have had access to the original version of Theon's *Progymnasmata*.[27]

Conclusion

The aim of this paper was to discuss how Byzantine scholars – the author of the treatise Περὶ τρόπων ποιητικῶν, three commentators on Aphthonius's *Progymnasmata*, and two commentators on Psedo-Hermogenes' treatise Περὶ μεθόδου δεινότητος – understood and adapted the theory of paraphrase created by Theon around the mid-first century AD. The discovery of the Armenian translation of his *Progymnasmata* which contains the chapter devoted to paraphrase allows us to state that Theon's work contributed to popularization of paraphrase as a rhetorical exercise, that he created a classification of different types of paraphrase, and that he was the creator of a most complete definition of this term. However, the success of later *progymnasmata* created by Pseudo-Hermogenes and Aphthonius, which did not include paraphrase as a separate exercise, reduced practice of and theoretical interest in it in subsequent centuries; consequently, for many centuries no one said about paraphrase anything which was not already said by Theon. All later ancient statements – by Quintilian, Pliny, or Pseudo-Hermogenes – are clearly inspired by his ideas.

There are also reasons to suppose that not only John the Deacon and Gregory of Corinth (as Oscar Hoppichler and Lydia Zimmermann believe), but also other Byzantine scholars who wrote about paraphrase (the grammarian Georius Choeroboscus and the three commentators on Aphthonius's *Progymnasmata*: John of Sardis, John Doxopatres, and an anonymous author) knew the lost chapter of Theon's *Progymnasmata* on paraphrase, if not directly, then through some summary of or a commentary on this text, created sometime between the fourth and the eighth century. The role of Pseudo-Hermogenes, who repeats Theon's description of paraphrase and then interprets it in his own way, should also not be overlooked. John the Deacon and Gregory of Corinth clearly

---

26 See: "Ceterum equidem opinor, ἀντίρρησιν , quam apud Gregorium Corinthium legimus, ipso ex Theone esse assumptam..." in: Oscar Hoppichler, *De Theone, Hermogene, Aphthonioque progymnasmatum scriptoribus* (Diss., Virceburgi, 1884), 49, note 1; Quotation from: Lydia Zimmermann, "Zur Überlieferung und Redaction von Theons 'Progymnasmata'," in *Collectanea Classica Toruniensia,* ed. by W. Appel, R. Jacobi, vol. 14 (Toruń, 2003), 94.

27 Lydia Zimmermann, "Zur Überlieferung...", 93–101.

believed that the author of the work they commented on was influenced by Theon, and they used Theon's work as an inspiration for their own reflections on the subject.

In both of these commentaries the element that undoubtedly comes from Theon's lost chapter on paraphrase is the modification of a text in different ways (κατὰ πολλοὺς καὶ ποικίλους τρόπους = διὰ τῆς τῶν σχημάτων μεταβολῆς = κατὰ τὰ σχήματα), which both authors consider as a sub-category of paraphrase.[28] Because of the presence of this method in both commentaries, Michael Roberts supposed that John the Deacon and Gregory of Corinth drew from the same source, which probably also contained examples of paraphrases from Μεταποιήσεις of Sopater, but he did not know that paraphrasing in various ways was also present in Theon's lost chapter on paraphrase.[29] It seems that this source could be a commentary on the original version of Theon's exercises. The hypothesis that these Byzantine scholars knew the original version of Theon's treatise or a commentary on it opens further research questions, namely, what importance the works of John and Gregory had in the process of transferring the ideas of Theon to the Western civilization and what impact they might have had on development of Western paraphrastical theory and practice in the sixteenth and seventeenth centuries. Undoubtedly, Byzantine commentaries discussed here go beyond discussions of paraphrase in Latin texts by Quintilian, Pliny, Priscian, Fortunatianus, and Augustine, and certainly could play a role in preserving Theon's theory. There is also an innovative element present in these commentaries, the authors of whichgive their own interpretations of the ancient treatise. Therefore, it should be assumed that Theon's text was preserved, either by itself or via comments and references of later authors, and that the Byzantine rhetors couldbecome familiar with its main assumptions. It can be clearly seen how this description of paraphrase from the mid-first century AD, so important for the rhetorical theory, survived up till the Byzantine period and how its content was preserved in Byzantine commentaries. After the release of the Armenian translation, we can compare them with Theon's chapter on paraphrase and see clearly that they are influenced by the theory created by the rhetorician of Alexandria.

---

28 Theon described modes of variation with a phrase "κατὰ πολλοὺς καὶ ποικίλους τρόπους" also in the chapter on narration (*Prog.* 86.1 Spengel); the same words probably appeared in his chapter on paraphrase in reference to paraphrasing.

29 Cf. Michael Roberts, *Biblical Epic...*, 26–27.

Ancient Commenting Literature
and the *Etymologies* of Isidore of Seville

Krzysztof Morta

The Institute of Classical, Mediterranean
and Oriental Studies, University of Wrocław

As he was writing his *Etymologiarum libri XX* [1], Isidore of Seville probably was not suspecting that his work would soon gain great popularity in Europe and that it would become the main textbook and source of knowledge of different areas for Latin scholars for many subsequent centuries. Even though he dedicated the text specifically to his friends, Sisebut, a Visigothic King, and Braulio, Bishop of Saragossa, he had chiefly in mind the needs of educated people of the Church in his native Spain. However, the concise form together with the abundance of information included (coming from a variety of disciplines, from the seven liberal arts through medicine, history, theology, zoology to such areas of knowledge as the military art, shipbuilding, and running a household) [2] appealed to the needs of the Western Europe of the time. Isidore's *Etymologies* became the second most frequently copied and read text, right after the Bible. [3] Even today, scholars value the work not only as a document of the state of knowledge of its period, but also, because of numerous quotations from non-extant texts, as a source of ancient knowledge, presented from the Christian perspective to the people of the Middle Ages. [4]

---

1   In the Renaissance, the text is frequently referred to under the title *Origines*; see Manuel C. Díaz y Díaz, "Introducción general a San Isidoro de Sevilla Etimologias," in San Isidoro de Sevilla, *Etymologias*, Josè Oroz Reta, (et al., eds. (Madrid 1982), 1: 170–172.

2   Around 7, 500 entries total.

3   There may have been around 10,000 manuscripts of the *Etymologies* in circulation in the Middle Ages (Jocelyn Nigel Hillgarth, "Isidore of Seville," in: *Dictionary of the Middle Ages*, ed. by Joseph Reese Strayer (New York: Scribner, 1985), 6: 564. At the beginning of the 12th century, the *Etymologies* were also available in the Capitular Library in Cracow (Adam Vetulani, "Krakowska biblioteka katedralna w świetle swojego inwentarza z roku 1110" ["Cracow Cathedral Library in the Light of its Inventory from 1110"], *Slavia Antiqua* 4 (1954): 163–192.

4   Klaus Karttunen, "*Phoebo vicinus Padaeus*: Reflections on the Impact of Herodotean Ethnography," in: *The Children of Herodotus: Greek and Roman Historiography and Related Genres*, ed. by Jakub Pigoń (Newcastle: Cambridge Scholars Publishing, 2008), 22.

As Isidore wished to encompass a huge variety of topics in the limited space, he must have employed certain procedures of selecting and cutting the material, which frequently exposed the source material to various distortions. Particularly interesting are the cases in which modification or distortion of information is a result of a mistake or misunderstanding of the source text (and not a result of supplementing the text with information coming from other textual sources or author's own experience, as, for instance, in Strabo's *Geography*, where a description of a rhinoceros coming from earlier accounts is supplemented by the author with his own arguments and additional, empirical information[5]).

A fourteenth-century fresco entitled "The Triumph of St. Thomas Aquinas" by Andrea da Firenze (Andrea di Bonaiuto), located in the Dominican church of Santa Maria Novella in Florence, is a good example of Isidore's uncritical approach to his source material and, at the same time, its reflection in art.

In the fresco we see, among others, personifications of the seven liberal arts together with their representatives. Starting from second figure from the left, there are: Arithmetic (represented by Pythagoras[6]), Geometry (Euclid),

---

5   See G. Malinowski, *Zwierzęta świata antycznego: Studia nad "Geografią" Strabona* [The Animals of the Antiquity: Studies in Strabo's "Geography"], (Wrocław: Wydawnictwo Uniwersytetu Wrocławskiego, 2003), 139, 141, where it has been proved that the rejection of the widely accepted idea that rhinoceros have yellow skin was a result of an empirical observation.

6   Pythagoras: "Numeri disciplinam apud Graecos primum Pythagoram autumant conscripsisse," (*Etym*.3.2).

Astronomy (Ptolemy[7]), Music (Tubal-cain), Dialectic (Aristotle[8]), Rhetoric (Cicero[9]), and Grammar (Priscian). Among these figures, the representative of Music stands out, both visually and culturally. Tubal-cain is represented as a sullen bearded man in a smith's apron, sitting next to an anvil, with two hammers in his hands. He is the only biblical character among the liberal arts' inventors.

Yet, it is hard to find a connection between Tubal-cain and the art of music. We read in the Book of Genesis (4:22): "Sella quoque genuit Thubalcain qui fuit malleator et faber in cuncta opera aeris et ferri soror vero Thubalcain Noemma."

Tubal-cain's appearance in the fresco, then, cannot be based directly on this passage because it does not draw any connection between him and music. It is in Isidore's *Etymologies* (III. 16.1) that we read: "Moyses dicit repertorem musicae artis fuisse Tubal, qui fuit de stirpe Cain ante diluvium." This passage indicates that even when discussing biblical characters, Isidore drew on other than biblical sources. According to the Bible, it was Jubal who was the father of music: "et nomen fratris eius[10] Iubal ipse fuit pater canentium cithara et organo," [Gen 4:21].[11]

We know that, because of his poor knowledge of Greek, Isidore made use of Latin works and translations[12], which were marred by frequent translating errors and misinterpretations. It is in a Latin translation of Flavius Josephus' Antiquities of the Jews that we find the mistake concerning the name of the father of music, later repeated by Isidore. In 1.64, Josephus wrote that Jubal was the inventor of music, but in the old Latin translation Jubal was turned into Tubal:

> Horum Iobal quidem fuit de Ada, tabernacula fixit et greges amavit; **Tubal consanguineus eius existens musicam coluit et psalterium citharamque laudavit.** Tubalcain, qui ex altera natus est, fortitudine cunctos excellens res bellicas decenter

---

7   Ptolemy: "sunt de astronomia scripta volumina, inter quos tamen Ptolemaeus rex Alexandiae apud Graecos praecipuus habetur," (*Etym.* 3.26).

8   *Etym.* 2.22.2.

9   Cicero: "... et translata in Latinum a Tullio videlicet" (*Etym.* 2.2.1).

10   Refers to Jabel (Latin Iabel).

11   There were attempts to connect Jubal with Thubalcain as the inventors of music, as evidenced by a medieval poem titled *Speculum humanae salvationis*: "Iubal et Tubalcain filii Lamech fuerunt, / Qui inventores artis ferrariae et musicae exstiterunt. / Quando enim Tubalcain cum malleis sonos faciebat, / Iubal ex sonitu malleorum melodiam inveniebat."

12   Despite the twelfth-century information that Isidore was *Latinis, Graecis et Hebraicis litteris instructus* (*Acta Sanctorum*, 1 Aprilis, col. 332), it is questionable whether he knew the language of the New Testament, not to mention Hebrew (cf. Jocelyn Nigel Hillgarth, "The Position of Isidorian Studies: a Critical Review of the Literature 1936 – 1975." *Studi Medievali* ser. 3, 24 (1983): 853).

exercuit, ex his etiam, quae ad libidinem attinent corporis, enutrivit; ferrariam artem
primus invenit, habuitque sororem nomine Noemma.

A juxtaposition of the sentence in bold and the relevant passage from the Greek
original clearly shows the mistake: "Ἰούβαλος δέ, ὁμομήτριος δ' ἦν αὐτῷ,
μουσικὴν ἤσκησε καὶ ψαλτήρια καὶ κιθάρας ἐπενόησεν. " [*Antiquitates*
1.64]. The original version of Flavius' work mentions Jubal, not Tubal. While in
the Greek the two names differ significantly, a spelling mistake was easy in
Latin (Iubal – Tubal).[13]

Isidore's use of secondary sources contributed to numerous errors. The
process of transmission of information was exposed to distortions at every stage,
usually due to misinterpretation of the text[14] or copyists' mistakes.[15] In
particular, such errors occurred frequently when a text was translated from one
language to another, in the case of Isidore's sources primarily from Greek into
Latin.[16]

As far as the *Etymologies* are concerned, the number of mistakes was
certainly influenced by a long time gap between the composition of this text
(completed in early 7th c. C.E.) and of its sources. Isidore did not use
comprehensive and detailed works dedicated to individual topics, but rather
drew from excerpts and summaries. It facilitated and accelerated his work on
entries (it still took him twenty years to finish the work), but at the same time
increased the risk of potential mistakes. Isidore copied errors from the excerpts,
scholia, and works of grammarians he used and also added new ones because of
misreading or unskilful abridgement. The bishop of Seville did not carry out a
profound research on his sources and did not approach them with a critical eye.

We do not find in the *Etymologies* any creative contribution of the author,
extending beyond the source material. Due to the massive scope of his work,

---

13 For a Latin speaker, the name Tubal resembled the term used for a trumpet, *tuba*.

14 Just like it happened to modern interpreters and researchers. Jean Hardouin (Johannes
Harduinus), a seventeenth-century French scholar, had problems with an ambiguous
fragment in Pliny the Elder (*NH* 6.200: "viros pernicitate evasisse"): "Viros non in
conspectum colloquiumque venisse, quoniam pernicitate summa avolarint. Alii sic
interpretantur, quasi feminae viros pernicitate evaserint" (Caii Plinii Secundi *Historiae
naturalis libri XXXVII, quos interpretatione et notis illustravit ... e Societate Jesu, Jussu
regis Christianissimi Ludovici Magni in usum serenissimi Delphini. Editio nova
emendatior et auctior*. Vol. 1 (Parisiis, 1741), p. 348, n. 7).

15 Cf. Cicero, who in a letter to his brother Quintus complains about numerous mistakes he
finds in books (*Ad Quintum fratrem* III, 5–6).

16 Lucio Russo (*The Forgotten Revolution: How Science Was Born in 300 BC and Why it
Had to Be Reborn* (Berlin, New York: Springer, 2004), 252) cites examples of erroneous
understanding of Greek sources by Pliny the Elder.

Isidore did not try to get to the core of issues discussed in the text. He did not even analyse them logically. The entry devoted to a parrot (12.7.24) reads:

> Psittacus Indiae litoribus gignitur, colore viridi, torque puniceo, grandi lingua et ceteris avibus latiore. Unde et articulata verba exprimit, ita ut si eam non videris, hominem loqui putes. Ex natura autem salutat dicens: 'have,' vel χαῖρε. Cetera nomina institutione discit. Hinc est illud:
>
>> Psittacus a vobis aliorum nomina discam;
>> hoc didici per me dicere: «Caesar, have»."[17]

Isidore's **misunderstanding of the hyperbolical compliment contained in Martial's epigram** resulted in the information that a parrot (an Indian bird for him) can greet in Latin and Greek by nature. It can be argued that the scope of the *Etymologies*, which cover a vast range of topics (though not comparable to Pliny's *Natural history*), went to some extent beyond Isidore's intellectual capabilities.[18]

Thus, Europe received an important textbook – a compendium of all knowledge, but created without critical review and deeper reflection on the collected material. Also quotes from the Church Fathers appearing in the *Etymologies* could in fact come from florilegia[19], where they might have been already altered. This is obvious, for instance, in case of a description of a mole (*Etym.*12.3.5), which was taken from the *Commentary on Isaiah* (*Commentaria in Isaiam*) by St. Hieronymus, where we read:

> Est autem animal absque oculis, quod semper terram fodit, et humum egerit, et radices subter comedens, frugibus noxium est: quod Graeci ἀσπάλακα vocant.[20]

Hieronymus's description contains more substantial information than that of Isidore of Seville, who quoted it in his *Etymologies* after the author of the Vulgate:

> Est etenim absque oculis, semper terram fodit, et humum egerit, et radices subter frugibus comedit; quam Greci ἀσφάλακα vocant."

---

17 Mart. 14.73

18 I agree with scholars who claim that Isidore was not directly familiar with Pliny's work (see Jacques Fontaine, *Chrześcijańska literatura łacińska: Rys historyczny* [*Christian Latin Literature: Historical Outline*], J. Słomka, (transl.), (Tarnów: Biblos, 1997), 197.

19 Patric Gautier Dalché, "Isidorus Hispalensis, De gentium vocabulis (*Etym.* IX. 2) quelques sourses non reperées." *Revue des Études Agustiniennes* 31 (1985): 278–285.

20 PL 24, 54B. The character of the description and its emphasis on damage done to crops indicates that an agricultural text was a source of the information. Hieronymus emphasizes that a mole damages crops because it eats plant roots – this is a perspective of a farmer or a gardener. We can compare the text with a description of a mole in a Persian treatise on agriculture (*Samuelis Bocharti Hierozoicon sive bipertitum opus de animalibus Sacrae Scripturae* (Londini 1663), 1: 1026a).

A change is introduced in the phrase: *et radices subter frugibus comedit* ("and eats roots under the plants"). Hieronymus's comment about the mole (*radices subter comedens*) was misunderstood by Isidore, who took *subter* not for an adverb, but for a preposition – hence *radices subter frugibus* in the *Etymologies*. Isidore abridged (by omitting the information about the damage caused by a mole – *noxium*) and slightly modified the source text (*frugibus* referring to *noxium* was connected with the preposition *subter*). The source vocabulary was almost entirely preserved in the process of alteration.

In the example above the meaning of the text was not significantly changed. However, in many cases next to abridgements we find alterations of source texts which must have resulted from misunderstanding and which have no parallel elsewhere in literature. In his description of dangers waiting for a daredevil who looks for gold in Indian mountains, Isidore enumerates dragons (large snakes) and griffins, as well as certain creatures of human shape and immense size: "Ibi sunt et montes aurei, quos adire propter dracones et gryphas, et immensorum hominum monstra impossibile est." [*Etym*. 14.3.7].

We are familiar with ancient legends, stories, and myths in which griffins and dragons are guardians of treasures. Yet, who were these giants and where did the bishop of Seville obtain this information from? As it turns out, it is Hieronymus's writings that were Isidore's source. Letter 125 reads as follows:

> montesque aurei, quos adire propter gryphas et dracones et immensorum corporum monstra hominibus impossibile est: ut ostendatur nobis, quales custodes habeat avaritia.[21]

According to Hieronymus, the access to the golden mountains is guarded by griffins, dragons, and other creatures of immense size; these guardians make it impossible for people to reach these areas. As we can see, Isidore misread and misunderstood this passage and connected people (*hominibus*) with the phrase *immensorum corporum monstra*, which appears in direct proximity. By changing the grammatical connections (in Hieronymus *hominibus* is linked to *quos adire ... impossibile est*) he radically distorted the meaning.

A similar case concerns the basilisk.[22] Earlier sources describe a characteristic white spot on the head of this snake in the shape of a diadem:

---

21 PL 22.1074.

22 Basiliscus Graece, Latine interpretatur regulus, eo quod rex serpentium sit, adeo ut eum videntes fugiant, quia olfactu suo eos necat; nam et hominem vel si aspiciat, interimit. Si quidem et eius aspectu nulla avis volans inlaesa transit, sed quam procul sit, eius ore conbusta devoratur. [7] A mustelis tamen vincitur, quas illic homines inferunt cavernis, in quibus delitescit; itaque eo visu fugit, quem illa persequitur et occidit. Nihil enim

candida in capite macula ut quodam diademate insignem (Plin. *NH*, 8. 78); *alba quasi mitrula lineatus caput* (Solin. 27.50). In Isidore, instead of a single spot we find multiple spots covering the basilisk's whole body – and this also how the animal is depicted in medieval bestiaries.[23]

Similarly, Isidore misreads an account concerning hissing (*sibilus*) of the basilisk which scares other snakes: "Sibilum eius etiam serpentes perhorrescunt et cum acceperint, fugam quaeque quoquo potest properant." [Solin. 26. 54]. And as a result, in the *Etymologies* he describes a snake called *sibilus*: "Sibilus idem est qui et regulus. Sibilo enim occidit, antequam mordeat vel exurat." [*Etym.* 12.4.9].

A piece of information frequently travelled for a very long time before it was included in the *Etymologies*. It was edited by numerous armchair scholars, whose work amounted to compiling and abridging earlier sources. The longer the process of transmitting information, the more intermediaries there were, and, as a result, the more accidental and unintended distortions occurred in the text (leaving aside the case of intendedones).

In this context the process of transmission of information about a carnivorous bull is particularly interesting. It was a fantasy creature, supposedly living among Troglodytes; stories about it must have been a product of indigenous legends. The first known description appeared in Agatharchides's work *On the Erythraean Sea* and was preserved in Photius' summary (*Biblioth.* cod. 250, 455B–456A), as well as in Diodorus (3.35.7–9) and Aelian (*NA* 17.45).

Because their descriptions roughly overlap and discuss the same characteristic features of this unusual creature, let us quote Photius' description as an example:

Πάντων δὲ τῶν εἰρημένων ἀγριώτατον καὶ δυσκατεργαστότατον τὸ τῶν ταύρων τῶν σαρκοφάγων γένος, ὃ τῷ μεγέθει μὲν ὑπάρχει τῶν ἡμέρων ἁδρότερον, τάχει δὲ ὑπερβάλλον, πυρρὸν δὲ ἐξαισίως. Καὶ τὸ μὲν στόμα μέχρι τῶν ὤτων αὐτῷ διέστηκεν, ὄμμα δὲ ὑποφαίνει γλαυκότερον λέοντος. Τὰ δὲ κέρατα τὸν μὲν ἄλλον χρόνον τοῖς ὠσὶ παραπλησίως κινεῖ, μάχῃ δὲ χρώμενον ἵστησιν ἀραρότως. Τὴν δ' ἐπαγωγὴν τῆς τριχὸς ἐναντίαν ἔχει τοῖς ἄλλοις. Τοῦτο δὲ τοῖς τε ἀλκιμωτάτοις ἐπιτίθεται καὶ κυνηγεῖ τὰ λοιπὰ τῶν ζῴων, καὶ τὰς ποίμνας τῶν ἐπιχωρίων μάλιστα κακοποιεῖ, καὶ μόνον ἐστὶν ἄτρωτον λόγχῃ καὶ τόξῳ. Διὸ καὶ ποιῆσαι μὲν ὑποχείριον οὐδεὶς πολλῶν ἐπιβεβλημένων κατίσχυσε, τὸ δ' εἰς ὄρυγμα ἐμπεσὸν ἤ τινα δόλον τούτῳ παραπλήσιον ὑπὸ τοῦ θυμοῦ συντόμως γίνεται περιπνιγές. Καὶ τὸ

---

parens ille rerum sine remedio constituit. Est autem longitudine semipedalis; albis maculis lineatus. (*Etym.* 12.4. 6–7).

23 See the image of a basilisk in the manuscript (Kongelige Bibliotek, MS Gl. kgl. S. 1633 4°, fol. 51r).

μὲν θηρίον εἰκότως κρίνεται παρὰ Τρωγλοδύταις ἀλκὴν μὲν ἔχειν λέοντος, τάχος δὲ ἵππου, ῥώμην δὲ ταύρου, σιδήρῳ δὲ οὐχ ὑπεῖκον. (76, *Geographi Graeci min.* ed. Muller, vol. 1, p. 160).

The description is created by combining together, against Cuvier's principle of correlation of parts, features of various African creatures, from the buffalo and the antelope to wild cats; as a result the wildest, hybrid creature is created. The fantasy bull was larger than the domesticated one (twice as big according to Aelian), it had a ginger coat and blue eyes. Supposedly it was the fastest animal. The description keeps adding the most extraordinary features: a mouth extended from ear to ear, moving horns that tighten in preparation for a fight, a coat growing in the other direction than in other animals, a skin so hard that it is impossible to wound it with a spear. This carnivorous bull hunts other wild animals and attacks even the strongest creatures; it also kills groups of local people. It is impossible to catch it alive because when it finds itself in a trap (such as a dug hole), it chokes on its own fury.

In the process of transmitting the information about this fantasy creature we can observe gradual purging the account of fantastic elements. Greek authors who abridged and summarized this description did not highlight the fantastic qualities of the animal but omitted them; as a result, the animal lost its most characteristic qualities. The description of a carnivorous bull in Pliny the Elder no longer contains the epithet σαρκοφάγος, but still preserves many of its features. Yet, the text is much more concise and does not include all the details:

> sed atrocissimos tauros silvestres, maiores agrestibus, velocitate ante omnes, colore fulvos, oculis caeruleis, pilo in contrarium verso, rictu ad aures dehiscente iuxta cornua mobilia. Tergori duritia silicis, omne respuens vulnus. Feras omnes venantur, ipsi non aliter quam foveis capti feritate semper intereunt.[*NH* 8.74]

Pliny also replaced a detailed list of various groups of animals hunted by the bull which appears in Greek sources (the strongest animals, other wild-living animals, domesticated animals) with "wild-living animals" (*feras omnes venantur*). It is not just an abridgement (in this case a generalisation would have been made – *animalia omnia*), but a selection of one portion of information. This procedure is also typical of the *Etymologies*.

In Solinus' *Collectanea rerum memorabilium* (52.36) we see a further stage of the transmission of the account of a carnivorous bull. Interestingly, in this work, which comes from the 3th century, the animal is referred to as "an Indian bull":

> Indicis tauris color fulvus est, volucris pernicitas, pilus in contrarium versus, hiatus omne quod caput. Hi quoque circumferunt cornua flexibilitate, qua volunt. Tergi duritia omne telum respuunt, et tam immiti feritate, ut capti animas proiciant furore.

What was changed here is the geographic location: in Solinus, the carnivorous bull, described by Agatharchides as an animal from the Troglodyte areas (Ethiopia), is moved to India. Probably someone who was preparing an excerpt from Pliny was mislead by the author's mention of Indian bulls (*boves Indici*) earlier in this passage (8.72). [24]

In Solinus's account we can also see clearly that many characteristic features of the bull were excluded from the description. [25] This includes, for example, the claim that it is the most dangerous animal and that it is larger than a farm bull. Also, there is no mention of the eye colour of the beast or that it attacks other animals. To sum up, in Solinus's description the bull is no longer a predator. As a result, the most important, defining feature of this animal is lost. However, the information regarding its moving horns was kept.

Following Solinus's version, Isidore repeats the erroneous topographic reference and speaks of "Indian bulls" (12.1.29):

> Indicis tauris color fulvus est, volucris pernicitas, pilis in contrarium versis, caput circumflectunt flexibilitate, qua volunt, tergi duritia omne telum respuunt immiti feritate.

It is worth pointing out that in Solinus we also find a problematic phrase: *hiatus omne quod caput* which appears in place of Pliny's *rictu ad aures*. A rather odd description of a gap of the mouth as wide "as the whole head" was probably difficult to understand for the readers. [26] In the *Etymologies*, the head (*caput*) became a direct object of the predicate *circumflectunt* ("move around"). [27] Isidore reads Solinus's text in the following manner: "caput hi quoque circumferunt cornua flexibilitate qua volunt." This made certainly more sense to the excerptor than the reading in which the verb would be linked with *cornua*,

---

24 Despite the information about Indian bulls, the entire passage refers to Africa (*Aethiopia generat*).

25 Features that were not reported in Solinus's account are marked in bold: "**sed atrocissimos** tauros **silvestres, maiores agrestibus**, velocitate ante omnes, colore fulvos, **oculis caeruleis**, pilo in contrarium verso, rictu ad aures dehiscente iuxta cornua mobilia. Tergori duritia silicis, omne respuens vulnus. **Feras omnes venantur, ipsi non aliter quam** foveis capti feritate semper intereunt.

26 An anonymous work *De bestiis et aliis rebus* ascribed to Hugo de Folieto shows that the image contained in the phrase *hiatus omne quod caput* was too bold for medieval naturalists: "Taurus [ταῦρος] nomen Graecum est, sicut et bos. Indicis tauris color fulvus est, volucris pernicitas, pilus in contrarium versus, hiatus magnus. Hi quoque circumferunt cornua, omnique caput flexibilitate qua volunt tergi duritia omne telum respuunt; tam immani sunt feritate, ut capti animas ne domentur proiiciant." [PL 177.89D]

27 Isidore replaced *circumferunt* with a synonymous *circumflectunt*.

the horns; as a result, the horns were left out by Isidore: "caput circumflectunt flexibilitate, qua volunt". Thus, not only was a distinctive and exceptional quality of carnivorous bulls (moving horns) left out, but also a new element was introduced in the description, namely the bull's ability to move its head in many directions. This new quality was a result of a mistake caused by vagueness of the source text.

What was also left out from the *Etymologies* is the end of Solinus's description: "ut capti animas proiiciant furore", which – together with the earlier part ("tam immani sunt feritate") – constitutes a subordinate consecutive clause: "and they are characterised by such great wildness (*abl. qualitatis*) that when they are caught they die in fury." In Isidore's account, which misses the last element of the sentence, *immiti feritate* perforce refers to "tergi duritia omne telum respuunt". In this way, we obtain the information that "they drive back any missile in cruel wildness by the hardness of the neck (*abl. instrumentalis*)".

The case of carnivorous bulls, which not only lose their predatory nature in the course of the transmission but, more generally, are deprived of their distinctive features, is a good example of a frequent practice of excerpting and summarising aimed at making a synthesis or highlighting the essential information. Though the vocabulary is kept, some elements are arbitrarily left out in order to shorten the text. As a result, words and phrases which were initially separated are now positioned next to each other and create a new meaning. The selection of the material was often a result of chance, misreading or misinterpretation.[28] Reliance on excerpts, scholia, and grammatical commentaries, which contained processed material taken from specialist works (on agriculture, natural science, medicine) and which often were themselves based on earlier extracts, led to further misunderstandings and distortions. Editing frequently consisted of copying sentences and occasionally changing the number or providing synonyms. As clauses were cut out and words omitted, new sentence structures and phrases were created, which resulted in corruption and alteration of information.

The material gathered in the *Etymologies* contains defects arising from the aforementioned reasons. As they prepared the entries, Isidore and his secretaries[29] did not correct or compare the texts they were using to other

---

28 E.g. the reading of name of the city of Pesaro from Servius's comment on the Aeneid (*Aen.* 6.825): *Pisaurum dicitur, quod illic aurum pensatum est*, as *pis aurum dicitur*, i.e. that *pis* means gold (*Etym.* 17.4.10) see *The Etymologies of Isidore of Seville*, Stephen A. Barney, (ed. and transl.), (New York: Cambridge Univ. Press, 2010), 18.

29 On the help Isidore received from a team of copyists, see Jacques Fontaine, "Isidore de Séville et la mutation de l'encyclopédisme antique." *Cahiers d'Histoire Mondiale* 9 (1966): 526.

sources; and frequently they further distorted them. The *Etymologies* provided Western Europe with a significant dose of knowledge of both pagan antiquity and Christian authors. However, due to Isidore's method and quality of his sources (which depended on a longer or shorter process of transmission), information enclosed in his text often distorted the original meaning – not because it was supplemented with additional facts found in other sources, but because of mistakes occurring in the process of transmission. In particular, abridgements of source texts led to various distortions and alterations of its contents. While Isidore retained in general the vocabulary and sentence structures and limited himself to cosmetic edits, the examples discussed above demonstrate how a removal or accidental omission of some part of a text led not only to reduction of information, but also to various distortions.

The popularity of the *Etymologies* in the Middle Ages (it was the basis of subsequent works, such as *De Universo* (On the Nature of Things) by Hrabanus Maurus[30]) led to further transmission and dissemination of such distorted information. In consequence European literature, culture, and its symbols were "enriched" by common mistakes and distortions rather than by new information, observations and theories.

---

30 See Maria Rissel, *Rezeption antiker und patristischer Wissenschaft bei Hrabanus Maurus: Studien zur karolingischen Geistesgeschichte.* Lateinische Sprache und Literatur des Mittelalters, vol. 7. (Bern: Peter Lang, 1976).

Commenting with Hexameter. The Imagery of Light and Darkness in Nonnus' Poetic Exegesis of John 3:1–21[1]

Filip Doroszewski

Institute of Classical Philology and Culture Studies,
Cardinal Stefan Wyszyński University in Warsaw

Nonnus of Panopolis, a Greek epic poet of the fifth century AD who was presumably bound up with the Alexandrian milieu,[2] is primarily known as the author of the *Dionysiaca*, a vast poem on Dionysus consisting of forty eight books. In the recent decades, however, also the poet's other epic work, the *Paraphrase of St. John's Gospel*, has been receiving an increasing amount of attention from scholars. It has been demonstrated that the *Paraphrase* is not just a mere retelling of a purely rhetorical character, but also provides the reader with numerous exegetical hints hidden between its lines. A closer analysis of the *Paraphrase* (henceforth abbreviated as *Par.*) shows clearly that Nonnus was familiar not only with the Bible but also with many patristic authors, especially with Cyril of Alexandria, whose immense commentary on John's Gospel has been proved to have had an important influence on Nonnus' work.[3] This paper aims at demonstrating Nonnus' exegetical approach by analyzing the imagery of light and darkness in his retelling of the Nicodemus pericope (John 3:1–21).

The opposition between light and darkness plays an essential role in John's Gospel. Light symbolizes Christ and his salvation (cf. John 1:1–13), and those who follow Christ are called the sons of light (cf. John 12:36). Darkness, by contrast, stands for the sphere of sin and the world hostile to Jesus and his actions.[4] In the third chapter, verses 1–21, the author of John's Gospel describes a night discussion between Jesus and Nicodemus the Pharisee in which the latter is taught about the need for a spiritual rebirth. Jesus reveals to Nicodemus the truth about the light that has come to earth in order to judge people's deeds. There is no doubt, in the context of the Gospel, that when Jesus speaks of the

---

1 This paper is a reworked version of my earlier article published in Polish as "Z mroku do światła. Jezus, Nikodem i Helios w Parafrazie Ewangelii św. Jana Nonnosa z Panopolis." *Meander* 64–67(2009–2012): 138–145.

2 See Livrea 1987, 440, 450–453; Gigli Piccardi 1993.

3 Golega 1930, 110–111, 127–130; Livrea 1987, 103–104; Livrea 1989, 30 n. 29; De Stefani 2002, 9.

4 See e.g. Barrett 1978, 158; McPolin 1984, 141–142; Beasley–Murray 1999, 11–12.

light, he refers to himself. Thus, it is also clear that Nicodemus, while coming to Jesus by night, leaves the world's darkness and enters into the circle of the true Light.[5]

An even greater emphasis on the opposition of light and darkness can be seen in Nonnus' retelling of the aforementioned account (*Par.* 3.1–109).[6] The opposition is reinforced not only by means of the accumulation of the imagery of light and darkness, but also by references to other texts in which the theme of light and darkness is of key importance. As a result, Nonnus creates a poetic image of passing from darkness into the light in which the moment of enlightenment is explicitly correlated with the sacrament of baptism and Jesus is correlated with the source of light.

The sun and the moon

Nonnus elaborates on the theme of light and darkness from the very first lines of his retelling. Whereas the beginning of John 3:2 reads simply οὗτος ἦλθεν πρὸς αὐτὸν νυκτός "This man [sc. Nicodemus] came to him by night"[7], Nonnus' relevant account reads (*Par.* 3.3–7):

> ἀμάρτυρος οὗτος ὁδίτης
> Χριστῷ νυκτὸς ἵκανε φυλασσομένῳ ποδὶ βαίνων·
> ἔννυχος εἰς δόμον ἦλθεν, ὅπη φάος· ἀνδρὶ δὲ πιστῷ
> Ἰησοῦς ἐνέπων βαπτίσματος ἔνθεον αἴγλην
> νυκτιφανῆ Νικόδημον ἑῷ φαιδρύνατο μύθῳ.

This traveler came unwitnessed during the night to Christ by walking on guarded foot. In the night he came to the house wherein was the light. And Jesus while addressing the faithful man about the inspired splendor of baptism, cleansed the nocturnal Nicodemus with his expression.[8]

In patristic exegesis Nicodemus' late visit was often taken symbolically as proof that the Pharisee's mind was darkened so that he could not understand who Jesus really was. Of particular interest is the following fragment of Origen's Commentary on John[9] regarding Nicodemus's night-time visit (fr. 34):

---

5   Brown 1966, 130; see also e.g. Beasley-Murray 1999, 47.
6   For a more general discussion of the imagery of light and darkness in the *Paraphrase*, see Ypsilanti 2014.
7   English quotations of John's Gospel are from the NRSV, sometimes adapted.
8   All translations of the *Paraphrase* are cited from Sherry 1991, sometimes adapted.
9   As Heine 1986, 131 argues, in most cases the catena fragments attributed to Origen cannot be ascribed to him. Here, however, the question of authorship is of less importance than the fact that the fragment seems to reflect the exegetical *opinio communis* of that time.

[Nicodemus] came by night, because he did not know God whom he approached, and was not yet enlightened (πεφώτιστο). For the Sun of Righteousness (ὁ τῆς δικαιοσύνης ἥλιος) which brings about the spiritual day had not yet risen (ἀνατετάλκει) for him.[10]

Both the image of the rising sun and the idea of enlightenment are essential in the Christology of the Early Church.[11] As we will see, the same symbolism can be found in Nonnus' retelling of John 3:1–21.

In Nonnus' retelling of John 3:2, he juxtaposes the expressions νυκτός ("by night"), ἔννυχος ("night-time"), and νυκτιφανῆ ("appearing by night") with the words φάος ("light"), αἴγλην ("brightness"), and φαιδρύνατο ("made bright"). Thus, he highlights the Johannine contrast between night and Jesus. Without any doubt, Nonnus alludes to the Johannine images such as the light that shines in the darkness (cf. John 1:5) and Jesus as the light of the world (cf. John 8:12, 9:5). Perhaps Nonnus also has in mind the synoptic parable of the lamp that illuminates the house.[12] Thus, the two sentences Χριστῷ [...] ἵκανε ("he came to Christ") and εἰς δόμον ἦλθεν, ὅπη φάος ("he came to the house wherein was the light") can be seen as fully synonymous. Nicodemus leaves the darkness of night and stands face to face with Jesus, "the light of the world".

In *Par.* 3.5–7 it is explicitly stated that the subject of the conversation which Jesus and Nicodemus are about to begin will be the baptism (βάπτισμα).[13] Undoubtedly, Nonnus follows here the Early Church tradition of interpreting John 3:1–21, specifically lines 3 and 5, in terms of baptismal initiation.[14] Jesus "enlightens" (φαιδρύνατο) Nicodemus, who is significantly described as "appearing by night" (νυκτιφανῆ), by his teachings of the "light" (αἴγλην) of baptism. The combination of φαιδρύνατο and αἴγλην contrasted with νυκτιφανῆ makes it obvious that it is Jesus who is the source of light which illuminates man through baptism.[15] A direct relationship between light, baptism, and the figure of Jesus is emphasized in other passages of the *Paraphrase*, too.

---

10 διὰ τοῦτο νυκτὸς προσελήλυθεν, ἐπείπερ ἄγνοιαν ἔχων τὴν περὶ θεοῦ ᾧ προσήρχετο οὔπω πεφώτιστο. οὐ γὰρ ἀνατετάλκει αὐτῷ ὁ τῆς δικαιοσύνης ἥλιος, ὁ ποιητικὸς τῆς νοητῆς ἡμέρας; tr. mine. Cf. e.g. Chrys. *In Io. hom.* 24: 3: σκοτοῦται δὲ [...] ἐκπίπτων τῆς πίστεως.

11 On Christ as ἀνατολή and the Sun of the Righteousness (cf. Mal 4:2), see e.g. Kantorowicz 1963, 135–149.

12 Matth 5:15; Mark 4:21; Luke 11:33.

13 Baptismal symbolism in the *Paraphrase* is discussed by Agosti 2003, 59–62.

14 On the sacramentalism in John's Gospel, see Brown 1966, CXI–CXIV (in general) and 141–144 (John 3:3 and 5); on John 3:1–21 understood in the early Church as a reference to baptism, see Koester 1965, 118.

15 Cf. Agosti 1998, 56.

In *Par.* 1.124–5 John the Baptist speaks of Jesus as the one who ἀφωτίστοισι φάος μερόπεσσιν ὀπάσσει / ἐν πυρὶ βαπτίζων καὶ πνεύματι, "grants light to unenlightened mortals by baptizing them in fire and Spirit". Additionally, in *Par.* 4.4–5 it is Jesus himself who εἰς φάος ἕλκων / [...] βαπτίζει „baptizes ... drawing to the light". This direct relationship is also mentioned in the later part of the conversation between Jesus and Nicodemus. In John 3:8, where the author of the Gospel writes οὕτως ἐστὶν πᾶς ὁ γεγεννημένος ἐκ τοῦ πνεύματος ("So it is with everyone who is born of the Spirit"), Nonnus instead writes (*Par.* 3.46–7): οὕτω παντὸς ἔφυ τύπος ἀνέρος ἐκ πυρὸς ὑγροῦ / πνεύματι τικτομένοιο ("Such is the shape of every man who has come into being from the liquid fire born by the Spirit"). As Koenraad Kuiper remarks, ὑγρὸν πῦρ, "liquid fire", is a metaphor of baptism as enlightenment (φωτισμός).[16] The idea of baptism as the sacrament of enlightenment, alluded to in the Fourth Gospel[17] and in the other books of the New Testament[18], was quickly elaborated upon by the early Church.[19] Justin Martyr, an apologist who lived in the first half of the second century AD, wrote that baptism is called φωτισμός because it enlightens the minds of those who undergo it.[20] Much in the same vein, Clement of Alexandria, a half century after Justin Martyr, wrote that baptism grants man the holy light of salvation that allows him to see God.[21]

Taking all of this into account, one may suppose that the epithet νυκτιφανής, which means both "appearing at night" and "shining by night", is not used to describe Nicodemus by mere accident. This uncommon adjective recurs once again in the *Paraphrase* as an epithet of the Morning Star[22], and, apart from Nonnus' poem, can elsewhere be found only five times.[23] Four of them just repeat the same line in which νυκτιφανής is used in the same metrical position as in *Par.* 3.7 and with regard to the moon.[24] An almost

---

16 Kuiper 1918, 245–246.

17 See the account of the man born blind (John 9:1–41) and Brown 1966, 380–382.

18 See Heb 6:4,10:32; 1 Pet 2:9.

19 See Lampe s. v. φώτισμα and φωτισμός.

20 Justn. *Apol.* 61,12: καλεῖται δὲ τοῦτο τὸ λουτρὸν φωτισμός, ὡς φωτιζομένων τὴν διάνοιαν τῶν ταῦτα μανθανόντων.

21 Clem. *Paed.* 1.6.26.1: φώτισμα δὲ δι' οὗ τὸ ἅγιον ἐκεῖνο φῶς τὸ σωτήριον ἐποπτεύεται, τουτέστιν δι' οὗ τὸ θεῖον ὀξυωποῦμεν.

22 *Par.* 20:4: νυκτιφανὴς ... ἑῶιος ... ἀστήρ; on that passage, see Agosti 1998, 56.

23 According to TLG.

24 *Corp. Herm.* fr. 29.1.3 = Stob. 1:5.14.3 = *Carm. Astrolog.* [Heitsch] 3 = App. *Anth.* 3.147.3: νυκτιφανὴς Μήνη, στυγνὸς Κρόνος, Ἥλιος ἡδύς.

identical epithet νυκτιφαής occurs in a fragment of Parmenides that, according to Plutarch, refers to the moon reflecting the light of the sun.[25]

An image of the moon illuminated by the sun is not only an ideal match for the scene set by Nonnus in *Par*. 3.3–7, but also a well-known theme in patristic writings. Origen compares Christ to the Spiritual Sun from which the Church, depicted as the Moon, owes its shine.[26] Methodius of Olympus also establishes a direct link between the moon and baptismal symbolism.[27] Thus, Nicodemus, whom Jesus is going to teach about baptism, appears by night like the moon to receive light from Christ the Spiritual Sun.

Continuing in a similar vein, Nonnus seems to allude in the following lines to the figure of Christ-Helios.[28] While paraphrasing John 3:13 καὶ οὐδεὶς ἀναβέβηκεν εἰς τὸν οὐρανὸν εἰ μὴ ὁ ἐκ τοῦ οὐρανοῦ καταβάς, ὁ υἱὸς τοῦ ἀνθρώπου [ὁ ὢν ἐν τῷ οὐρανῷ] "No one has ascended into heaven except the one who descended from heaven, the Son of Man [who is in heaven]"[29], the poet retells John's words in six lines of which the last two read (*Par*. 3.69–70):

ἀνθρώπου μόνος υἱός, ὃς ἀστερόεντι μελάθρῳ
πάτριον οὖδας ἔχων αἰώνιος αἰθέρα ναίει

The divine son of man, who has his paternal ground in a starry hall and eternally inhabits the aether.

The expression αἰθέρα ναίει, "inhabits the aether", is a variation of Homeric αἰθέρι ναίων, "inhabiting the aether"[30]; apart from the *Dionysiaca*, Nonnus'

---

25 Parm. fr. 14 ap. Plut. *Mor*. 1116 a (*Adv. Col*. 15): νυκτιφαὲς περὶ γαῖαν ἀλώμενον ἀλλότριον φῶς.

26 Or. *In Jo*. 1:164–165: Ὁ δὲ σωτήρ, «φῶς» ὢν «τοῦ κόσμου», φωτίζει οὐ σώματα ἀλλὰ ἀσωμάτῳ δυνάμει τὸν ἀσώματον νοῦν, ἵνα ὡς ὑπὸ ἡλίου ἕκαστος ἡμῶν φωτιζόμενος καὶ τὰ ἄλλα δυνηθῇ βλέπειν νοητά. Ὥσπερ δὲ ἡλίου φωτίζοντος ἀμαυροῦται τὸ δύνασθαι φωτίζειν σελήνην καὶ ἀστέρας, οὕτως οἱ ἐλλαμπόμενοι ὑπὸ Χριστοῦ καὶ τὰς αὐγὰς αὐτοῦ κεχωρηκότες οὐδέν τινων διακονουμένων ἀποστόλων καὶ προφητῶν δέονται – τολμητέον γὰρ λέγειν τὴν ἀλήθειαν – οὐδὲ ἀγγέλων, προσθήσω δὲ ὅτι οὐδὲ τῶν κρειττόνων δυνάμεων, αὐτῷ τῷ πρωτογεννήτῳ μαθητευόμενοι φωτί.

27 Meth. *Symp*. 8:6: τούτῳ γὰρ καὶ σελήνη κέκληται τῷ τρόπῳ ἡ περὶ τὸ λουτρὸν αὐτῆς ἐνέργεια, ἐπειδὴ νέον σέλας ἀνανεασθέντες οἱ ἀναγεννώμενοι λάμπουσιν, ὅ ἐστι νέον φῶς, ὅθεν καὶ νεοφώτιστοι καλοῦνται.

28 On the figure of Christ-Helios in the *Paraphrase*, see Accorinti 1996, 198–199.

29 The words put in the square brackets appear only in some manuscripts of John's Gospel. However, Nonnus clearly paraphrases them.

30 *Il*. 2.412, 4.166, *Od*. 15.523 (always with regard to Zeus).

                        Filip Doroszewski

other poem, where it takes the form of αἰθέρα ναίειν, "to inhabit the aether"[31], it can be found only in the poetry of Isidorus of Fayum, an author of four hymns to the goddess Isis, dated to the 1st century BC.[32] Isidorus, an Egyptian and an author of hexametric poetry, even if not an outstanding representative of the genre,[33] may have been well known to such an erudite as Nonnus surely was.[34] In lines 13 and 14 of his second hymn, Isidorus addresses the goddess with the words similar to these of *Par.* 3.69–70:

> καὶ Ἀγχόης ὁ σὸς υἱός, ὃς οὐρανοῦ αἰθέρα ναίε[ι
> ἥλιος ἀντέλλων ἐσθ', ὃς ἔδειξε τὸ φῶς.

And Anchoes your son, who inhabits the aether, is the rising sun who shows forth the light.[35]

This passage occurs just after the expression οὐρανοῦ ἀστερόεντος, "starry sky", in line 11 which can be paralleled with ἀστερόεντι μελάθρῳ, "starry abode", in *Par.* 3.69.

Having a predilection, like many Christian poets in antiquity, for the technique of *Kontrastimitation*, consisting of – among other things – attributing to Jesus the epithets and features of pagan deities[36], Nonnus uses it quite often in his evangelical poem.[37] In fact, if we accept that *Par.* 3.69–70 is an allusion to Isidorus' hymn, the passage in question should also be considered an example of this technique. The sentence υἱός, ὃς ... αἰθέρα ναίει, "son who inhabits the aether", in the *Paraphrase* describes Jesus, whereas Isidorus uses the sentence to describe Anchoes, the son of Isis, who is identified with the rising sun. Isidorus' passage corresponds very well both to the enlightenment theme occurring in *Par.* 3.1–109 as well as to the context of John 3:13. Jesus, the one who descends from heaven and returns there in order to be at his Father's side, is paralleled with Anchoes-Helios who reigns in heaven with his mother Isis. Moreover, the expression ἥλιος ἀντέλλων, "the rising sun", makes one think of the figure of Jesus as the Sunrise (ἀνατολή), a popular theme in baptismal imagery of the early Church.[38]

---

31 See e.g. *Dion.* 2.569, 8.133, 8.164 etc.
32 However, see also an interestingly similar passage *Orac. Sib.* 3.16–17: ἀλλ' αὐτὸς μόνος οἶδεν ὁ ποιήσας τάδ' ἀπ' ἀρχῆς // ἄφθαρτος κτίστης αἰώνιος αἰθέρα ναίων.
33 Vanderlip 1972, 3.
34 On Nonnus' wide reading and poetic erudition, see e.g. Hollis 1994, 43–62.
35 Tr. V. F. Vanderlip 1972.
36 On the *Kontrastimitation* technique in the Christian poetry, see Van der Laan 1993, 151–164.
37 Some examples can be found in Agosti 2003, 89–94.
38 See e.g. Kantorowicz 1963, 137–138.

The mysteries of light and darkness

As in John's Gospel (cf. John 3:19–21), Nonnus' retelling of the Nicodemus account ends with a division of people into those who love the light and do God's will, and into those who prefer darkness because their deeds are bad. A man from the latter group is presented as follows (*Par.* 3.104–106):

> ἄξια νυκτὸς ἔχων στυγέει φάος· οὔποτε βαίνει
> εἰς φάος ἀγχικέλευθος, ὅπως μὴ φέγγος ἐλέγξῃ
> ἔργα, τάπερ τελέει κρυφίῃ κεκαλυμμένα σιγῇ.

> Who has deeds worthy of the night, he loathes the light. He never will walk on a close path to the light, in order that the light not rebuke the deeds he has veiled in the hidden silence.

Conversely, the lines regarding a man who prefers the light read (*Par.* 3.108–109):

> ἵξεται αὐτοκέλευστος, ὅπῃ φάος, ὄφρα φανείη
> ἔργα, τάπερ ποίησε θεοῦ τετελεσμένα βουλῇ.

> He shall come self-bidden to where the light is, in order that the deeds which he had done through the will of God be made manifest.

The expression ἄξια νυκτός, "worthy of the night", as well as the forms τελέει, "performs", and τετελεσμένα, "the things that have been performed", allow us to assume that Nonnus makes here a reference to a passage from Clement of Alexandria's *Protrepticus* in which the pagan mysteries, celebrated in the night, receive harsh criticism: Ἄξια μὲν οὖν νυκτὸς τὰ τελέσματα... "These mysteries are truly worthy of the night...".[39]

Nonnus' interest in the mystery cults, at least at the terminological level, is conspicuous in his *Paraphrase*, and should not be surprising as he was a Christian poet from Alexandria, where the use of mystery terminology in interpreting the Bible dates back at least to Philo the Jew.[40] In the above comparison of men who love the light and those who prefer darkness, Nonnus renders the Johannine verses in such a way as to make a subtle allusion to the idea of the mystery cults or, more precisely, to the two kinds of mysteries: the godly and the ungodly. The latter, which I suggest should be identified with the pagan mysteries mentioned by Clement, are performed in the dark and need to be kept secret (κρυφίῃ κεκαλυμμένα σιγῇ), whereas the former take place in bright light and are pleasant to God (θεοῦ ... βουλῇ). Since the whole dialogue

---

39   Clem. *Prot.* 2.22.1; tr. ANF, adapted.
40   General remarks on the mystery terminology in the *Paraphrase* can be found in Wójtowicz 1980, 131–141 and Vian 1988, 408–409. For a more detailed discussion, see Caprara 1999, 200–202; Livrea 2000, 303–304; Agosti 2003, 426; Caprara 2005, 15–18, 216–217, 223–224, 227, 228, 292; Doroszewski 2014.

between Jesus and Nicodemus as retold by Nonnus carries baptismal undertones, it seems likely that the godly mysteries alluded to by the poet are meant to evoke the theme of baptism, known in the Early Church, as we have seen, as the sacrament of enlightenment and the Christian initiation.[41] Be that as it may, the godly mysteries surely evoke the general idea of Christian mysteries consisting not of secret cult practices, as in the pagan religions, but rather of exploring the mysteries of the Christian faith.

Conclusions

To sum up, Nonnus' retelling of John 3:1–21 is an excellent example of his exegetical approach. It shows clearly that Nonnus' *Paraphrase* is not just John's Gospel retold, but that it contains a commentary to the Johannine text, too. Step by step, Nonnus explains the reader how the light of Jesus as well as Jesus, who himself is the Light, find their way to the man who takes pains to leave the darkness. This commentary consists of references to the Scriptures and Church Fathers, as well as to the non-Christian tradition, both of which Nonnus creatively introduces into his narration. As a matter of fact, the harmonious combination of these elements in Nonnus' poem must be seen against the background of the culture of fifth-century Egypt, which – although predominantly Christian – was firmly rooted in the classical tradition. Significantly, the references to the non-Christian tradition in Nonnus' *Paraphrase* do not distort the message of the Gospel, nor make the poet's interpretation of the Gospel unorthodox. Quite the opposite as they always serve one purpose: to make the message of the Gospel, as understood in Nonnus' times, clearer and more appealing.

Abbreviations

Ancient authors are cited according to the abbreviations in the LSJ and Lampe.
ANF = A. Roberts, J. Donaldson (eds.) 1885–1896, *The Ante-Nicene Fathers: Translations of the Writings of the Fathers Down to A.D. 325*, Bufallo.
Lampe = Lampe, G. 1961, *A Patristic Greek Lexicon*, Oxford.
LSJ = Liddell, H. G., R. Scott, H. S. Jones ⁹1996, *A Greek-English Lexicon, with a Revised Supplement*, ed. by P. G. W. Glare. Oxford, ⁹1996.

---

41 Christian sacraments, baptism included, quite often are described by the Fathers as τελετή „initiation into mysteries", see Lampe s.v.

NRSV = *New Revised Standard Version of the Bible*, copyrighted, 1989 by the Division of Christian Education of the National Council of the Churches of Christ in the United States of America.

TLG = *Thesaurus Linguae Graecae* (http://www.tlg.uci.edu).

Bibliography

Accorinti, D. 1996, *Nonno di Panopoli, Parafrasi del Vangelo di San Giovanni. Canto XX.* Pisa, 1996.

Agosti, G. 1998, "L'alba notturna (ἔννυχος ἠώς)." *Zeitschrift für Papyrologie und Epigraphik* 121 (1998): 53–58.

Agosti, G. 2003, *Nonno di Panopoli, Parafrasi del Vangelo di San Giovanni. Canto Quinto.* Firenze, 2003.

Barret, C.K. 1978, *The Gospel According to St. John: An Introduction with Commentary and Notes on the Greek Text*, 2nd edn. London, 1978.

Beasley-Murray, G. R. 1999, *John* (Word Biblical Commentary 36), Nashville, 1999.

Brown, R.E. 1966, *The Gospel According To John, vol. I–II, Introduction, translation and notes* (Anchor Bible Series 29), New York, 1966.

Caprara, M. 1999, "Nonno e gli Ebrei. Note a Par. IV.88–121." *Studi Italiani di Filologia Classica* 17 (1999): 195–215.

Caprara, M. 2005, *Nonno di Panopoli, Parafrasi del Vangelo di San Giovanni, Canto IV.* Pisa, 2005.

De Stefani, C. 2002, *Nonno di Panopoli, Parafrasi del Vangelo di S. Giovanni. Canto I.* Bologna, 2002.

Doroszewski, F. 2014, "Judaic Orgies and Christ' Bacchic Deeds: Dionysiac Terminology in Nonnus' *Paraphrase of St. John's Gospel*", in: K. Spanoudakis (ed.), *Nonnus of Panopolis in Context: Poetry and Cultural Milieu in Late Antiquity*, Berlin, 2014, 287–301.

Gigli Piccardi, D. 1993, "Nonno, Proteo e l'isola di Faro." *Prometheus* 19 (1993): 230–234.

Golega, J. 1930, *Studien über die Evangeliendichtung des Nonnos von Panopolis.* Breslau, 1930.

Heine, R. E. 1986, "Can the Catena Fragments of Origen's Commentary on John Be Trusted?" *Vigiliae Christianae* 40 (1986): 118–134.

Hollis, A. 1994, "Nonnus and Hellenistic Poetry", in: N. Hopkinson (ed.) *Studies in the Dionysiaca of Nonnus*, Cambridge, 1994.

Kantorowicz, H. 1963, "Oriens Augusti. Lever du Roi." *Dumberton Oaks Papers* 17 (1963): 135–149.

Koester, H. 1965, "History and Cult in the Gospel of John and in Ignatius of Antioch." *Journal for Theology and the Church* 1 (1965): 111–123.

Kuiper, K. 1918, "De Nonno Evangelii Johannei interprete." *Mnemosyne* 46 (1918): 223–270.

Livrea, E. 1987, "Il poeta e il vescovo: la questione nonniana e la storia." *Prometheus* 13 (1987): 97–123.

Livrea, E. 1989, *Nonno di Panopoli. Parafrasi del Vangelo di S. Giovanni, Canto XVIII. Introduzione, testo critico, traduzione e commentario.* Napoli, 1989.

Livrea, E. 2000, *Nonno di Panopoli, Parafrasi del Vangelo di s. Giovanni. Canto B*. Bologna, 2000.

McPolin, J. 1984, *John* (New Testament Message 6). Wilmington, 1984.

Sherry, L. F. 1991, "The Hexameter Paraphrase of St John Attributed to Nonnus of Panopolis. Prolegomenon and Translation." Ph.D. diss., Columbia, 1991.

Van der Laan, P. W. A. Th. 1993, "Imitation créative dans le Carmen Paschale de Sédulius." In *Early Christian Poetry: A Collection of Essays*, ed. by J. den Boeft, A. Hilhorst. Leiden, 1993.

Vanderlip, V. F. 1972, *The Four Greek Hymns of Isidorus and the Cult of Isis*. Toronto, 1972.

Vian, F. 1988, "Les cultes païens dans les Dionysiaques de Nonnos: étude de vocabulaire." *Revue des Études Anciennes* 90 (1988): 399–410.

Wójtowicz, H. 1980, *Studia nad Nonnosem*. Lublin, 1980.

Ypsilanti, M. 2014, "Image-Making and the Art of Paraphrasing: Aspects of Darkness and Light in the *Metabole*." In K. Spanoudakis (ed.), *Nonnus of Panopolis in Context. Poetry and Cultural Milieu in Late Antiquity*. Berlin 2014, 123–137.

Some Remarks on the *Super Esaiam*
of Pseudo–Joachim of Fiore

Adam Poznański

The Institute of Classical, Mediterranean
and Oriental Studies, University of Wrocław

Some time ago, while browsing medieval collections in the Wrocław University
Library, I came across a thirteenth-century Latin manuscript which contained
several intriguing images. Among them, there were some simple diagrams
consisting of geometric shapes (circles and squares), as well as decorative
illustrations of instruments (trumpet, psaltery) and dragons. All of them were
accompanied by numerous captions and marginal glosses. It turned out that the
manuscript (signature: Mil. II 8 membr.) originally belonged to Johann Gottlieb
Milich's Library in Görlitz and was relocated after the Second World War.[1] It is
divided into two parts: the first one contains a collection of figures presenting
the doctrine of Joachim of Fiore (so called *Praemissiones*); the other one is a
composite work including commentary on some chapters of Isaiah (*Super
Esaiam* or *Super Prophetas*), previously attributed to Joachim of Fiore (†1202),
but now recognized as written by one of his followers in the mid-thirteenth
century. This unexpected encounter aroused my interest and I decided to learn
more about the works included in the manuscript.

The *Praemissiones*, extant in various manuscripts,[2] are composed of eight to
eleven various figures with marginal glosses and short descriptions. Researchers
dealing with the legacy of the Calabrian abbot consider it to be a post-
Joachimian collection prepared on the basis of genuine figures from the *Liber
Figurarum*.[3] Both figure collections and their relationship have been thoroughly

---

1 For more information about Milich's collection, see: Robert Joachim, *Geschichte der
  Milich'schen Bibliothek und ihre Sammlungen,* Thl. I–II, (Görlitz: Jungandreas, 1876–
  1877).

2 The list of manuscripts including *Praemissiones* and *Super Esaiam* can be found in:
  David Morris, "A Census of Known 'Super Prophetas' Manuscripts", *Oliviana*
  [Online] 4 (2012). Accessed March 15, 2014. http://oliviana.revues.org/530.

3 *Liber Figurarum* is a collection of diagrams illustrating the original views of Joachim of
  Fiore. For a long time, it was considered to be lost, but then was discovered
  (independently) in manuscripts from Reggio Emilia (published in 1939) and Oxford
  (published in 1942). The edition based on all known manuscripts was prepared in 1953
  by Leone Tondelli, Marjorie Reeves and Beatrice Hirsch-Reich, (eds.), "*Liber*

examined by Marjorie Reeves and Beatrice Hirsch Reich[4] (who, however, were convinced that the Milich's manuscript was lost).

The *Super Esaiam*, which also includes its own figures, has not yet drawn much attention of scholars.[5] In manuscripts, it is usually preceded by the *Praemissiones* and in such combination the two texts were published in Venice in 1517.[6] After having studied that edition (I will refer to it throughout this whole article), I decided to share my reflections on the text, especially on the comments on Isaiah. I will begin with a short overview of two issues concerning the *Super Esaiam*, namely the text's origin and content. The first point was recently discussed by David Morris who collected and compared all existing studies on the *Super Esaiam*.[7] According to him, it is impossible to determine whether the work comes from the Cistercian or the Franciscan milieu, since the teachings of Joachim of Fiore spread in both communities in southern Italy. As for the dating, Morris argues for 1260s as the most probable time.

In terms of content, one can distinguish three main parts of the *Super Esaiam*. The first one begins with a short prologue addressed to Joachim's companion, Rainer of Ponza (fol. 1r), which is followed by a commentary on chapters 1–9 and 11 of Isaiah (fols. 1r–9r). As for the format, the commentary is a freestanding lemmatic one: the biblical text is not quoted in its entirety, but single words or short extracts (*lemmata*) are cited. They are provided with explanations containing many references to various chapters of Isaiah and the other books of the Bible. There are also numerous marginal glosses with further explanations and biblical references. It is significant that only selected verses of each chapter of Isaiah are analyzed; for instance, in the first chapter, sixteen verses out of thirty-one are explicated, and in the fifth one, only six out of thirty. The author himself writes about these omissions and justifies them, stating that his intention was to shed light on what was obscure, and leave out what was

---

Figurarum". *Il libro delle Figure dell'abate Gioacchino da Fiore*, (Torino: Società editrice internazionale, 1953). The individual figures from this collection are described in detail in: Marjorie Reeves, Beatrice Hirsch-Reich, *The "Figurae" of Joachim of Fiore* (Oxford: Clarendon Press, 1972).

4   Marjorie Reeves, Beatrice Hirsch-Reich, "The 'Figurae' of Joachim of Fiore. Genuine and Spurious Collections." *Mediaeval and Renaissance Studies* 3 (1954), 170–199.

5   Ibid., 285–288; David Morris, "The Historiography of the 'Super Prophetas' (also known as 'Super Esaiam') of Pseudo-Joachim of Fiore", *Oliviana* [Online], 4 (2012). Accessed March 15, 2014. http://oliviana.revues.org/512.

6   Pseudo-Ioachimus Florensis, *Scriptum super Esaiam Prophetam* (Venetiis: Lazaro de Soardis, 1517).

7   See: Morris, "The Historiography… ," 25–34.

lucid.[8] All the comments are primarily of a typological character, i.e. the author attempts to present prefigurations of the New Testament events in the text of Isaiah. For example, seven women, who are taking hold of one man in Isa. 4:1 provide a parallel to seven gifts of the Holy Spirit in Acts 2:1–13.[9]

The second part, entitled *De oneribus sexti temporis*, describes the tribulation which will be sent by God upon the mankind during the sixth *tempus*. It may be useful here to summarize briefly the view of the Calabrian abbot on stages in the world's history. Joachim believed that there are two different, but complementary, historical patterns: *prima diffinitio* and *secunda diffinitio*.[10] The first one refers to the Holy Trinity: there are three ages (*status*) that correspond to the Father, the Son, and the Holy Spirit. There are also three orders, related to each *status* respectively: the married laity (*ordo coniugatorum*), the clergy (*ordo clericorum*), and the monks (*ordo monachorum*). The age of the Father encompassed the period from Adam until the birth of Jesus; the age of the Son lasted up until the time of Joachim; the final one, the age of the Holy Spirit, which has yet to come, will lead the believers to the summit of the spiritual life. It is significant that the last *status* will take place on the earth, before the end of the world. These ages, however, are not sharply separated, but overlap to some extent. For instance, some signs of the second *status* appeared already in the first one, and so forth.[11]

The second pattern, *secunda diffinitio*, is based upon the seven days of creation. This idea was not new, since already Saint Augustine proposed it in the *De Civitate Dei*[12], but Joachim developed it. According to him, there are two *tempora*, each divided into seven *etates*. The first *tempus* corresponds to the first *status*, and the second *tempus* to the second *status* (except for the seventh *etas* of the second *tempus* – the sabbath, which is identified with the third *status*, the age

---

8   *Super Esaiam* (Wrocław University Library MS Mil. II 8, fol. 8r): "In premisso capitulo plura dimisimus, sicut et in locis aliis, quia patent. Sufficit enim si illa solummodo illucescere facimus que obscurioribus sunt sensibus involuta."

9   Ibid., fol. 4v: "'Apprehenderunt septem mulieres virum unum in die illa' [Isa. 4:1]. Nonnulli putant septem mulieres totidem donationes spiritus designare [...]."

10 These patterns can be seen on the figures: the *Seven Etates* and the *Trinitarian Circles* of the *Liber Figurarum*, see: Reeves, Hirsch-Reich, *The "Figurae"…*, 120–129, 192–198.

11 These patterns are much more complicated, for details, see E. Randolph Daniel, "The Double Procession of the Holy Spirit in Joachim of Fiore's Understanding of History," *Speculum* 55, 3 (1980): 469–483; idem, "Joachim's Unnoticed Pattern of History: The Second Diffinitio," in *Joachim of Fiore and the Influence of Inspiration: Essays in Memory of Marjorie E. Reeves (1905–2003)*, ed. by J. E. Wannenmacher (Farnham: Ashgate, 2013), 3–13.

12 Aug. *Civ. Dei* 11.8. See Paul Archambault, "The Ages of Man and the Ages of the World. A Study of two Traditions," *Revue des Études Augustiniennes* 12 (1966): 200–206.

of the Holy Spirit). One of the most crucial elements of Joachim's doctrine is the assumption that the events from the Old Testament have their counterparts in the New Testament and also in the events which will come in the future. Consequently, it is possible to deduce the future by interpreting the Old Testament.[13] The seven *etates* of the first *tempus* in the *secunda diffinitio* are parallel to the seven *etates* in the second one. Since Joachim claimed to be living in the fifth *etas*, one would expect events similar to those described in the Old Testament to happen. Each *etas* (in both *tempora*) was also associated with the opening of one of the seven seals. Furthermore, in every *etas* there is a king who inflicts persecution on the believers.[14] The four kings of the second *tempus* were: Herod, Nero, Constantius the Arian (Constantius II), and Chosroes (Khosrau II, King of the Persians who invaded the Byzantine Empire) – each *etas* experienced an inevitable tribulation. *Liber de Concordia Novi ac Veteris Testamenti*, one of Joachim's essential works, is entirely devoted to this problem.[15]

The text particularly appreciated by the Calabrian abbot as a source for the motifs and symbolic numbers was the Apocalypse. According to his own testimony, he experienced enlightenment while working on the commentary on the Book of Revelation, which led to his understanding of the relation between the two Testaments.[16] Take the *secunda diffinitio* as an example: the openings of the seals refer to the book with seven seals in Apoc. 6–8, whereas the seven kings represent the seven heads of the Apocalyptic Dragon in Apoc. 12–13.[17]

Let us come back to the *Super Esaiam*. The part *De oneribus sexti temporis* describes the persecution in the sixth *etas* of the second *tempus* (using the original Joachim's terminology), which is yet to come. In order to predict the future, the author chose the Old Testament's *onera*, 'the burdens', as parallels. According to Isaiah and three minor prophets, they were to be sent upon various

---

13   Also the author of the *Super Esaiam* expresses this belief: "Videsne, lector, quomodo sunt involuta mysteria scripturarum, ubi per ea, que facta sunt, futura alia prenoscuntur?" (*Super Esaiam*, fol. 31r)

14   This idea is also presented in the *Super Esaiam*, fol. 50v: "Synagoge per septem libri signacula et tempora pressurarum; fluvius vero Novum Testamentum est continens septem apertiones sigillorum que facte sunt per totidem draconis capita in ecclesia militanti."

15   Abbot Joachim of Fiore, *Liber de Concordia Novi ac Veteris Testamenti*, ed. E. R. Daniel, Transactions of the American Philosophical Society, vol. 73, 8 (Philadelphia, 1983).

16   The *Expositio in Apocalypsim*, published in Venice in 1527, is one of the key works of Joachim of Fiore.

17   There is a figure of the Dragon with Seven Heads both in the *Liber Figurarum* and in the *Praemissiones*, see: Reeves, Hirsch-Reich, *The "Figurae" of Joachim of Fiore*, 146–152.

tribes and regions as a punishment for their sins. In the *Super Esaiam*, the 'burdens' consisted primarily of invasions and persecutions by heretics and pagans.

The section under discussion begins with a figure of concentric circles on fol. 9v. In the middle of it, there is a caption: *Visio super Hierusalem* ('vision of Jerusalem'), which is surrounded by another caption: "Hierusalem in medio gentium posita est sicut onus lapidis." This is, arguably, a reference to Zech. 12:3:

> "Et erit: In die illa ponam Ierusalem lapidem oneris cunctis populis: omnes, qui levabunt eam, concisione lacerabuntur; et colligentur adversus eam omnia regna terrae".[18]

The outermost circle contains fourteen *onera* – eleven from Isaiah and three from minor prophets (Nahum, Habakkuk, Malachi). This figure has a short explanation indicating regions or people to whom particular *onera* refer.[19] Next, there is a brief introduction (fol. 10r–v), followed by seventeen folios of simple geographic diagrams (fols. 11r–27v), presenting probably all the places of the world known to the author of the *Super Esaiam*. They are provided with numerous marginal glosses, mainly with the Bible references. Their role is to illustrate all the regions that are to be affected by the *onera*. At the end of this "geographic" section, a justification of such a great punishment is presented: since all people together distanced themselves from God (*communis excessus omnium*), the affliction would spread over the entire world (*universalis transitus*

---

18 "And it shall come to pass in that day, that I will make Jerusalem a burdensome stone to all people: all that shall lift it up shall be rent and torn, and all the kingdoms of the earth shall be gathered together against her." (Zech. 12:3)

19 *Super Esaiam*, fols. 9v–10r: "Onus verbi Domini [Mal. 1:1], quod replicat Malachias ultimus prophetarum, tangit Iudeos et populum gentium seculi lubricum et tripudium salvandorum. Onus Babylonis [Isa. 13:1] secundum concordiam tangit Romam sicut Caldea Alemaniam Onus Philistiim [Isa. 11:14]: secundum concordiam Lombardos et alios Italos et Guilelmandalos. Onus Moab [Isa. 15:1] et filiorum Amon [Isa. 11:14]: principes Latinos et Grecos. Onus deserti maris [Isa. 21:1]: Affricanos et alios Saracenos. Onus Duma [Isa. 21:11] vel Idumee tangit Iudeos negociatores. Onus maris [in the Venetian edition "os mare"] et terre [Isa. 24:15–16]: sapientes et legistas et Grecos. Onus in Arabia [Isa. 21:13] Hyspanos et Marchianos. Onus vallis visionis [Isa. 22:1]: cuiuscunque ordinis regulares. Onus Tyri [Isa. 23:1]: Siculos et regnicolas sibi subiacentes. Onus Egypti [Isa. 19:1]: Iudeos, Danaos et Francos. Onus iumentorum austri [Isa. 30:6]: clericos, prelatos, rectores eorum ubique diffusos. Onus Damasci [Isa. 17:1] tangit Thuscos et Ligures in gladio verbi Domini et ferro effundendos et conterendos. Onus Ninive [Nah. 1:1]tangit mundum pollutum sanguine peccatorum: ecclesiam tam in Greco populo quam Latino ; Assyricos atterendum exterminium. Onus Abacuch [Hab. 1:1] tangit peccatores seculi, trangressores legis et fidei, Iudeos, Italicos, adventum Christi in carne, crucis patibulum, vocationem paganorum."

flagellorum).[20] Nevertheless, after these hardships the sabbath, the time of peace and rest (*pacis et ocii sabbatismus*) will come to chosen places.[21] The section that follows contains descriptions of individual *onera* (fols. 28r–49v). Their order, however, differs from the one presented in the figure of concentric circles, which I find difficult to explain.

The third and last part also has its own title: *De septem temporibus ecclesie* (fols. 49v–59v); it refers to the *secunda diffinitio* and seven *etates* of the second *tempus*. David Morris, in the article mentioned above, suggests that this part is "a separate tract".[22] One should, however, pay particular attention to its opening, in which we read: "Ecce ab oneribus omnibus expediti..." (*Super Esaiam*, fol. 49v) – "Here, having freed ourselves from all burdens..." These words might indicate a connection with the previous part. The beginning continues: "[...] quibus orbis in suis urbibus eque pro peccatis affligitur, ut facilius corrigatur [...]" (*Super Esaiam*, fol. 49v), "with which the world in its cities is everywhere equally oppressed for its sins, in order that it may be easier corrected [...]". This might refer to the world represented in the above-mentioned geographic diagrams. This part also includes a figure (fol. 50v): it depicts the Old Testament Tabernacle with two captions in the middle (one above the other): "Longos fac funiculos tuos et clavos tuos consolida" (in the Venetian edition, we find twice "tres" instead of "tuos" and "curvos" instead of "clavos"; evidently in the manuscript the sentence accompanying the drawing had been written with smaller letters, and the printer had troubles reading it) and "forma tabernaculi federis" (a figure of the Tabernacle of the Convenant). The first one is a paraphrase of Isa. 54:2:

> "Dilata locum tentorii tui, et pelles tabernaculorum tuorum extende, ne parcas; longos fac funiculos tuos, et clavos tuos consolida."[23]

Below these captions, there is another one: "Sacra pagina" – the Bible. Marjorie Reeves and Beatrice Hirsch-Reich argue that the Holy Scripture is symbolized by the fundament on which the Tabernacle is based[24], whereas in my opinion the Bible, as an object of great value and importance, is rather stored in the

---

20 Ibid., fol. 27v: "Non ambigimus omnes seculi per circuitum regiones propter malitiam sexti temporis et etatis a gentibus infidelibus feriendas ; et iccirco quia communis excessus est omnium, universalis erit et transitus flagellorum."

21 Ibid., fol. 27v: "Post exterminium harum omnium regionum succedet electis reliquiis pacis et ocii sabbatismus."

22 See Morris, "The Historiography...'," 3.

23 "Enlarge the place of thy tent, and stretch out the skins of thy tabernacles, spare not: lengthen thy cords, and strengthen thy stakes." (Isa. 54:2)

24 See Reeves, Hirsch-Reich, *The "Figurae" of Joachim of Fiore*, 287.

Tabernacle, which plays similar function as the Ark of the Covenant. Besides, the Old Testament Tabernacle served as a place of encounter with God and reading of the Bible is such an encounter to some extent. The four sides of the figure are indicated by the four directions of the world, which represent the four senses of Scripture.[25] However, they were not exactly the same as those transmitted by the patristic tradition, because the Calabrian abbot invented his own sophisticated "system" of biblical exegesis.[26] In his teachings, he distinguishes four main senses (*intellectus*): typological (with seven sub-categories), historical, moral, and allegorical (with three subdivisions). Altogether, they are twelve in number, and in the *Super Esaiam* they are compared to twelve different characters from the Old Testament, whose task, within the context of this figure, is to guard the Tabernacle.[27] Their names are also enumerated around the figure.

The rest of the third part of the *Super Esaiam* deals with the seven *etates* of the second *tempus*, which are called "the seven *tempora* of the church" (*septem tempora ecclesie*) here. Although all seven are introduced, only six of them are discussed. The reason might be that during the sixth *etas* the climax of tribulation was to take place and this was the main topic of the whole work. In this part, number seven is used in other contexts as well. The author mentions seven 'sub-senses' of the typological sense of Scripture, seven synagogues and, significantly, seven streams (*septem rivi*) from Isa. 11:15:

> "Et desolabit Dominus linguam maris Aegypti, et levabit manum suam super flumen
> in fortitudine spiritus sui; et percutiet eum in septem rivis, ita ut transeant per eum
> calceati."[28]

---

25 *Super Esaiam*, fol. 50r: "Et in evangelio Joannis: 'Ego sum ostium, per me si quis intraverit, salvabitur et ingredietur et pascua inveniet' [John 10:9], scilicet spiritualium lectionum. Habet enim volumen divine pagine quadruplicem intellectum: moralem ab oriente, hystoricum ab occidente, typicum ab aquilone, allegoricum ab austro, et ascensiones notate sunt successive." The creator of this figure might have been inspired by the *Rotae of Ezekiel* from the *Liber Figurarum*, see: Reeves, Hirsch-Reich, *The "Figurae" of Joachim of Fiore*, 224–231.

26 See Herbert Grundmann, *Studien über Joachim von Fiore. Mit einem Vorwort zum Neudruck. (Unveränderter reprographischer Nachdruck der Ausgabe Leipzig 1927)* (Stuttgart: Teubner, 1966), 18–55; Henri de Lubac, *Exégèse médiévale: les quatre sens de l'Écriture*, I, 2 (Paris: Aubier, 1961), 437–558.

27 Ibid., fol. 50r: "Sic ad custodiam tabernaculi federis in plagis suis viri duodecim deputantur ad instar totidem intellectuum... ."

28 "And the Lord shall lay waste the tongue of the sea of Egypt, and shall lift up his hand over the river in the strength of his spirit: and he shall strike it in the seven streams, so that men may pass through it in their shoes." (Isa. 11:15)

This division of the river into seven streams symbolizes the division of the God's revelation into seven parts (*particule*), so that each part could be revealed during each of the seven *tempora ecclesie* (or *etates*).

It should be added that the Venetian editors made a mistake while dividing the text into sections. Their edition consists of seven parts, although there should be only three: the commentary on Isaiah, *De oneribus sexti temporis* and *De septem temporibus ecclesie*. The reason is that the third one was incorrectly split into five parts, which were entitled *secunda pars libri, tertia pars libri* and so on, up to *sexta pars libri*. *De oneribus sexti temporis* is called *prima pars* in the Venetian edition, while the first part of the whole text – the commentary on Isaiah – has no number. However, the expression *tertia pars libri* ("the third part of the book") does not refer to the part of work as a whole, but only to the opening of the third seal of the apocalyptic book which is described there; it is indicated by the fact, that the openings of the first and second seals are mentioned right above.[29] Similarly for the *quarta pars libri* and so on.

Turning to the role of Isaiah in the text, I assume that the author, as a follower of Joachim of Fiore, wished to propagate the teachings of his master and that this was his main goal in all three parts of the *Super Esaiam*. In my opinion, he wanted to explicate the sense of history to his contemporaries, so that they were prepared for the imminent persecutions and aware that after the great suffering, the age of the Holy Spirit will eventually come. For a supporter of Joachim's, the most proper way to present such matters was to refer to the harmony of the two Testaments. So, assuming that all present and future events have their prefigurations in the Old Testament, he had to find an adequate passage, one containing warnings and threats of future tribulation. For this purpose, the Book of Isaiah was, indeed, a right choice, since it includes a great deal of oracles against Judah and other nations. In general, its themes are the wrath of God, the judgment over Israel, and the punishment for its perfidiousness – but also hope for the future time of peace, which was to emanate from the New Jerusalem. As one can see, all these prophecies may be useful while referring to the teachings of Joachim of Fiore, especially in the context of the sixth *etas* and the age of the Holy Spirit. In my opinion the chapters of Isaiah that are included in the commentary might have been chosen intentionally. They all concern persecutions and the final liberation of the God's

---

29 *Super Esaiam,* fol. 51r: "Igitur sub apertione primi signaculi vel sigilli ordo apostolicus in albo equo designatus exivit: qui ad regnandas animas errore pollutas datus est arcus celestis eloquij et irrefragabilis corona triumphi. [...] In secunda parte libri soluto secundo signaculo sub secundo draconis capite seviente interfecti sunt Christi martyres a paganis: sicut antiqua Madianitarum Philistiimque prelia protestantur."

chosen nation, and therefore may be seen as relevant for the situation of the Roman Church in the time between the sixth and seventh *etas*. Therefore, the first part of the *Super Esaiam* is closely related to the second one, *De oneribus sexti temporis*, which also describes the imminent affliction and also draws much from Isaiah. Unlike these two, the third one is based rather on the Apocalypse, although there is one remarkable reference to a passage from the Isaiah – the one concerning the seven streams (Isa. 11:15), which was already discussed. Nevertheless this part has a similar goal – it continues to present the sense of history according to views of Joachim of Fiore.

On the whole, I think that the *Super Esaiam* is an interesting example of various methods being used to demonstrate and explain certain elaborate views. The first one is the biblical exegesis. Considering the first part of the *Super Esaiam*, we may suppose that the author's final intention was not just to comment on Isaiah, but rather to use the commentary form as a means to an end. The second part consists of the marginal glosses. They occur throughout the entire work and, since they are a special feature of ancient and medieval commentaries, they serve as an aid to present all the unclear words and expressions. Finally, there are figures, the most original aspect of abbot's of Fiore works. The author of the *Super Esaiam* probably came across that reader-friendly way of illustrating complex patterns while he was studying the teachings of his master. That might have encouraged him to provide the text with his own diagrams and thereby enrich one of the secondary sources of Joachim's thought.

Aristotélisme ou thomisme? La dispute sur le caractère du discours de l'éthique dans le *Commentaire* de saint Thomas à *L'Éthique à Nicomaque*

Izabella Andrzejuk

La Chaire d'Histoire de la Philosophie Ancienne et Médiévale
L'Université Cardinal Stefan Wyszyński à Varsovie

Notre attitude à l'égard de la philosophie morale de saint Thomas a été, pour une large part, déterminée par deux historiens éminents de la philosophie : Étienne Gilson et Fernand van Steenberghen. Les deux savants exprimaient des opinions bien divergentes à propos des textes où, d'après eux, Thomas aurait exposé d'une façon la plus complète sa philosophie morale. Steenberghen était en effet d'avis que l'éthique thomasienne est présente principalement dans son *Commentaire à l'Éthique à Nicomaque* d'Aristote tandis que Gilson indiquait surtout la *Somme théologique* et la *Somme contre le païens* comme la source la plus intégrale et la plus mûre de la pensée éthique d'Aquinate.

Il est frappant de constater que jusqu'à présent, à vrai dire, personne n'a pris de position décidée et significative à propos de cette controverse. Ainsi, la discussion entre Gilson et Steenberghen n'a pas été fermée et les deux savants sont restés sur leurs positions. Il semble que le manque d'une continuation de cette « dispute » présente une certaine lacune dans le discours sur l'importance des commentaires de saint Thomas aux œuvres d'Aristote. Et bien que le but du présent article ne soit nullement d'établir d'une façon définitive lequel des savants avait raison, nous voudrions tout au moins jeter une lumière sur les coulisses de cette dispute et élucider des raisons potentielles qui ont amené les deux grands philosophes à prendre des positions différentes.

L'objet de cette discussion, le *Commentaire à L'Éthique à Nicomaque* a été écrit dans les années 1271–1272 à l'époque où Thomas était le professeur de l'Université de Paris. La constatation de ce fait a falsifié l'opinion selon laquelle les commentaires d'Aristote avaient été créés au séminaire dominicain de Sainte-Sabine et d'autre part, a mis fin à la période de sous-estimation de ces textes, traités jusqu'alors seulement comme un moyen d'expliquer pensée difficile d'Aristote aux jeunes séminaristes. René-Antoine Gauthier a démontré que le *Commentaire à L'Éthique à Nicomaque* a été écrit parallèlement à *II-II*

Summa theologiae[1] tandis que le texte de *L'Éthique à Nicomaque* qui a servi de base à Thomas dans sa rédaction des commentaires est une version corrigée de la traduction de Robert Grosseteste.[2]

Il faut aussi ajouter qu'autant en rédigeant les commentaires Thomas suivait les règles[3] étant en vigueur dans ce domaine au Moyen Âge, autant dans le *Commentaire à L'Éthique à Nicomaque* il est allé plus loin en essayant de lier une présentation détaillée des thèses d'Aristote à ses propres idées éthiques. Ce qui – semble-t-il – n'a pas rendu difficile la distinction entre les idées de Stagirite et celles d'Aquinate même.

1. La position de Fernand van Steenberghen sur la question du *Commentaire* Thomasien *à L'Éthique à Nicomaque*

Steenberghen situe les *Sommes* de Thomas au rang des œuvres théologiques tandis que ses commentaires aux œuvres d'Aristote – au rang des œuvres philosophiques (dont aussi le *Commentaire à L'Éthique à Nicomaque*).[4] Analysant la présence de la philosophie dans les œuvres théologiques de Thomas, Steenberghen admet que l'on peut parler de deux façons de lier ces disciplines : soit c'est une inclusion d'un sujet philosophique « en entier » à des considérations philosophiques, soit la philosophie fonctionne comme un outil rationnel servant à élaborer les traités *stricte* théologiques. Et il paraît évident que la première méthode est plus propice pour distinguer les opinions philosophiques de l'auteur.

Steenberghen – semble-t-il – range *La Somme théologique* dans la deuxième catégorie de textes et par conséquent ne la considère pas comme la meilleure source des idées philosophiques de saint Thomas. Il est d'avis qu'Aquinate a procédé à la rédaction des commentaires aux textes de Stagirite dans le seul but d'expliquer à fond ses propres idées et de démontrer qu'elles n'étaient pas en

---

1   Il nous paraît significatif que cette partie de *Summa theologiae* contient aussi la problématique éthique, p. ex. la question des vertus cardinales.

2   R.-A. Gauthier, « La date du *Commentaire* de saint Thomas sur *l'Éthique à* Nicomaque », *Recherches de Théologie Ancienne et Médiévale* 18 (1950), pp. 66–105 ; James A. Weisheipl, *Friar Thomas D'Aquino, His Life, Thought and Works* (Washington, D.C, 1983), p. 283.

3   Bien qu'il semble avoir apporté les soins particuliers à commenter justement les textes d'Aristote. Pour plus d'informations consulter : F. van Steenberghen, *La Philosophie au XIIIe siècle. Deuxiéme éd., mise à jour* (Louvain–Paris, 1991), pp. 294–297.

4   Ibidem, pp. 280–281.

opposition avec la Révélation.[5] Établissant sa distinction entre les œuvres théologiques et philosophiques, Steenberghen a essayé de la légitimer en citant le Docteur Angélique même, qui avait défini sa *Summa theologiae* comme l'œuvre dans laquelle il voulait avant tout parvenir à la vérité de la religion chrétienne.[6] Pour Steenberghen, il reste donc douteux que *La Somme théologique* puisse être une source riche et complète de la philosophie de saint Thomas. Aussi se penche-t-il plutôt vers les commentaires thomasiens aux textes philosophiques en y voyant dans une plus large mesure la source des idées du grand philosophe. Steenberghen qualifie les commentaires mêmes d'Aristote de « magnifiques » en tant que textes où Aquinate avait réussi à réaliser deux objectifs à la fois : exposition du texte et présentation de ses propres opinions sur le sujet traité. Thomas, en voyant dans les idées d'Aristote une vraie et solide philosophie, aurait été convaincu, que moyennant ses commentaires, il enseignant une vraie philosophie. Suivant Steenberghen, nous pouvons indiquer des traits caractéristiques du travail de commentateur d'Aquinate :

– Thomas garde un objectivisme bienveillant à l'égard de l'œuvre commentée : Il essaie de dissiper les doutes dans le texte en faveur de Stagirite. Mais s'il trouve une solution erronée, il ne cherche pas à la justifier à tout prix ;
– Grâce à l'explication littérale du texte, Thomas essaie de parvenir à l'intention réelle de l'auteur ;
– À ce but précis servent les divisions du texte commenté grâce auxquelles le sens des fragments abordés et plus compréhensible.[7]

En concluant en quelque sorte sur cette caractéristique du style d'Aquinate, Steenberghen ajoute que cette « habile » et « profonde » interprétation d'Aristote avait surtout pour but de dégager de ses textes tout ce qui en était digne et de laisser à l'ombre toutes les opinions qui pourraient induire le lecteur en erreur. Selon lui, les traits énumérés des commentaires donnent à l'activité de Thomas « l'attribut de la gloire ». Il semble que pour lui ce qui est essentiel ce n'est pas seulement la pensée de saint Thomas (soit philosophique, soit théologique), mais aussi sa stratégie d'élaborer les textes de Stagirite grâce à

---

5   Les opinions semblables quant aux motifs de la création des commentaires aux œuvres d'Aristote ont exprimé J. A. Weisheipl et, c'est surprenant, É. Gilson. Voir: É. Gilson, *Le Thomisme. Introduction au système de saint Thomas d'Aquin.* Cinquième éd. revue et augm. (Paris, 1947), p. 15 ; et aussi : J. A. Weisheipl, *Friar Thomas d'Aquino*, p. 283.
6   Voir : F. van Steenberghen, *La Philosophie au XIIIe siècle*, p. 282.
7   Il faut souligner que Steenberghen n'est pas seul à penser ainsi. Son point de vue sur les méthodes de commenter adoptées par Thomas partagent M.-D. Chenu, *Introduction à l'étude de saint Thomas d'Aquin.* Deuxième éd. (Montreal–Paris, 1954), pp. 173–198.

laquelle, à l'occasion de commenter les textes de Stagirite, il présentait en plus ses propres idées philosophiques, en tirant des conceptions d'Aristote des conséquences perspicaces et en approfondissant leur sens et leur signification. Toutes ces traits caractéristiques ont amené Steenberghen à appeler les commentaires d'Aristote effectués par Thomas « la somme philosophique pour les débutants ».[8] La façon spécifique de commenter ce groupe de textes adoptée par Thomas fait d'eux un témoignage important et significatif de propres idées philosophiques d'Aquinate.

Parmi les œuvres d'Aristote commentées par Thomas une place exceptionnelle – selon Steenberghen – occupent les textes éthiques. Car, à son avis, l'éthique de Thomas est « le couronnement de la philosophie ». Dans les considérations éthiques d'Aquinate il distingue également des thèmes clé tels que :

a) La Divine Providence en tant que le point de départ de l'éthique ;
b) L'homme en tant que personne (avec l'accent mis sur sa liberté, sa responsabilité et sa vocation à l'éternité) – comme le deuxième, à côté de la Divine Providence, pilier de l'éthique ;
c) L'adoption de l'autonomie de l'ordre pratique (l'éthique a ses propres principes et son objet est l'expérience humaine) ;
d) L'accentuation de l'importance de la raison en tant que pouvoir permettant d'identifier les principes de la loi naturelle.[9]

L'opinion de Steenberghen sur l'autonomie de l'éthique paraît intéressante d'autant plus qu' il en déduit la thèse selon laquelle il n'est pas possible de conclure sur la doctrine philosophique de la morale en se référant à la métaphysique. Une telle position est inquiétante dans la mesure où elle pourrait aboutir à la conviction que la métaphysique de Thomas ne serait pas la base de son éthique. Steenberghen remarque aussi que le *Commentaire à l'Éthique à Nicomaque* se caractérise souvent par une fine frontière, parfois presque impossible à délimiter, entre l'éthique en tant que science philosophique et théologie morale.[10]

2. La position d'Étienne Gilson sur la question de *Commentaire Thomasien à l'Éthique à Nicomaque* d'Aristote

Steenberghen et Gilson avaient des opinions différentes sur beaucoup de questions liées à la doctrine de saint Thomas. Ils étaient pourtant tous les deux

---

8   Steenberghen, *La Philosophie au XIIIᵉ siècle*, p. 297.
9   Ibidem, pp. 309–310.
10 Ibidem, p. 309.

d'accord sur le fait que chez Aquinate on peut apercevoir une forte liaison entre la philosophie et la théologie.[11]

Gilson construit sa position à l'égard de la philosophie contenue dans les textes de Thomas à la base de sa propre conception de la philosophie chrétienne qui admet que la Révélation vient en aide à la raison dans la connaissance. Il est évident que pour Gilson cette « coopération » de la Révélation et la raison ne signifie pas l'effacement de certaines délimitations ou compétences de la connaissance aussi bien naturelle que surnaturelle mais seulement une sorte d'interaction.[12] C'est pour cette raison que – selon Gilson – les textes d'Aquinate les plus originaux et créateurs sont ceux qui présentent des conceptions philosophiques comme « enclaves » sur le terrain des considérations théologiques.

On peut aussi constater que de ce point de vue c'est justement les textes situés à la charnière entre la théologie et la philosophie qui devraient être l'objet du plus grand intérêt des chercheurs. Une telle position implique la conséquence : la reconnaissance de la supériorité des *Sommes* sur les commentaires des textes d'Aristote.[13]

Analisant le patrimoine d'Aquinate, Gilson arrive à la constatation que celui-ci étudiait Aristote uniquement pour renforcer les fondements de sa propre activité scientifique, qui, par principe, devait concerner la théologie. Ainsi, l'attitude de Thomas à l'égard de la philosophie d'Aristote aurait été purement instrumentale. D'ailleurs, son attitude envers la relation théologie-philosophie était telle – ce qu'a souligné Gilson – que Thomas avait traité avec le plus grand soin ces parties de sa philosophie qui auraient pu lui servir au plus haut dégré, à élaborer sa doctrine théologique.[14] Selon E. Gilson ces raisons suffisent pour qu'on soumette le discours philosophique de Thomas à sa disposition des considérations théologiques.

---

11 Au sujet de l'approche spécifique de la philosophie et théologie au Moyen Âge voir : É. Gilson, « Les recherches historico-critiques et l'avenir de la scolastique », *Antoninianum* 26 (1951), pp. 40–48.

12 Voir: É. Gilson, *L'Esprit de la philosophie médiévale.* Deuxième éd. revue (Paris, 1948), pp. 34–35.

13 Gilson le dit clairement quand il constate: « Les *Commentaires* de saint Thomas sur Aristote sont pour nous des documents très précieux, dont la perte eût été déplorable. Pourtant, s'ils s'étaient tous perdus, les deux *Sommes* nous permettraient encore de connaître ce qu'il y a de plus personnel et de plus profond dans sa philosophie; mais si les ouvrages théologiques de saint Thomas s'étaient perdus, serions-nous aussi bien renseignés sur sa philosophie par ses commentaires sur Aristote ?». Consulter: É. Gilson, *Le Thomisme*, p.15.

14 « La théologie de saint Thomas est d'un philosophe, mais sa philosophie est d'un saint », Ibidem, p. 16].

Gilson, voyant la plus grande valeur et profondeur intelectuelle dans les textes où la théologie est la plus étroitement liée à la philosophie, est d'avis que c'est justement les deux *Sommes* qui sont la source la plus riche et le plus complète de la philosophie de saint Thomas. Gilson met aussi en valeur une sensibilité exceptionelle de saint Thomas qui tout en liant ces deux disciplines prenait soin de ne pas faire disparaître l'essence même de la philosophie. Le but essentiel de Thomas était pourtant – selon Gilson – d'expliquer la Révélation sans tomber en contradiction avec la raison.[15] De plus, Gilson avance une thèse qu' aucune des œuvres de Thomas ne renfermerait une exposition complète de sa philosophie car, s'il en était autrement, ce texte aurait été tout simplement examiné séparément. Cela concerne également les commentaires thomasiens sur Aristote qui ont été finalement subjugués à la disposition des problèmes imposés par Stagirite.

Thomas est donc tout d'abord théologien et après seulement philosophe. Son œuvre principale, *Somme théologique,* contient les idées philosophiques mais démontrées en accord avec l'ordre théologique (bien que les justifications elles-mêmes appartiennent du point de vue de la méthodologie à la philosophie). Dans le texte ainsi construit Gilson indique un ordre spécifique des sujets éthiques abordés par Aquinate[16] :

a)   Les actes humains orientés sur le but (Dieu) ;
b)   La liberté et l'intelligence des actes humains (le problème du but final – qui est nécessaire et celui buts occasionnels qui ne sont pas nécessaires) ;
c)   Les aptitudes et les vertus (le problème du mal et du bien moral) ;
d)   Les lois ;
e)   L'amour et les sentiments ;
f)   La vie privée de l'homme ;
g)   La vie sociale de l'homme ;
h)   La vie religieuse de l'homme ;
i)   Le but final.

Il faut remarquer qu en adoptant un tel ordre des idées éthiques de Thomas Gilson n'est pas fidèle à ses propres constatations car cette proposition est déjà une certaine perturbation de l'ordre original utilisé par Thomas dans *la Somme.*[17]

---

15   Ibidem, pp. 18–19 [*Tomizm*, p. 20].
16   Ibidem, pp. 351–496 [*Tomizm*, p. 294–409].
17   Comme on l'a signalé avant, selon Gilson, les questions philosophiques dans *Summa theologiae* devraient être considérées dans l'ordre indiqué par la théologie et non en essayant de décortiquer des fragments philosophiques des textes théologiques de Thomas pour en déterminer le système philosophique d'Aquinate. Voir: Ibidem, p. 16.

L'ordre de ces sujets établi par Thomas se présenterait en effet de la façon suivante :

a)   Le but final de l'homme et y étroitement liée la question du bonheur ;
b)   La volonté libre et l'absence de liberté dans les actes humains ;
c)   La volonté et ses fonctions ;
d)   Le bien et le mal dans les actes humains ;
e)   Les sentiments et le sujet des sentiments ;
f)   L'amour ;
g)   Les aptitudes ;
h)   Les vertus et les vices (en général) ;
i)   Les lois (dont la Grâce en tant que le nouvelle loi) ;
j)   Les vertus théologiques ;
k)   Les vertus cardinales et les vices ;

Même si en écrivant sur la vie privée, sociale et religieuse Gilson pouvait penser aux vertus et capacités précises, il nous serait difficile – semble-t-il – d'approuver l'ordre des sujets qu'il a proposé. Thomas en effet parle des vertus théologiques avant d'énumérer les vertus cardinales. De plus, il soulève le sujet des vertus deux fois : tout d'abord quand il présente leur spécificité à l'occasion de traiter les questions liées aux aptitudes et ensuite en parlant des vertus particulières. D'autre part, les questions liées à la loi apparaissent dans la *Somme* plus tard que le voudrait Gilson. Enfin, la problématique de l'amour apparaît aussi deux fois dans la Somme : au moment où Thomas parle du fonctionnement des sentiments en l'homme et quand il soulève la question de l'amour de l'homme pour Dieu.

Les divergences observées entre Thomas et Gilson dans leur façon de mettre en ordre les questions soulevées démontreraient que Gilson dans sa proposition essaie plutôt d'établir l'ordre probable des questions éthiques chez saint Thomas que de présenter l'ordre que celui-ci avait effectivement utilisé dans ses considérations éthiques.

Conclusion

La première question qui paraît digne d'être accentuée dans le cadre de la conclusion est le point de départ commun de Steenberghen et de Gilson. En effet il paraît intéressant que les deux historiens de philosophie ont constaté unanimement que le Moyen Âge ne connaissait pas de distinction entre la philosophie et la théologie dont la preuve est par exemple *Summa theologiae* mais qu'ils ont abouti à des conclusions bien différentes s'il s'agit de la valeur des œuvres de Thomas comparées. Si l'on essaie de trouver les causes des positions divergentes de Gilson et de Steenberghen au sujet du *Commentaire à L'Éthique à Nicomaque* et à la *Somme théologique* il faut, semble-t-il, indiquer tout d'abord la conception de la philosophie chrétienne de Gilson. Dans cette perspective, les textes les plus intéressants paraissent ceux dans lesquels le philosophie-chrétien élargit les horizons de la philosophie grâce à la Révélation. Mais ayant adopté une telle position Gilson aboutit à rétrécir en quelque sorte les compétences philosophiques de Thomas. Ainsi, quand il s'exprime en tant que théologien philosophant – il est intéressant, original et authentique mais quand il prend la parole en tant que philosophe – il est imitatif.

Steenberghen, bien qu'il traite la philosophie et la théologie médievales comme un certain monolith, accomplit finalement une division assez rigide des textes d'Aquinate. La *Somme* est une œuvre théologique, et par conséquent, orientée vers la problématique théologique accompagnée à peine de philosophie. *Le Commentaire*, par contre, est un texte philosophique et en tant que tel contient toutes les idées de valeur de saint Thomas. Il paraît que c'est cette catégorique distinction méthodologique qui a amené Steenberghen à considérer *La Somme* comme l'œuvre philosophique de moindre importance.

De même, il serait difficile de partager l'opinion de Steenberghen selon laquelle l'éthique de Thomas est à tel point autonome qu'elle ne puise pas à sa métaphysique. Or, il suffit de regarder la structure même de *la Somme* pour voir qu'Aquinate considère les premières questions éthiques seulement après avoir présenté le sujet de Dieu et de l'homme.

Le Commentaire à L'Éthique à Nicomaque est dans son essence quelque chose de plus qu'une simple présentation de l'éthique d'Aristote. Car Thomas, tout en la commentant, construit sa propre philosophie morale, en commençant par la définition de son objet et de sa méthode. Il est vrai que certaines questions y sont moins développées que dans *la Somme* mais cela ne change rien au fait que le Commentaire contient la base des principaux sujets désignant l'éthique thomasienne.

La conclusion ultime de nos considérations peut être la constatation que les deux chercheurs se sont partiellement trompés : Sans *le Commentaire à L'Éthique à Nicomaque* nous n'aurions pas de la définition thomasienne de l'objet de la philosophie morale ainsi que de riches considérations sur l'amitié en tant que l'une des variantes de l'amour. D'autre part, sans *la Somme théologique* il nous manquerait des fondements antropologiques de la philosophie morale de même que la situation exacte de Dieu au centre de cette philosophie en tant que la fin de toute chose.

Le commentaire de Thomas d'Aquin à *Liber de causis* – odyssée de textes et de conceptions à travers les cultures, les époques et les écoles philosophiques

Artur Andrzejuk

La Chaire d'Histoire de la Philosophie Ancienne et Médiévale
L'Université Cardinal Stefan Wyszyńskià Varsovie

Liber de causis(*Le Livre des Causes*) c'est une suite d'extraits *d'Éléments de théologie* de Proclos commentés par un auteur arabe anonyme. Ce texte, traduit du latin par Gérard de Crémone avant l'an 1187, était, jusqu'à la parution en 1272 de son commentaire effectué par Thomas d'Aquin, attribué à Aristote. Malgré une immense littérature concernant la paternité de *Liber de causis* une « prudente » opinion de Thomas reste en vigueur[1] :

> Le livre du platonicien Proclus constitué de deux cent onze théorèmes et intitulé *Éléments de théologie* avait été écrit en grec et ainsi divulgé. Par contre, le livre, connu parmi les latinistes sous le titre *Liber de causis* et à propos duquel on sait qu'il avait été écrit avec une complète méconnaissance de la version grecque, n'existe qu'en version arabe. Il est donc fort probable qu'il ait été rédigé par des philosophes arabes sous forme d'un résumé effectué à la base du livre mentionné de Proclus ce qui prouve le fait que tout ce qui est contenu dans ce livre est contenu de façon plus complète et plus élaborée dans l'autre.[2]

Le texte en version arabe a paru probablement à Toledo au début du XIIIe siècle ou peut-être encore plus tôt à « l'époque des traductions » initiée par le calife abbasside al-Mamun, fondateur de la « Maison de la sagesse » à Bagdad (vers 830). Pourtant, ce n'est pas cela qui est le plus important. Or la grande « renommé » de ce texte résultait du fait que l'on avait attribué à Aristote même. Et cela n'aurait rien de spécial si on ne savait pas que le véritable auteur des idées contenues dans *Liber de causis* – Proclos (412–485) – était l'un des plus éminents philosophes néoplatoniciens, réformateur de l'Académie de Platon, bref, quelqu'un se situant presque aux antipodes du Lycée d'Aristote. Il a écrit l'œuvre intitulée *Éléments de théologie* (*Stoichéiosis theologiké*, lat. *Elementatio theologica*) en s'appuyant avant tout sur Plotin et Porphyre. C'est de la partie

---

1   Comp. M. Olszewski, *Liber de causis* [*Le Livre des causes*], in *Powszechna encyklopedia filozofii*, vol. 6 (Lublin, 2005), pp. 390–393.

2   Thomas d'Aquin, *Super Librum de causis expositio*. Ed. H.-D. Saffrey (Friburgi, 1954), Prooemium, p. 4.

centrale de cet ouvrage qu'on avait compilé *Liber de causis*. Cette renommé du
Livre qui paraît imméritée récapitule brillamment Paweł Milcarek :

> *De causis* est un texte *par excellence* néoplatonicien. Par contre, ses relations avec
> l'aristotélisme sont presque paradoxales : presque aussi fortes qu'irréelles. Car d'une
> part, dans *De causis* il n'y a pas du tout de références à la philosophie d'Aristote et
> la doctrine de cette œuvre nous paraît la plus éloignée possible de la tradition
> aristotélicienne que nous connaissons. D'autre part, dans la tradition latine, on
> considérait *De causis* comme l'achèvement de la *Métaphysique* d'Aristote et cela
> même après avoir rejeté l'opinion érronée selon laquelle ce premier texte appartenait
> à l'œuvre du Philosophe. On pourrait dire que dans la relation des latinistes avec
> *Liber de causis* s'est réalisée d'une façon assez singulière une ancienne ambition du
> néoplatonisme : l'aboutissement réussi d' une synthèsedu platonisme et de
> l'aristotélisme! Et pourtant dans *De causis* l'aristotélisme n'a pas reçu même ce que
> l'on lui avait attribué dans beaucoup d'autres versions du néoplatonisme et il paraît
> que ses relations avec Aristote ne sont à vrai dire que purement extérieures à l'égard
> du texte et de la doctrine réels.[3]

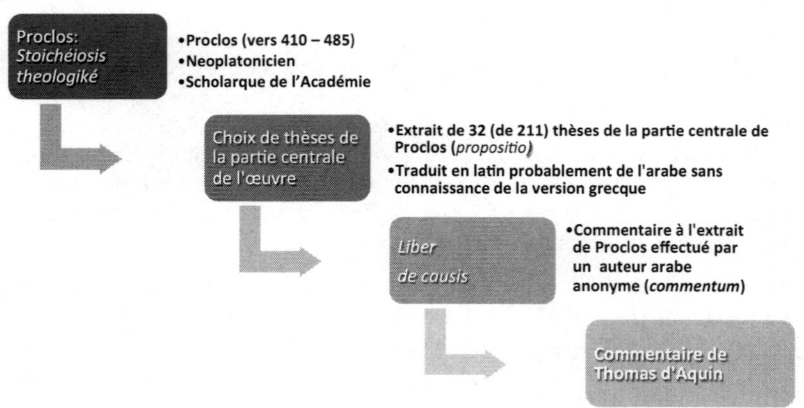

Dessin 1. « Chronologie » du Commentaire thomasien à Liber de causis.

La genèse de *Liber de causis* et de son commentaire thomasien influence le texte.
En effet, la philosophie que nous découvrons dans ce texte est extraordinaire.
Dans la première version, celle de Proclos, nous retrouvons le classique
néoplatonisme grec, polythéiste et radicalement païen, mais considérablement

---

3   P. Milcarek, *Od istoty do istnienia. Tworzenie się metafizyki egzystencjalnej wewnątrz
     łacińskiej tradycji filozofii chrześcijańskiej* [*De l'essence à l'existence. Formation d'une
     métaphysique existentielle au sein de la tradition latine de la philosophie chrétienne*]
     (Warszawa, 2008), p. 423.

émoussé par le choix approprié de thèses de *Stoichéiosis theologiké* et le commentaire arabe écrit dans un ésprit monothéiste et créationniste.

C'est ce texte néoplatonicien que commente par la suite Thomas d'Aquin – le plus célèbre partisan de l'école d'Aristote au Moyen Âge, à qui la doctrine contenue dans *Liber de causis* devrait être extrêmement étrangère. Thomas ne le dissimule pas en exposant dans l'introduction ses constatations concernant l'attribution de *Liber de causis*. Néanmoins, il trouve dans le *Livre* des questions qui l'intéressent.

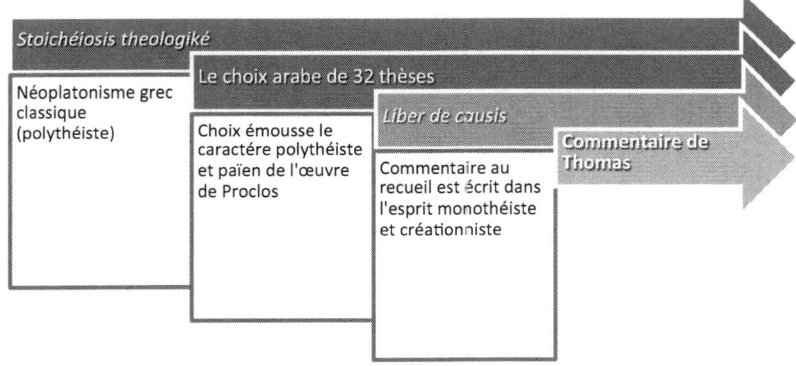

Dessin 2. Les « couches » philosophiques dans le commentaire thomasien à Liber de causis.

L'une des questions qui intéressent Aquinate est sûrement la problématique de *esse* – de l'existence. Aquinate interprète *esse* du *Livre des causes* dans l'esprit de sa propre métaphysique, ce qui nous fait apparaître la couche suivante du texte celle de l'approche philosophique.

Cette structure complexe du texte n'est pas facile à examiner ni à interpréter. La première méthode, qui s'impose ici presque spontanément, est l'analyse contextuelle du contenu de toutes les couches du *Commentaire*. À une telle démarche incite Thomas lui-même qui, dans ses commentaires, situe souvent les thèses de *Liber de causis* dans leur contexte plus large, celui de *Elementatio theologica*. L'analyse contextuelle se concentre sur la genèse des thèses successives. Cette méthode aboutit à démontrer que le sujet du *Livre* est la causalité qui constitue l'œuvre de la cause première située au-dessus de l'Un, du Bien et de l'Éternité. Car, elle contient en elle-même toutes ces perfections et les dépasse immensément. En créant son système Proclos, ainsi que Plotin et beaucoup d'autres néoplatoniciens, cherchait à l'opposer au monothéisme et au créationnisme du christianisme. Pourtant, ce système – le néoplatonisme – a subi, tout d'abord dans les esprits des chrétiens syriens et puis dans ceux des mahométans arabes, des modifications dont le témoignage est le *Livre de causes* : la triade néoplatonicienne c'est « l'ensemble des êtres liés l'un à l'autre, qui par la création même appartiennent directement à Dieu ». Dans le *Livre* on souligne pour autant que la création ne converne pas encore chaque être, mais uniquement *prima rerum creatarum* (la première chose créée), à savoir *esse* qui, depuis, constitue ensemble l'objet d'intérêt des commentateurs, y compris Thomas d'Aquin.

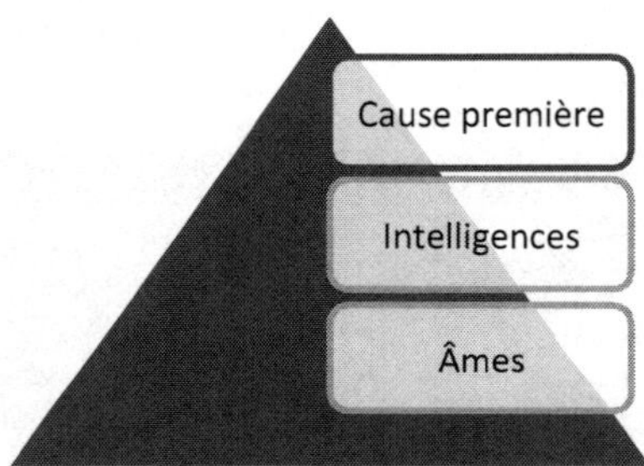

Dessin 3. Le schéma des causes dans Liber de causis, qui constituent les sujets d'études.

Le deuxième moyen d'analyser *le Livre des causes* consiste à saisir d'une façon immanente le contenu du texte. Dans cette méthode, les sources et « l'arrière » philosophique nous intéressent beaucoup moins que leur situation et leur rôle dans le *Commentaire* même. Car, il s'avère qu'Aquinate modifie assez souvent la signification de la terminologie empruntée à d'autres auteurs, qu'il change aussi leur situation au sein des problèmes abordés. Ceci donne comme résultat une autre répartition des accents dans le *Commentaire* et aboutit à ce que le sujet principal de celui-ci, c'est-à-dire la causalité, signifie plutôt l'attribution de « esse » que le fait de causer les êtres.

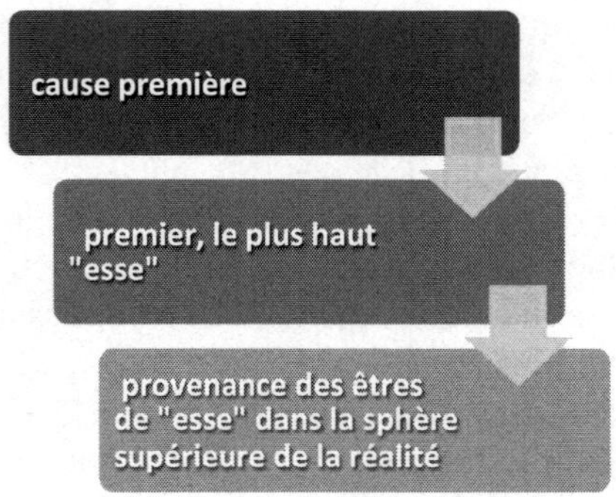

Dessin 4. Le schéma de la causalité de esse dans Liber de causis.

1. La conception de la cause première dans *Liber de causis,* rappelons-le, semble résulter davantage du monothéisme de l'auteur que du néoplatonisme de Proclos. Car elle dépasse sous plusieurs aspects le Un néoplatonicien. La cause première est absolument transcendante à l'égard du monde créé par elle-même, et en même temps, elle est immanente dans les êtres, en tant que ses conséquences.

2. *Esse*, en tant que la première chose créée, est un être spirituel (l'intelligence) qui est le plus simple et constitue l'unité au plus grand dégré du possible parmi les êtres créés. Cette simplicité n'est pas dérangée par le fait que *esse* se compose de ce qui est fini et en même temps de ce qui est infini (*finitum et infinitum*). C'est la base des multiplications parmi les êtres provenant de *esse primum.*

3. Le premier *esse* se divise en formes intellectuelles qui constituent la sphère du monde supérieur. Ce n'est pas pourtant une désunion, mais une imitation, l'empreinte du premier *esse* constituée de telle façon que dans ces copies reste sa marque. Cette marque constitue en même temps la relation de la forme donnée avec *esse*. Et les premières formes intellectuelles (les intelligences) émanent d'elles-mêmes les âmes les plus hautes qui dirigent les corps célestes. Tout cela, en somme, à savoir les intelligences, les âmes les plus hautes et les corps célestes constituent la sphère supérieure de la réalité.

4. La sphère inférieure est une imitation particulière de la sphère supérieure. Il y a donc ici les intelligences inférieures desquelles découlent les âmes inférieures qui, à leur tour, dirigent les corps destructibles. La sphère inférieure de la réalité est donc constituée de ces intelligences inférieures, des âmes inférieures et des corps corruptibles. Pourtant, *le Livre des causes* ne s'intéresse pas au monde destructible.

Étudions maintenant « l'histoire » de la thèse la plus célèbre de *Liber de causis* qui parle de l'existence en tant que la première chose créée[4] :

---

4   Je m'aide du synopsis mis en parallèle par P. Bany. Voir P. Bany, *Problem esse i partycypacji w Komentarzu św. Tomasza z Akwinu do Liber de causis*, Warszawa 2002, manuscrit à la Bibliothèque principale de UKSW, p. 151. Je profite de la version électronique du texte grec de Proclos: TLG (Thesarus Lingue Graecae) Workplace 8.0. La version latine provient de la traduction de Guillaume de Moerbecke. Quant à *Liber de causis* je me sers de Tomasz z Akwinu, *Księga o przyczynach* [*Le Livre de causes*], trad. Z. Brzostowska, M. Gogacz (Warszawa, 1970); quant au commentaire thomasien, j'utilise la traduction citée d'Adam Rosłan.

Stoichéiosis theologiké **nr 138**	
pantôn tôn metechontôn tês theias idiotêtos kai ektheoumenôn prôtiston esti kai akrotaton to on.	L'être est la première et la plus haute chose parmi toutes celles qui participent à la divinité et grâce à cela éprouvent la théosis.
Omnium participantium divina proprietate et deificatorum primum est et supremum ens.	

Il est difficile de remarquer dans le texte de Proclos les moindres traces de la pensée existentielle. Le néoplatonicien parle de la participation à la divinité et de ce que la première chose qui participe à la divinité est l'être. L'être désigne littéralement : *to on*, ce que Guillaume de Moerbecke traduit correctement comme *ens*. Évidemment l'être est toujours ce que la chose est, mais au néoplatonisme il ne constitue que l'une des hypostases (la première dans le système de Proclos) tandis que ce qui est vraiment important c'est la divinité, à savoir une certaine puissance de la cause première, qui émane sur les suivantes hypostases. L'existence ou l'être ne semblent pas préoccuper l'auteur d'*Eléments de la théologie*.

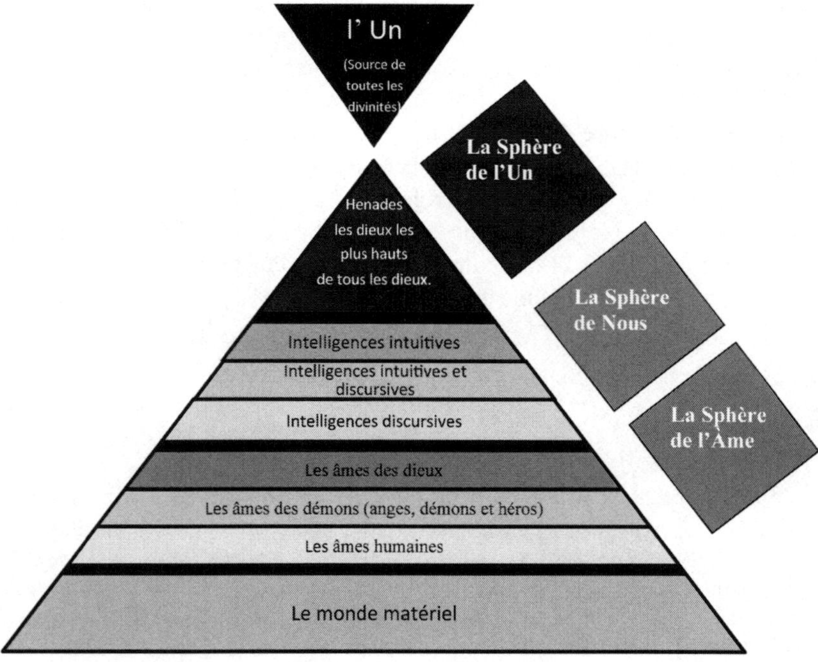

Dessin 5. Le schéma de l'émanation dans l'ontologie de Proclos.

Dans le schéma connu de l'émanation dans l'ontologie de Proclos, *ens* appartiendrait à la sphère de l'Un et serait la première des hénades divines – émanantes de Un. Dans le système polythéiste du néoplatonicien d'Athènes *ens* est tout simplement l'un des dieux.

Liber de causis – **IV proposition (l'extrait de *Stoichéiosis theologiké*)**	
IV. Prima rerum creatarum est esse et non est ante ipsum creatum aliud.	IV. La première des choses créées est l'être et il n'y a rien d'autre créé avant lui

Cette thèse subit la première modification dans l'extrait qui est « la base » de *Liber de causis*. Nous nous rappelons que l'auteur anonyme du *Livre* l'avait compilé des thèses contenues dans la partie centrale de l'œuvre de Proclos de telle façon que son polythéisme radical ne soit pas visible. Mais cela n'a pas suffi car ce polythéisme nous épatait dans la plupart des fragments d'*Éléments de la théologie*. Le compilateur arabe avait donc effectué certaines modifications terminologiques : il a décidé de transmuer l'attribution de la divinité en création et semblait comprendre la création même comme le « passage » de « l'existence » à l'inexistence. Pour cela, à la place de *ens* qui indique plutôt une unité, il préférait dire que la première chose créée est *esse* en tant que ce qui distingue l'existence de l'inexistence.[5] Il est possible de commenter cette phrase aussi bien dans l'esprit néoplatonicien ce que fait l'auteur de *Liber de causis,* ou bien dans la perspective plus substantialiste, à savoir plus aristotélicienne, ce qu'essaie de faire Thomas d'Aquin.

Liber de causis – **IV proposition (commentaire)**	
38. Quod est quia esse est supra sensum et supra animam et supra intelligentiam, et non est post causam primam latius neque prius creatum ipso.	38. Il est ainsi car l'être est au-dessus des sens et au-dessus de l'âme et au-dessus de l'intelligence et que (après la cause première) il n'y a rien de plus complet ni créé antérieurement.

---

5   Evidemment, il reste encore la traduction de ces termes. Ainsi Pierre Duhem est d'avis que *esse* c'est tout simplement l'existence. Il attire l'attention sur le fait que pour les néoplatoniciens arabes, aussi bien l'être que l'existence et l'essence sont synonymes. Pour Étienne Gilson *esse* de *Liber de causis* c'est l'être. Cela n'explique pas pourtant *esse* d'une façon univoque, mais seulement analogique c'est pourquoi Mieczysław Gogacz a proposé d'introduire le terme «entité» [bytowanie]. C'est ce terme qui a employé par Adam Rosłan dans sa traduction de thomasien *Expositio*.

39. Propter illud ergo factum est superius creatis rebus omnibus et vehementius unitum.	39. À cause de cela donc il est devenu supérieur à toutes les choses créées et quelque chose de plus unique.
40. Et non est factum ita nisi propter suam propinquitatem esse puro et uni et vero in quo non est multitudo aliquorum modorum.	40. Et il n'est devenu ainsi qu'à cause de sa proximité avec l'Être pur, unique et vrai, en qui il n'y a aucune multiplicité.
41. Et esse creatum quamvis sit unum, tamen multiplicatur, scilicet quia ipsum recipit multiplicitatem.	41. Et bien que l'être créé soit un, pourtant il se multiplie ce qui résulte du fait qu'il reçoit lui-même la multiplicité.

Dans ce passage de *Liber de causis* il est bien visible que la thèse de Proclos, très polythéiste et suggérant l'émanation, dans la version présentée par le *Livre des causes* a le ton nettement créationniste et ne possède aucune trace de panthéisme. L'explication qui suit cette thèse affermit une telle image de *esse*, en conservant la néoplatonicienne structure hiérarchique des êtres, en remplaçant le polythéisme par le monothéisme et l'émanation par la création. Nous voulons le souligner encore une fois : le commentateur arabe ne renonce pas au hiérarchisme néoplatonicien des êtres ; il cherche plutôt à l'interpréter uniquement dans la perspective néoplatonicienne et créationniste. Cette manière de voir va de pair avec la façon d'interpréter la philosophie néoplatonicienne que nous rencontrons chez les adeptes des religions monothéistes : juifs, chrétiens et musulmans. Car d'une part, le néoplatonisme empregné de mysticisme était pour eux une interprétation très attirante du monde, et d'autre part il demandait pourtant des corrections de son polythéisme et émanationisme selon lequel les hypostases successives surgissaient d'elles-mêmes dans le processus nécessaire de l'émanation de l'Un à la matière. De plus, les adaptes de la « religion du Livre » ne pouvaient aussi accepter le fait que le monde est créé de façon nécessaire, et non par l'effet de la décision libre de Dieu.

Mieczysław Gogacz assemble les traits du néoplatonisme classique et du néoplatonisme médiéval de façon suivante[6] :

	Les traits du néoplatonisme classique	Les traits du néoplatonisme médiéval
1	La hiérarchie nécessaire des hypostases.	L'orde hiérarchique des êtres entre Dieu et la matière.
2	Chaque hypostase est la cause productive essentielle de l'hypostase inférieure.	La cause productive de chaque être à un degré donné de l'échelle est Dieu.

---

6   M. Gogacz, *W kierunku tomizmu konsekwentnego. Opera philosophorum medii aevi,* t. 11 (Warszawa, 2012), p. 56.

3	La causalité consiste dans l'émanation des êtres.	La causalité consiste dans la création.
4	Les différences entre les hypostases consistent dans la distance de l'Un et non dans le contenu intérieur de la conséquence.	Les différences entre les êtres consistent dans la ressemblance à Dieu et du même contenu de la conséquence dans chaque être.
5	Le chemin qui mène de l'Un est l'acquisition quantitative de la multiplication ; le chemin vers l'Un est la réduction de ces multiplications et par conséquent la transformation en hypostase supérieure.	La raison de l'imperfection, à savoir le manque de la ressemblance des êtres, à Dieu est leur implication dans la matière ; le retour à Dieu consiste dans la domination ascétique de la matière par l'âme.

Dans le passage cité du *Livre* nous remarquons facilement certaines différences indiquées dans le tableau. Le commentaire de Thomas d'Aquin est – comme on l'a déjà dit – *expositio* (exposition)[7] ; on y ressent une grande distance de Thomas à l'égard de son contenu, lié clairement par lui-même avec les idées des « platoniciens ». Le contenu du *Livre* même est expliqué en général par le biais des références à Proclos : il présente soigneusement la source de cette thèse, à savoir le texte de Proclos, il compare les théorèmes de celui-ci avec d'autres versions du néoplatonisme – les textes de Pseudo-Denis, afin de les ramener au niveau de la substance.

Commentaire de Thomas d'Aquin : L 4	
Videtur tamen non esse eius intentio ut loquatur de aliquo esse separato, sicut Platonici loquebantur, neque de esse participato communiter in omnibus existentibus, sicut loquitur Dionysius, sed de esse participato in primo gradu entis creati, quod est esse superius. Et, quamvis esse superius sit et in intelligentia et in anima, tamen in ipsa intelligentia prius consideratur ipsum esse quam intelligentiae ratio, et similiter est in anima; et propter hoc praemisit quod est supra animam et supra intelligentiam.	Il semble pourtant que l'intention de l'auteur n'est pas parler d'un être séparé comme le faisaient les platoniciens ni comme de l'être dans lequel participent toutes les choses qui existent, comme le fait Denis, mais plutôt comme de l'être se trouvant au premier degré de l'être créé, qui est l'être supérieur. Et bien que l'être supérieur se trouve aussi bien dans l'intelligence que dans l'âme, c'est dans l'intelligence même que l'être même est tout d'abord considéré, avant le principe de l'intelligence ; et de même est avec l'âme. C'est pour cette raison que l'auteur a dit qu'un être pareil se trouve « au-dessus » de l'âme et « au-dessus » de l'intelligence.

---

7   Édition critique H. D. Saffrey (ed.) (Friburgi, 1954) porte le titre: *Sancti Thomae de Aquino Super Librum de causis expositio.*

Il faut remarquer la démarche interprétative de Thomas : il ne cherche pas à faire de ce texte néoplatonicien un autre traité, aristotélicien ou substantialiste. Il est tout à fait conscient du caractère néoplatonicien du livre commenté, mais il fait attention au problème de *esse* et à différentes possibilités de son interprétation, aussi dans les textes de provenance platonicienne. Ainsi, il constate que l'auteur de *Liber de causis* ne parle pas plutôt de l'être séparé comme c'est le cas dans la phrase respective de *Stoichéiosis theologiké*, il ne parle pas non plus de la sphère de l'être où, comme dans le sol vivifiant, sont enracinés les êtres réels. Mais il dit qu'aussi bien dans l'intelligence que dans l'âme – par quoi il faut comprendre l'*essence* de certains êtres – *esse* est quelque chose de connu avant. Et c'est à cet ordre de connaissance qu'Aquinate semble ramener le hiérarchisme néoplatonicien du texte *Liber de causis*.

* * *

« L'histoire de la philosophie a son sens philosophique » – a écrit Gilson dans *L'introduction* à *L'unité de l'expérience philosophique*.[8] Il est pourtant très rare que l'on puisse en un seul texte passer par plusieurs sphères de la pensée et de la langue ainsi que par quelques frontières qui les séparent. Nous pouvons aussi examiner comment la problématique qui nous intéresse se transformait depuis la classique version grecque dans *Stoichéiosis theologiké* de Proclos, à travers les transformations d'un auteur arabe anonyme dans *Liber de causis*, jusqu'à la version de Thomas d'Aquin dans son commentaire latin. Nous avons aussi « chemin faisant » deux, peut-être trois traductions de l'œuvre de Proclos : du grec à l'arabe (il n'est pas exclu que « entre » elles il existait aussi une version syrienne) et ensuite une traduction de l'arabe au latin.

Dans les recherches historiques de même que historico-littéraires et surtout – semble-t-il – en médiévistique, depuis un certain temps est à la mode une catégorie de la « zone frontalière ». Dans l'histoire universelle, elle consiste le plus souvent à explorer des terrains très différents où se mélangent, se combattent ou bien se complètent différentes tendances : culturelles et civilisationnelles, nationales, sociales et économiques. Dans l'histoire de la philosophie, cette catégorie peut s'avérer très utile ; elle consiste dans la translation de la problématique et de la langue de la philosophie. Et il ne s'agit pas ici des traductions des textes philosophiques particuliers ou même des traductions contemporaines des œuvres latines ou grecques, mais des actions organisées de traduction ayant pour but de interpréter toute une théorie

---

8   É. Gilson, *The Unity of Philosophical Experience* (New York, 1950).

philosophique déterminée d'une langue et culture à l'autre. Dans l'historie de la philosophie antique et médiévale on peut indiquer au moins quatre processus de ce genre : la charnière gréco-romaine, gréco-syrienne, syriano-arabe, arabo-latine. Pourtant,il arrive rarement que dans un seul texte nous puissions étudier presque tous ces processus et toutes ces transformations. Un tel texte est sans doute le *Commentaire* thomasien à *Liber de causis*.

Features of an *Explanatio* in Three Commentaries from Around the End of the Middle Ages. Some Observations on *Commentum* of John of Dąbrówka and on Commentaries on *Theodulus* and *Facetus* (Lyon 1514)

Dorota Gacka

The Institute of Literary Research
of the Polish Academy of Sciences, Warsaw

In the introduction to my article, I wish to say a few words about the *Theodulus*, the *Facetus* and the *Chronicle* of Vincentius Kadłubek – texts which were commented on in the 15th century and in the beginning of the 16th century; then I will discuss commentaries on them, with which I became acquainted when I was translating the first two works for the series Bibliotheca Litterarum Medii Aevi, published in Warsaw by the Institute of Literary Research of the Polish Academy of Sciences. I will discuss them in chronological order.

The *Ecloga Theoduli* is the oldest of the three texts. It was written probably in the 9th century by a Carolingian writer, who was educated in Italy as a child and then in Greece as a young man. In Athens, he witnessed disputes between pagans and Christians; subsequently, he gathered and combined their arguments and created an allegorical eclogue. The *Ecloga Theoduli* consists of two parts. The first one is idyllic: in rural scenery, two shepherds take part in a singing competition. One of them, named Alithia, plays on the zither and sings about persons and events described in the *Old Testament*. The other one, Pseustis, plays on a rustic pipe and sings about heroes of the Greek and Roman mythology. Fronesis, who is the judge of the *agon*, listens to both of them. The second part consists of songs of Alithia and Pseustis. It is divided into four-line stanzas; every stanza refers to a biblical story or to a myth and has its heroes and internal action. Alithia, who is the personification of the truth, wins the competition, which demonstrates the superiority of Christianity over the ancient culture.[1]

---

1   See: Theodulo, *Ecloga. Il Canto della Verità e della Menzogna*, ed. Francesco Mosetti Casaretto (Firenze: SISMEL-Edizioni del Galluzzo, 1997), 1–48; George Rigg, (transl.), *The "Eclogue" of Theodulus. A Translation with an Introduction*, on-line edition: http://medieval.utoronto.ca/ylias/web-content/theoduli.html. Accessed May 15, 2014.

The *Facetus* was probably written by John, a Cistercian monk, in 1192. The author conceived the text as a continuation of the *Disticha Catonis* – a collection of moral sentences compiled around the end of the 4th c. The *Facetus* contains rules which a medieval man should observe at home, in church, in court, at school, at a marketplace, as a guest, and as a traveller. Therefore, it was named "the medieval book of good manners." The *Facetus* is written in hexameters, which are connected by rhymes. The composition opens with a short preface in which the author enumerates reasons for writing the poem and compares his text to "a little garden" which yields fruits and flowers, and to "a goblet, which smells sweet of wine": pupils, who want to become acquainted with good manners, should drink from it.[2]

The third composition is the *Chronica Polonorum* by the bishop Vincentius Kadłubek, which was composed between 1190 and 1223. Vincentius wrote it on the order of the duke Casimir II the Just. The *Chronica Polonorum* includes events since the prehistoric origins of the Polish state up to year 1202. It consists of a preface and four parts, three of which contain a dialogue between John, the archbishop of Gniezno, and Matthew, the bishop of Cracow. The fourth part is a narration.[3]

I turn now to commentaries which were written on these works; I will discuss them in chronological order. The *Commentum* of John of Dąbrówka was written between year 1431 and 1436. Its aim was to present the *Chronica Polonorum* to young people studying in cathedral schools and in the Cracow University, and it was subsequently, in fact, read and discussed together with the *Chronica* for many years. The *Commentum* contributed to enriching the knowledge of the medieval Poles about their history and therefore it is regarded the first handbook of Polish history. It is a medieval commentary, but with a feel of a new era.[4]

Commentaries on the *Facetus* and on the *Theodulus* which we find in the *Auctores octo* (Lyon 1514) are teachers' commentaries. Their aim was to instruct young people (*iuvenes*) to comment (*glossare*) on texts on their own. The title card says that the contents of the commentaries is easy (*facilis*), short

---

2   See: Leopold Zatočil, *Cato a Facetus: Pojednání a texty. Zu den deutschen Cato- und Facetusbearbeitungen: Untersuchungen und Texte*, Opera Universitatis Masarykianae Brunensis. Facultas Philosophica, 48 (Brno, 1952), 287–293 (the part of this publication containing the edition of the *Facetus* is available online: http://www1.uni-hamburg.de/disticha-catonis/homepage/zatocil.html; accessed May 15, 2014).

3   See: Marian Plezia, (ed.), *Magistri Vincentii dicti Kadłubek "Chronica Polonorum"*, Monumenta Poloniae Historica: Nova Series, vol. 11 (Kraków, 1994).

4   See: Ioannes de Dąbrówka, *Commentum in Chronicam Polonorum Magistri Vincentii dicti Kadłubek*, ed. Marian Zwiercan, Monumenta Poloniae Historica: Nova Series, vol. 14 (Kraków, 2008), 1–279.

(*tenuis*), and nice (*familiaris*). They are composed according to the rules of display rhetoric (*rem demonstrativam*). They were probably created in France in the end of the 15th century – they contain references to the French life and quotations from works of scholars who taught at the University of Paris. Some passages indicate that the Reformation is approaching, but the overall spirit is still medieval. For instance, in the commentary on the *Theodulus*, the author discusses four levels of interpretation of biblical texts and announces that his work will proceed according to the method of biblical exegesis, i.e. it will include a literal, an allegorical, a moral, and an anagogical interpretation.[5]

After this lengthy preface, I turn now to a discussion of the *explanatio* of the commentaries. The structure of the *explanatio* resembles a block construction. Like a child building a block structure, the commentator uses more elements if he wishes to create a more complicated construction, and less if he desires it to be simple. The commentary on the *Facetus* is short and simple, on the *Commentum* – more intricate, and on the *Theodulus* – the most complicated of the three. The complexity of a commentary depends on the level of education of the target audience and on the contents of the commented text. If the text contains hidden meanings and its language is rich, the commentary is longer and more complicated. If we wanted to name these blocks, we should enumerate:

– four types of interpretation established in biblical exegesis: a literal, an allegorical, a moral, and an anagogical interpretation;
– interpretations specific to various scientific disciplines, especially to the *septem artes liberales*, but not only;
– divisions of a composition and discussion of *numerus et ordo librorum*;
– enumeration of author's sources and inspirations;
– enumeration of commentator's sources and inspirations;
– demonstration of analogies between various parts of the composition or between various compositions;
– various explanations concerning style and language.

As I said, the commentary on the *Facetus* is of the simplest construction. Examination of the contents reveals that there are two types of interpretation present: a literal and a moral one. The reader finds the literal interpretation in the commentary on the *Prologue*[6], where the commentator repeats the author's words, discusses the reasons for writing the poem, and compares it to "a little garden" and to "a goblet, which smells sweet of wine". On the other hand, explanations of distichs almost always include a moral interpretation. For instance the distich:

---

5   See: *Auctores octo cum commento*, [Lyon: Jacques Myt,], pp. [45]–[103].
6   Ibid., p. [91].

> Solum crede Deum, quem credis, semper adora,
> Et quicquid facias, quod Ipsum spectat, honora.[7]

has the following interpretation:

> Hic auctor dicit, quod tu debes credere in unum solum Deum, qui est Pater, Filius et
> Spiritus Sanctus, et Illum adorare, et non idola vel alias creaturas, et quicquid tu
> facias, tu debes facere propter honorem Dei. Et debes honorare omnes res, que Deo
> pertinent.[8]

Sometimes moral interpretation is supported by quotations from the Bible[9], more rarely by quotations from the *Disticha Catonis*.[10] If a moral interpretation cannot be provided for a particular distich, then a literal interpretation is offered.

In the commentary on the first distich, the commentator attempts to show the main *divisiones* of the composition. He says that the first part of the *Facetus* relates to God, the second – to fellow creatures, and the third – to us.[11] Although it is not true, we can see that the commentator makes an effort to discuss the main parts of the composition. He does not discuss *numerus et ordo librorum* because of the poem's brevity.

The third element of the commentary on the *Facetus* is constituted by linguistic and stylistic explanations. As a rule, they begin with a word *construe*, which introduces logical and grammatical analysis. Here the commentator gives the prosaic order of the words and provides synonyms for the vocabulary. He is particularly fond of explaining negations, for instance:

> "ne pro non", "ne pro ut non", "nihil pro non et aliquid", "numquam pro non et
> umquam".[12]

It seems, therefore, that the text was intended for introductory-level pupils. Sometimes a use of a word is illustrated by a proverb.

John of Dąbrówka construes his *explanatio* of the *Chronica Polonorum* of Vincentius Kadłubek in the following way. First, he summarizes the events described by the chronicler. It is a literal interpretation, yet he does not proceed here uncritically. He corrects and supplements the work of Vincentius with information which he found in the *Dzierzwa's Chronicle* and in the *Chronicle of Greater Poland*; consequently, his summaries include dates and details which are not to be found in Kadłubek's work. The summary of the historical narrative

---

7   Ibid., p.[92].
8   Ibid., p. [92].
9   Ibid., pp. [92], [93], [94].
10   Ibid., p. [99].
11   Ibid., pp. [91]–[92].
12   Ibid., pp. [92], [93], [94].

is followed by two kinds of explanations: *circa litteram*[13] and *circa vocabula*[14]. All chapters contain long explanations *circa litteram*, which contain philosophical and moral interpretation of the events. For instance, when Kadłubek writes about a rebellion which started because of a strong government of Mieszko III the Old and which was joined by Odon of Poznań, Mieszko's son, John of Dąbrówka gives a long lecture about love we owe our parents, filled with quotations from numerous ancient, medieval, and humanistic authors. These quotations contribute to the commentary's mosaic or patch-work character. Sometimes the commentator makes use of a method of threefold argumentation: he presents a thesis and supports it with three arguments.[15]

John of Dąbrówka provides explanations *circa vocabula* only sporadically. They are shorter than explanations *circa litteram*; they appear more often, and are longer, in the first book than in the later parts of the text. They include:

– synonyms of words used by Kadłubek: "scateo, -es, -re, id est ebulire, fervere, erumpere, emanare";
– cognate words: "scaturigo, -inis … venit enim a scateo, -es, -re";
– descriptive explanations of words: "scateo, -es, -re, id est … , quod aqua facit, dum decurrit inter angusta";
– classification of words as parts of speech: "Tyrius, -a, -um – nomen gentile vel patrium", "Lar, -artis est proprium nomen regis", "a cachinor, -aris, verbo deponentiali, venit cachinus";
– information about declensions: "lar, -aris – masculini generis".[16]

A question of sources used by John of Dąbrówka for his explanation of vocabulary is an important one. We can answer it thanks to the edition of Marian Zwiercan and his team. Most often the commentator uses *Catholicon* of John of Genoa, *Vocabularium* of Papias, *Liber derivationum* of Hugh of Pisa, *Etymologiarum libri* of Isidore of Seville, *Graecismus* of Evrard of Béthune.[17] He also quotes *Institutiones grammaticae* of Priscian (twice), *Summa super Priscianum* of Peter Helias (once), and *De orthographia* of the Venerable Bede (once).[18] He cites frequently proverbs which were considered an important mnemotechnical tool, for instance:

---

13   See for instance: Ioannes de Dąbrówka, *Commentum in Chronicam Polonorum*, 23, 30, 32, 34, 35.
14   See for instance ibid., 39, 40, 43.
15   Ibid., 228–233.
16   Ibid., 39, 43.
17   Ibid., 25–27, 30–31, 33, 39, 49, 52–53, 55, 59, 73, 80, 93–94, 101, 186.
18   Ibid., 41, 49, 53, 73.

> lar, laris [...] est domus vel ignis, sicut dicitur proverbialiter: 'Vidi larem in lare, id
> est ignem in domo.'

Sometimes, though not frequently, he embellishes his explanations with words of ancient (Vergil, Ovid, Lucan, Juvenal)[19] and Christian poets (Saint Ambrose, Prudentius, Theodulus).[20]

The commentary on the *Theodulus* is the most complicated of the three discussed here. It is constructed of numerous elements. Firstly, the commentator takes into account the four levels of textual interpretation taken over from biblical exegesis. The whole poem is provided with a literal interpretation. For the lines of the poem in which the characters are described, an allegorical interpretation is given. For instance Pseustis, who herds bad-smelling goats, represents the false teaching or the devil, who gathers the men of sin.[21] Alithia, the personification of the truth or of the Church, herds sheep, i.e. the faithful Christians. As she teaches the truth, the sheep, hearing her song, stop eating grass; this image represents Christians who abandon earthly pleasures.[22] The myth of Daedalus is provided with a similar interpretation:

> Per Dedalum intelligimus peccatorem, quem Minois, hoc est diabolus, implicat et
> illaqueat in laberintho negociorum mundanorum,"[23]; and also the story about
> Abraham: "Per Abraam intelligitur Pater ille noster celestis, gloriosus, qui Filio
> etiam proprio non pepercit.[24]

The verses about Fronesis are given a moral interpretation. The commentator gives us a lecture about the just judge.[25] In the myth of Daedalus he finds two moral lessons: one about the obedience due to parents, and another about keeping close to the centre, because the virtue is always in the centre.[26] The story of Abraham is provided with the following moral explanation:

> Ibi instruuntur parentes diligere filios suos, sed propter Deum, et ergo Deum magis
> diligere, ut semper sint prompti etiam de propriis filiis disponere secundum
> beneplacitum Dei.[27]

---

19   Ibid., 145, 157, 174, 186, 194, 237.
20   Ibid., 107, 116, 186, 187.
21   See: *Auctores octo cum commento*, p. [47].
22   Ibid., p. [48].
23   Ibid., p. [57].
24   Ibid., p. [58].
25   Ibid., p. [49].
26   Ibid., p. [57].
27   Ibid., p. [58].

An example of anagogical interpretation can be found in the comment on the stanza about Daedalus, who is compared to a man flying to God on wings of contemplation.[28]

Apart from the four types of interpretation taken over from biblical exegesis, the commentary also provides interpretations which draw from various branches of science. For instance, when discussing stanzas about Saturn and Mercury, the commentator refers to astronomy, one of the *septem artes liberales*, and says that Saturn and Mercury are not only mythological gods but also planets[29]; then he gives a short description of these planets. The theme of Mercury's eloquence inspires him to lecture about the mechanism of speaking:

> Et Mercurius est mentis currus, scilicet sermo humanus. ... Hunc lactavit Iuno uberibus suis, quia cum loquimur, attrahimus aerem inferiorem, quo attracto aspiramus, et mentis conceptum exprimimus.[30]

In his interpretation of the myth of Proserpine, the commentator refers to botanical imagery: Ceres's daughter is compared to a seed of a podded plant. The seed should be sowed in the soil if it is to sprout.[31]

An important task of a commentary is to establish the sources which the author used and which inspired him. In some passages which I have translated the commentator states that, in respect to mythology, the *Theodulus* was inspired by Ovid (*Metamorphoses*)[32] and Vergil (*Aeneid, Eclogues*).[33] Biblical stories, on the other hand, were taken directly from the *Old Testament*. The commentator not only lists the author's sources, but also studies them in detail in order to deepen the reader's knowledge of the topic. When the *Theodulus* mentions a mythical or biblical event, the commentator relates what happened before and after it. Sometimes he also refers to iconographic sources: for instance, when he discusses Saturn and Mercury, he opens his explanation with words: "Saturnus depingitur...,"[34] "[Mercurius] pingitur autem...".[35]

In addition, the commentator sometimes mentions his own sources and inspirations. In moralizing passages he quotes the ethical writings of Aristotle, *Liber Psalmorum, De civitate Dei* of Saint Augustine, and *De regimine*

---

28   Ibid., p. [57].
29   Ibid., p. [50], [72].
30   Ibid., p. [72].
31   Ibid., p. [88].
32   Ibid., pp. [50], [57], [72], [87].
33   Ibid., pp. [47], [57], [72], [88].
34   See: ibid., p. [50].
35   Ibid., p. [72].

principum of Giles of Rome (13th/14th c.)[36]; this last text was also used frequently by John of Dąbrówka.

An important element of the commentary on the *Theodulus* are *divisiones* of the poem. In the commentary on the *Prologue* they divide the text into logical and syntactic units[37], which is particularly useful as punctuation in the incunable is problematic. The commentator also distinguishes longer compositional units, especially in the second part of the composition[38] which, as has been mentioned above, consists of songs of Pseustis and Alithia.

In the commentary on the *Theodulus*, linguistic and stylistic explanations are equally frequent as explanations of literary matters. The commentator provides:
–   cognate words: "incola […] de incolo, –lis";
–   synonyms: "incola, id est inhabitans";
–   descriptive explanations of words: "emittens, id est extra mittens";
–   justification of use of a word: "posteritas sentit, […] quod parentes nostri commisere, quia ibi non fuit peccatum omissionis, sed commisionis";
–   explanations of Greek words: "sophie, id est sapientie, Grecum nomen est";
–   etymologies (frequently erroneous): "fistula a phonos, sonus";
–   explanations of mythological and biblical characters: "Saturnus, id est ille rex vel deus primus", "primus homo, scilicet Adam";
–   at times, information about gender and age of characters: "Dedalus, iste vir…", "Proserpina, illa puella…";
–   geographical explanations: "Athene nomen est civitatis in Grecia";
–   astronomical explanations: "iste stelle sunt plures, que dicuntur Maior Ursa et Minor Ursa";
–   instructions about pronunciation or spelling: "gemuit, id est trissyllabum", "scribitur oris sine h";
–   information about vowel quantity: "decoravit – secunda brevis";
–   classification of words as parts of speech: "mille – nomen numerale";
–   information about declension type: "mille – indeclinabile, bene reperitur milia declinabile";
–   past tense forms: "attigit – in preterito";
–   explanations of syncopated words: "superum, id est supernorum per sincopam";
–   explanations of Greek forms: "aëra – accusativus Grecus est";
–   explanations of diminutive words: "capellas, id est parvas capras";

---

36   Ibid., pp. [49], [50], [73].
37   Ibid.: pp. [47], [48].
38   Ibid.: pp. [50]–[51].

- explanations of onomatopoeic words: "balo, -as significat clamare et pertinet ad oves, sicut grunire ad porcos";
- explanations of conjunctions: "-que pro et";
- explanations of prepositions: "pro iudice, id est loco iudicis";
- in case of relative pronouns, information to which noun the pronoun relates: "cuius, scilicet David, habens cytharam";
- explanations of uses of the ablative case: "virga, id est cum virga";
- instructions of how to use the ablative case (with or without a preposition): "templo dicitur, a templo non est in usum";
- instructions of how one should connect words in translation: "ore perfidie, id est ore perfido et perverso, alii adiungunt verbum perfidie cum verbo gustum, gustu ...";
- explanations of metaphors and other rhetorical figures: "fistula, inquam, emittens sonitum per mille foramina vocum, ponitur numerus finitus pro numero infinito";
- examples of word usage in literature and science: "[natus] aliquando reperitur participium, ut apud Vergilium primo libro Eneidos: 'Nate dea' etc.";
- remarks derived from other literary and scientific works: "[Mulier]. De qua Hieronimus, *Contra Iovinianum*: pulchra, facile adamatur; quod plures amant, difficile custoditur ...".[39]

Sometimes the commentator explicitly quotes the source of his explanations. In the passages he quotes *Catholicon* of John of Genoa most often.[40] This work was also used by John of Dąbrówka in the *Commentum*. He also quotes once the *Doctrinale* of Alexander de Villa Dei.[41]

---

39 These examples come from: *Auctores octo cum commento*, pp. [47]–[51], [57]–[58], [72]–[74], [87]–[89].
40 For instance see ibid., pp. [73], [88].
41 Ibid., p. [58].

Commentaries on the *Decalogue* in the Late Middle Ages: Between Method and Catechesis. Poland in the European Context. The State of Research and Perspectives

Krzysztof Bracha

The Tadeusz Manteuffel Institut of History,
Polish Academy of Sciences, Warsaw

The subject and the purpose of catechesis in the late Middle Ages were exceptionally clearly presented by Jean Gerson, the Parisian chancellor, very influential in the 15th century. Using evocative medical rhetoric, he recommended in his *Epistola de reformatione theologiae*:

> it would certainly be practical, as it once was during the Black Death epidemic when the medical faculty formulated scripts to instruct people, if nowadays the theological faculty or someone on its behalf prepared similar scripts teaching the main rules of our faith, to instruct common believers, especially though", as Gerson clearly emphasized, "teaching about the Ten Commandments (*specialiter de praeceptis*)".[1]

In these words of counsel Gerson referred to the centuries-lasting process in which the *Decalogue* had been exalted. The process had been intensified since the half of the 13th century due to the change of Church's pastoral tools introduced in the resolutions of the Fourth Lateran Council from 1215 (Can. 21).[2] However, it was Augustine who, as one of the first, defined the special role of the *Decalogue*. In *Quaestionum in Heptateuchum libri VII* he lectured: "Omnia cetera, quae praecepit Deus ex illis decem praeceptis (...) pendere intelliguntur (...), quomodo haec ipsa rursus decem praecepta ex duobus illis, dilectione scilicet Dei et proximi, in quibus tota lex pendet et prophetae".[3]

---

1   "Item forte expediret sicut olim tempore quarumdam pestilentiarum facultas medicorum composuit tractatulum ad informandum singulos, ita fieret per facultatem vel de mandato eius aliquis tractatulus super punctis principalibus nostrae religionis, et specialiter de praeceptis, ad instructionem simplicium, quibus nullus sermo aut raro fit, aut male fit", Jean Gerson, *Oeuvre épistolaire*, in Palemón Glorieux, (ed.), *Oeuvres completés* (Paris–New York, 1960), 28.

2   Antonio García y García, (ed.), *Constitutiones Concilii quarti Lateranensis una cum Commentariis glossatorum*, Monumenta Iuris Canonici. Ser. A. Corpus Glossatorum, vol. 2 (Città del Vaticano, 1981), 67–68.

3   Cf. Mt 22:39. Augustinus, *Quaestiones in Exodum* 2. 140 (emphasized the double command of love appearing in the Decalogue: "dilectione scilicet dei et proximi" in the order where three of them refer to God, and seven to people (Ex. 20:1–17; Deut. 5: 6–

Resolutions of the Fourth Lateran Council assigned a special role to the two most important instruments of religious instruction which were closely linked to each other: the sermon and the confession. The sermon became a means of converting to one's confessor. The council thus brought a vital transformation of the tasks and the role of clergy in the ministry. Until then, a priest remained in remote contact with believers and served as a dispenser of Holy Sacraments, measuring sins and misdemeanours according to fixed sets of atonement and punishment. Now, thanks to the individual confession, he could come into a spiritually intimate contact with a penitent and act more like a doctor than a judge or a lawyer, study the state of the soul, penetrate the world of beliefs and the level of religious sensitivity, and at the end apply appropriate antidotes, consistent with the Christian norms. Contrary to the previous period dominated by baptism, the most important place was now assigned to the act of atonement. In this context, the confession became a moral exploration of a penitent's consciousness and was supposed to reinforce humbleness, raised to the role of a rudimentary Christian virtue.[4] This breakthrough also opened the way to the *Decalogue*'s exaltation, which was closely related to the practice of individual confession and atonement and became, besides *Pater Noster, Apostolicum,* seven deadly sins and seven sacraments, the elementary theme in religious instruction. Final changes in this matter were brought about in the times of deep intellectual re-evaluations at the end of the Middle Ages. The discourse of the Ten Commandments, incorporated into the triad of the elemental texts of the

---

21), then he influenced the depiction of sins in the following scheme: 9 someone else's sins, 4 crying for vengeance from God, and 6 against the Holy Ghost. Cf. Rudolf Suntrup, Burghart Wachinger, Nicola Zotz, "Zehn Gebote (deutsche Erklärungen)" in vol. 10 of *Die deutsche Literatur des Mittelalters: Verfasserslexikon* (Berlin–New York, 1999), col. 1485.

4   Jerzy Wolny, "Z dziejów katechezy" [From the History of Catechesis] in *Dzieje teologii katolickiej w Polsce* [The History of Catholic Theology in Poland], vol. 1: *Średniowiecze* [The Middle Ages], ed. by Marian Rechowicz (Lublin, 1974), 181; Nicole Bériou, "Autour de Lateran IV (1215): La naissance de la confession moderne et sa diffusion," in *Pratiques de la confession: des Pères du désert à Vatican II: quinze études d'histoire,* ed. by Groupe de la Bussière (Paris, 1983), 73–93; Stanisław Bylina, "Spowiedź jako instrument katechezy i nauki współżycia społecznego w Polsce późnego średniowiecza" [Confession as a Tool of Catechesis and Instruction of Social Co-existence in the Late Medieval Poland, in Polish Medieval Society], in *Społeczeństwo Polski średniowiecznej,* ed. by Stefan K. Kuczyński, vol. 5 (Warszawa, 1992), 255–265; Antonio García y García, "The Fourth Lateran Council and the Canonists," in *The History of Medieval Canon Law in the Classical Period: 1140–1234: From Gratian to the Decretals of Pope Gregory IX,* ed. By Wilfried Hartmann, Kenneth Pennington (Washington, D.C, 2008), 367–378.

religious instruction, in some catechisms even gained priority over *Credo* and *Pater Noster*. The growing position of the *Decalogue* in the late medieval catechesis is without question an effect of reformatory tendencies of the Church of these times and of the new theology oriented towards practical knowledge of a moral and ethical nature, non-speculative contemplation of the essence of faith, pious acts of construction and persuasion, specific human deeds, daily religious practice and its classification pursuant to the duties and obligations of every Christian determined by the *Holy Bible* and the *Decalogue*. The policy of moral and customary rebirth in the Church that was preached at the time drew the attention of many church reformers towards the purity of the original Church, and towards the true origins of faith – postulated in the nominalism of Biblical commands, laid down by God by the law of revelation *potestatis ordinariae*, in other words, the *Decalogue*.[5]

A particular emphasis was at the time put on the normative side of the *Decalogue*, which manifested itself among others in a tumultuous development of pastoral (penitential) literature, focused on the confession and the atonement, which was helpful to clergymen. There were composed, on the one hand, special treatises on virtues and sins (*De virtutibus et de vitiis*)[6], on the other hand, more

---

5   Cf. *Handbuch der Kirchengeschichte*, vol. 3, part 2, ed. by Hubert von Jedin, (Freiburg im Breisgau, 1968), 426–438, and Stefan Swieżawski, *Między średniowieczem a czasami nowymi: sylwetki myślicieli XV wieku* [Between the Middle Ages and the New Times] (Warszawa–Kraków, 1983), 49–58; idem, *Bóg* [God], vol. 4 of *Dzieje filozofii europejskiej XV wieku* [The History of European Philosophy of the 15th Century] (Warszawa, 1979), 228–234; idem, *U źródeł nowożytnej etyki. Filozofia moralna w Europie XV wieku* [At the Sources of Modern Ethics. Moral Philosophy in the 15th Century Europe] (Kraków, 1987), 36–51, 122–126.

6   Elementary repertories: Morton W. Bloomfield, "A Preliminary List of Incipitis of Latin Writings on the Virtutes and Vices, Mainly of the 13th, 14th, 15th Century", *Traditio* 11 (1955): 259–379; Morton W. Bloomfield, Bertrand-Georges Guyot, Donald R. Howard, Thyra B. Kabealo, *Incipits of Latin Works in the Virtues and Vices 1100 – 1500 A.D.* (Cambridge Massachusetts, 1979); Richard Newhauser, Istvan P. Bejczy, *A Supplement to Morton W. Bloomfield et al., Incipits of Latin Works on the Virtues and Vices 1100–1500 A.D.*, Instrumenta Patristica et Mediaevalia, vol. 50 (Turnhout, 2008); Richard Newhauser, *A Catalogue of Latin Texts with Material on the Vices and Virtues in Manuscripts in Hungary,* Gratia: Bamberger Schriften zur Renaissanceforschung, vol. 29 (Wiesbaden, 1996) and the history of the genre: idem, *The Treatise on Vices and Virtues in Latin and the Vernacular,* Typologie des sources du Moyen Âge occidental, vol. 68 (Turnhout, 1993), 21–54; Johannes B. Schneyer, *Repertorium der lateinischen Sermons des Mittelalters für die Zeit von 1150–1350,* vols. 1–8, Beiträge zur Geschichte der Philosphie und Theologie des Mittelalters: Texte und Untersuchungen, vol. 43, fasc. 1–8 (Münster, 1969–1978); idem, *Repertorium der lateinischen Sermones des Mittelalters für die Zeit von 1350–1500* (Ruhr, Münster, 2001) – CD. In Polish collections numerous

practical texts, remaining under the former's influence, such as confession manuals and casuistic summas: *Summa casuum, Summa de casibus conscientiae, Confessionale, Poenitentiale* etc.[7], and finally, especially interesting for us, treatises *De decem praeceptis* coming into being in large numbers in the late Middle Ages.[8] From the beginning, in the Christian

---

copies have been found, among others of *Summa de vitiis et virtutibus* by Wilhelm Perald, one of the more influential works of this genre, moreover treatises by Alcuin, Alain of Lille or William of Auvergne. Cf. Jerzy Wolny, *Z dziejów katechezy* [From the History of Catechesis], 201, n. 35; Krzysztof Bracha, *Casus pulchri de vitandis erroribus conscientiae purae. Orzeczenia kazuistyczne kanonistów i teologów krakowskich z XV w.* ['Casus pulchri de vitandis erroribus conscientiae purae': Casuistic Predications of Cracow Canonists and Theologians from the 15th Century] (Warszawa, 2013).

7 Johann Friedrich von Schulte, *Die Geschichte der Quellen und Literatur des canonistischen Rechts*, vols. 1–2, (Stuttgart, 1875–1878); Johannes Dietterle, "Die Summae confessorum (sive de casibus conscientiae) von Ihrem Anfängen an bis zu Silvester Prierias," *Zeitschrift für Kirchengeschichte* 24, (1903): 353–374, 520–548; 25 (1904): 248–272; 26 (1905): 50–81, 349–362; 27 (1906): 70–78, 166–188, 296–310, 431–442; 28 (1907): 401–431; Stephan Kuttner, *Repertorium der Kanonistik (1140–1234): Prodomus corporis glossarum*, Studi e testi, 71 (Città del Vaticano, 1937); Pierre Michaud-Quantin, *Sommes de casuistique et manuels de confession au Moyen Âge (XII–XVI siècles)*, Analecta Mediaevalia Namurcensia, 13 (Louvain–Lille–Montreal, 1962); Jiří Kejř, *Summae confessorum a jiná díla pro foro interno v rukopisech českých a moravských knihoven* (Praha, 2003), 37 –118. On this literary genre's history: Winfried Trusen, "Forum internum und gelehrtes Recht im Spätmittelalter: Summae confessorum und Traktate als Wegbereiter der Rezeption," *Zeitschrift der Savigny-Stiftung für Rechtsgeschichte, Kanonistische Abteilung* 57 (1971): 83–126; Frederick Broomfield, "Introduction: The Historical Background", in Thomas of Chobham, *Summa confessorum*, XI–XVII; Joseph Goering, "The Internal Forum and the Literature of Penance and Confession," in *The History of Medieval Canon Law in the Classical Period*, 379–428; Cyrille Vogel, *Le pécheur et la pénitence au Moyen Âge*, Traditions chrétiennes, vol. 5 (Paris, 1982); Henry Ansgar Kelly, "Penitential Theology and Law at the Turn of the Fifteenth Century," in *A New History of Penance*, ed. by Abigail Firey (Leiden, 2008), 239–318.

8 Dieter Harmening collated a comprehensive list of German commentaries, *Superstitio. Überlieferungs- und theoriegeschichtliche Untersuchungen zur kirchlich- theologischen Aberglaubensliteratur des Mittelalters* (Berlin, 1979), 272, n. 55; idem, "Spätmittelalterliche Aberglaubenskritik in Dekalog- und Beichtliteratur", in *Volksreligion im hochen und späten Mittelalter*, ed. by Peter Dinzelbacher, Dieter R. Bauer (Paderborn, 1990), 249–250; idem, "Katechismusliteratur Grundlagen religiöser Laienbildung im Spätmittelalter," in *Wissensorganisierende und wissensvermittelnde Literatur im Mittelalter: Perspektiven ihrer Forschung: Kolloquium 5.–7. Dezember 1985*, ed. by Norbert Richard Wolf, Wissensliteratur im Mittelalter, vol. 1 (Wiesbaden, 1987), 96–97. The basic texts were edited by Joseph Geffcken, *Der Bildercatechismus*

catechesis, which was under the influence of the *Decalogue* and the authority of the *Holy Bible* (Lm 21:8; Prov 12:28; Mt 7:13–14), the norms of Christian behaviour were presented in the form of a contrast between vices and virtues. Bright and dark sides of human nature were presented by means of the so-called "two ways", life and death, and the universal symbolism of light contrasted with darkness was used.[9] In this case, catechesis had used ancient models already

des fünfzehnten Jahrhunderts und catechetischen Hauptstücke in dieser Zeit bis auf Luther (Leipzig, 1855), moreover Franz Falk, *Drei Beichtbüchlein nach den zehn Geboten aus der Frühzeit der Buchdruckerkunst*, Reformationsgeschichtliche Studien und Texte, vol. 2 (Münster Westf., 1907) and Karin Baumann, *Aberglaube für Laien: Zur Programmatik und Überlieferung spätmittelalterlicher Superstitionenkritik*, Quellen und Untersuchungen zur europäischen Ethnologie, vol. 6 (Würzburg, 1989), 2: 493–831; Gabriele Baptist-Hlawatsch, *Das katechetische Werk Ulrichs von Pottenstein: Sprachliche und rezeptionsgeschichtliche Untersuchungen*, Texte und Textgeschichte: Würzburger Forschungen, 4 (Tübingen, 1979). Cf: Egino Weidenhiller, *Untersuchungen zur deutschsprachigen katechetischen Literatur des späten Mittelalters* (München, 1965); Rudof Suntrup, Burghart Wachinger, Nicola Zotz, *Zehn Gebote (deutsche Erklärungen)*, col. 1484–1503; Edmond Dublanchy, "Décalogue," in *Dictionnaire du théologique catholique*, vol. 4, 161–176; Bertrand-Georges Gyot, *Quelques aspects de la typologie du Commentaires sur le Credo et le Decalogue*, in *Les genres littéraires dans les sources théologiques et philosophiques médiévales. Définition, critique et exploitation. Actes du colloque internationale de Louvain-la-Neuve 1981*, ed. by Robert Bultot (Louvain-la-Neuve, 1982), 239–248; Joseph Anthony Slattery, "The Catechetical Use of the Decalogue from the End of the Catechumenat trough the Late Medieval Period," (Ph. D. diss., Washington, 1979); Joseph Goering, "Pastoralia: The Popular Literature of the Care of Souls," in *Medieval Latin: An Introduction and Bibliographical Guide*, ed. by Frank Anthony Carl Mantello, George A. Rigg (Wahington D.C., 1996), 675–676; Robert J. Bast, *Honor your Fathers: Catechisms and the Emergence of a Patriarchal Ideology in Germany, c. 1400–1600*, Studies in Medieval and Reformation Thought, 71 (Leiden, 1997); idem, "From Two Kingdoms to Two Tables: The Ten Commandments and the Christian Magistrate," *Archiv für Reformationsgeschichte* 89 (1998): 79–95; idem, "Honor your Fathers: Reform Movements, Catechisms and 'the Civilizing Process' in "Late Medieval and Early Modern Germany." *Amsterdams Sociologisch Tijdschrift* 21, 4 (1995): 116–125; Lesley Smith, "The Ten Commandments: Interpreting the Bible," in the Medieval World, Studies in the History of Christian Traditions, vol. 175 (Leyden, 2014), and the project in progress by Marta Bigus: *The Ten Commandments and the Ideal of Introspective Individuation in the Late Middle Ages (c. 1300 – c. 1550)*.

9   The two ways are already present in Arkadiusz Lisiecki, transl. and ed., "Nauka Dwunastu Apostołów," [The Teachings of the Twelve Apostles] in idem., transl. and ed., Pisma Ojców Apostolskich [Scripts of the Apostolic Fathers] (Poznań, 1924), 22–30. Cf. Johannes B. Schneyer, *Die Unterweisung der Gemeinde über die Predigt bei scholastischen Predigern*, Veröffentlichungen des Grabmann-Instituts zur Erforschung der mittelalterlichen Theologie und Philosophie, Neue Folge 4 (München–Wien, 1968),

since the early Middle Ages: the works of Prudentius or Cassianus described the battle between virtues and vices, or the therapy of vices by means of virtues, in a manner consistent with the medical principle "contraria contrariis sanantur", which was adopted by Christianity, among others by Isidore of Seville and his successors.[10] Moral teaching belonged to the basic triad beside rudimentary prayers and baptism already in the Patristic Period, and later also in the Missionary Period.[11] The first way was laid out with seven cardinal virtues adopted into the Christian ethics by Ambrose, with the Seven Acts of Mercy, the Beatitudes, and the Seven Gifts of the Holy Ghost, whereas the second way was laid out with vices classified in long lists of different sin categories, with *septem peccata capitalia* at the lead.[12] Although the contents of these moral schemes were changing, they were always presented by means of contrast. Mutual neutralization of virtues and vices was emphasized, as was the possibility of

---

91 ff.; Hervé Martin, *Le métier de prédicateur à la fin du Moyen Âge: 1350 –1520* (Paris, 1988), 282; André Vauchez, *Les laïcs au Moyen Âge: Pratiques et expériences religieuses* (Paris, 1987), 127; Jerzy Wolny, *Z dziejów katechezy* [From the History of Catechesis], 155. Cf. Krzysztof Bracha, *Nauczanie kaznodziejskie w Polsce późnego średniowiecza: "Sermones dominicales et festivales" z tzw. kolekcji Piotra z Miłosławia* [Preaching in Late Medieval Poland: 'Sermones dominicales et festivales' from the so-called Collection of Peter of Miłosław] (Kielce, 2007), 321–324.

10 Isidore of Seville, *Sententiarum libri tres*, II.37.2, Jacques-Paul Migne, ed., *Patrologia Latina*, vol. 83 (Paris, 1850), col. 638; idem, *Differentiae*, Lib. II, c. 40, ed. ibid., col. 95–98.

11 Honoratus Millemann, Caesarius von Arles und frühmittelalterliche Missionspredigt," *Zeitschrift für Missionswissenschaft und Religionswissenschaft* 23 (1933): 12–27; Anton Freitag, "Die Erziehung der Taufkandidaten im altchristlichen Katechumenat", *Zeitschrift für Missionswissenschaft und Religionswissenschaft* 17 (1927): 186; Heinrich Holtzmann, "Die Katechese des Mittelalters," *Zeitschrift für praktische Theologie* 20 (1898): 11–12 and a different perspective on modern literature with a demarcation line shift to the 5th century: Pierre Michaud-Quantin, "Les méthodes de la pastorale du XIIIe au XVe siècle," in *Methoden in Wissenschaft und Kunst des Mittelalters*, ed. by Albert Zimmermann, Miscellanea Mediaevalia, vol. 7 (Berlin, 1970), 76; *Handbuch der Kirchengeschichte*, vol. 3, part 1, 344–345.

12 Peter Göbl, *Geschichte der Katechese im Abendlande vom Verfalle des Katechumenats bis zum Ende des Mittelalters*, Kempten 1880, 197–211; Pierre Michaud-Quantin, *Les méthodes*, 86; Jean Delumeau, *Grzech i strach. Poczucie winy w kulturze Zachodu XIII – XVIII w.* [La Peur en Occident XIVe – XVIIIe siècles: Une cité assiégée] (Warszawa, 1994), 271 ff.; Morton W. Bloomfield, "The Origin of the Concept of the Seven Cardinal Sins," *Harvard Theological Review* 34 (1941): 121–128; idem, *The Seven Deadly Sins: An Introduction to the History of Religious Concept* (East Lansing, Michigan, 1952); Carla Casagrande, Silvana Vecchio, *Histoire des péchés capitaux au Moyen Âge* (Paris, 2009), 275 ff.

regression or progression in one's actions. These tendencies were systematised after the Fourth Lateran Council in the form of arithmetic constructions.

*

When studying catechetical literature of the end of the Middle Ages one can simply get the impression that the *Decalogue* overshadows other sources of religious substance of those days. The *Decalogue* was commented on or explained in numerous catechistic textbooks, comprehensive treatises, minor issues and sermons; its content was taught by means of prosaic or poetic texts intended for mnemonic purposes; moreover, especially frequently, it was represented in iconography, on murals, on tablets, and even on stone reliefs. It is precisely at that time that tablets presenting the meaning of the Ten Commandments, numerously funded and intended especially for the illiterate, appear in churches and cloisters (e.g. the *Ten Commandments table* from the BVM parish church in Gdańsk, ca. 1480, *Heidelberger Dekalog* from MS. Heidelberg Universitätsbibliothek Pal. germ. 438, ca. 1455 – 1458).[13] Drastic scenes, which are simple illustrations of contrasting bad and good deeds, were to suggestively interact with the believers and to encourage the choice of behaviour according to prescribed Christian standards. One must also not forget that the *Decalogue*, like the whole catechistic literature, owes its growing position to the invention of print and the stormily developing production of books. We know book illustrations based on the motifs from the *Decalogue* from these times, executed firstly with a drawing pen, and then rendered in the technique of wood engraving. The *Decalogue* provided the first incentive to use wood engravings as a means of religious teaching. The postulate of the *Decalogue*'s privileged position can also be found in normative church sources, particularly in numerous

---

13 Adam S. Labuda, "Cnota i grzech w gdańskiej Tablicy Dziesięciorga Przykazań, czyli jak rzeczywistość przedstawienia obrazowego s(po)tyka się z rzeczywistością miasta późnośredniowiecznego" [Virtue and Sin in the Gdańsk Table of Ten Commandments: The Reality of Pictorial Representation and the Reality of a Medieval City] *Artium Quaestiones* 7 (1995): 65–102; Maria Otto-Michałowska, *Gotyckie malarstwo tablicowe w Polsce* (Warszawa–Berlin–Budapeszt, 1982), no. 19; *Die Zehn Gebote: Faksimilie eines Blockbuches*, kommentiert von Wilfried Werner (Zürich, 1971); http://digi.ub.uni-heidelberg.de/diglit/cpg438/0337. Cf. Dieter Harmening, "Bildkatechese," in vol. 2 of *Lexikon des Mittelalters* (München–Zürich, 1983), col. 153 ff.; Geffcken, *Der Bildercatechismus*, il. 1–10; Gertrud Schiller, *Die Kirche,* vol. 4.1 of *Ikonographie der christlichen Kunst,* (Güttersloh, 1976), 121–134.

synodal resolutions and in statements by many church writers from the 15th century.

Starting from the 13th century, the commands of the church synods often reminded of the duty of teaching (among others of the *Decalogue*) by parish clergy during the Sunday mass, although with regards to the Polish land, a trace of teaching can already be found in "The Life of St. Otto of Bamberg" (1124)[14], in the description of a missionary expedition to Pomerania. *Decem praecepta* can furthermore be found in the oldest collations of Polish texts intended for teaching the faith, right after the sermon, during *exhoratio*, i.e. the supplement to the sermon, presented within the "general confession" (according to Bishop Świnka's decretal from 1285 starting from the words: "Kajam się Bogu..."). They were said after the remembrance of the faithful departed, at the end of the 13th century in Latin, and in the beginning of the 15th century in Polish. The remembrance of the faithful departed already known in *The Prayers of Princess Gertrude*, is, according to Paweł Sczaniecki, a researcher who made an inventory of Polish collections and discussed 20 texts from the years 1415 – 1500, the first form of church prayers in vernacular.[15] It was also in the 15th century that numerous prose and rhymed *Decalogues* in Polish appeared.[16]

The *Decalogue* was then the basis of Christian moral teaching and became completely conventional. The meaning of the *Decalogue* as a foundation of

---

14   August Bielowski, (ed), *Herbordi vita Ottonis episcopi Babenbergensis,* Monumenta Poloniae Historica, vol. 2 (Warszawa, 1961), 79; Ferdinand Cohr, "Zur Katechese am Ende des Mittelalters," *Zeitschrift für praktische Theologie* 20 (1898): 293–294.

15   *Liber precum Getrudae ducissae e Psalterio Egberti cum Kalendario: Modlitwy księżnej Gertrudy z Psałterza Egberta z Kalendarzem*, Małgorzata H. Malewicz, Brygida Kürbis, (eds.) (Kraków, 2002), 166–169; Paweł Sczaniecki, *Służba Boża w dawnej Polsce: studia o Mszy św.,* ser. 2 [Divine Service in Old Poland] (Poznań–Lublin, 1966), 116–120; Jerzy Wolny, *Z dziejów katechezy* [From the History of Catechesis], 193, n. 59; Ludwik Biernacki, "Najdawniejszy pomnik katechizmu polskiego," [The Oldest Monument of Polish Catechism] *Pamiętnik Literacki* 9 (1910): 31–319; Maria Kowalczyk, "Wypominki Uniwersytetu Krakowskiego z lat 1431/1432, 1453 i 1458," [The Remembrance of the Faithful Departed of Jagiellonian University from the Years 1431/1432,1453 and 1458] *Studia Warmińskie* 9 (1972): 523–534. On Teaching Rudimentary Prayers in Church: Marianne G. Briscoe, *Artes Praedicandi,* Typologie des sources du Moyen Âge occidental, 61 (Turnhout, 1992), 18, n. 10 (Constitutiones from 1281 by Archbp. Peckham); George H. Russell, "Vernacular Instruction for the Laity in the Later Middle Ages," *Journal of Religions History* 2 (1962): 98–119; Hervé Martin, *Le métier de prédicateur*, 295–315; Jean-Claude Schmitt, "Du bon usage de 'Credo'," in *Faire Croire: Modalités de la diffusion et de la réception des messages religieux du XIIe au XVe siècle*, Collection de l'École Française de Rome, 51 (Rome 1981), 349.

16   See below, n. 50.

ethical norms of each Christian was emphasized by many theologians of the times. A Czech protagonist of the reformatory movement, Matthew of Janov, repeatedly compared the meagerness of all later *"mandata et adinventiones hominum"* with the letter of the *Decalogue,* comprehended by him *"quasi decem gubernacula vitae hominis"*.[17] Others, on the other hand, cautioned against ignorance and viciousness. Martin of Amberg (b. ca. 1340), a preacher and inquisitor, the author of the German *Commentary on the Ten Commandments*, reminded that observing the commandments is a condition for redemption.[18] Others still, in order to easier reach the beliefs and consciences of broader circles of believers, resorted to didactical measures and symbolism which were peculiar in their simplicity. Marquardt (Marcus) of Lindau (d. 1392) perceived the God's warning against failing to keep the Ten Commandments in the obvious number of ten fingers and ten toes.[19] Gottschalk Hollen stressed the informative and juridical character of the *Decalogue* in his commentary entitled *Praeceptorium*, for, as he lectured in the introduction, "ignorantia facti non iuris excusat". That is why "divina legis" are according to him "addiscenda, opere

---

17 Jana Nechutová, "Kategorie zákona božího a M. Matěj z Janova," *Sborník Prací Filosofické Fakulty Brnénské University* 16, Řada Archeologicko-klasicka, E 12, 213. The great spokesman of *Decalogue* was John Hus, author of "Expositio Decalogi," in vol. 1, Fasc. 1 of *Mag. Joannis Hus Opera omnia*, Vaclav Flajšhans, (ed.) (Prag, 1903); idem, "Výklad na desatero příkázanie," in *Expositiones bohemicae: Výklady,* vol. 1 of *Magistri Iohannis Hus Opera omnia*, Jiří Daňhelka, (ed.) (Praha, 1975), 327. Cf. František Šmahel, "Słowo pisane i mówione w służbie reformy husyckiej" [Writing and Oral Words in Hussite Reform] in *Kultura pisma w średniowieczu: znane problemy: nowe metody*, ed. by Anna Adamska, Paweł Kras (Lublin, 2013), 184. On the wall painting in the Bethlehem Chapel in Prague only *Credo* and *Decalogue* (*Desatero*) were written in Czech, B. Ryba, ed., *Betlemské texty* (Praha, 1951), 37–38.

18 "Und wer der eines zwpricht und pust sein nicht der gesicht got nymmer froleichen: Warm an ir behaltnus mag nyemand kegen hymel chomen", Martin of Amberg, *Der Gewissenspiegel*, Stanley Newman Werbow, (ed.), *Texte des späten Mittelalters*, 2.7 (Berlin, 1958), 40. See also K. Baumann, *Aberglaube für Laien*, 1: 215–217.

19 Weidenhiller, *Untersuchungen zur deutschsprachigen katechetischen Literatur*, 20. See also K. Baumann, *Aberglaube für Laien*, 1: 220–221. Similar comparison in a German adaptation of "Praeceptorium" by Henry of Friemar (under the name Nicholas of Lyra), Geffcken, ed., *Der Bildercatechismus*, Beilagen, 21: "Diese gebot sint geschrieben an dryen stetten des libes, in den henden, by den zehen fingern, an den fussen by den zehen und an unsern funf sinnen uszwendig und inwennig. Darumb die gebot sollen in uns schicken die werk unser hend, die weg unser begirde, und messen und bruchen unser synne und unser wandel, also das in alien unsern werken gemeinet werdet gotlich ere, in aller unser begirde gotlich lob geubet werde, und in allem unserm wandel bezeichniss eines heiligen lebens bewiset werde."

adimplenda i nunquam obliviscenda".[20] The universalism of the *Decalogue*, in which the entirety of possible human vices and susceptibility to sin are reflected, was also emphasized. John Wolff of Frankfurt, one of the better known German commentators of the *Decalogue* in the second half of the 15th century, was therefore often described with a nickname *doctor decem praeceptorum*. He explained that the God's commandments contain all the sin categories distinguished in the Church's teaching, where each of the sins is at the same time a sin against the Ten Commandments.[21] Nicholas of Dinkelsbühl in the German commentary *Von den czehen poten* included all the commandments in a meaningful and voluminous triad: *moralia, cerimonialia* and *judicalia*.[22] All possible human moral dilemmas of worldly life were solved according to the God's commandments, which constituted the fundamental criterion of good and evil. In this way the symbolism of the *Decalogue* was referred to as *res significata* in explanations of the meaning of objects and events which contain the number 10, especially in reference to the relation between the 10 Commandments and the 10 plagues of Egypt. Presentation of the 10 plagues of Egypt as a God's punishment for breaching the *Decalogue* can be found in literature and iconography starting from early-Christian literature up until the late Middle Ages. In this context the *Decalogue* is understood as *medicina decem plagarum*.[23] This Old Testament interpretation was continued by, among others, Thomas of Chobham in *Summa confessorum*.[24]

The rhetoric of the times, often using the symbolism of a mirror, also follows this semantics. Many commentaries on the *Decalogue* were willingly named "mirrors", e.g. *Speculum aureum decem praeceptorium Dei, Speculum Christiani, Eyn speyghel des cristen ghelouen, Speygel der Christen mynschen, Spiegel christlicher walfart, Der speygel der leyen, Spiegel des Sünders, Gewissenspiegel, Der dreieckecht Spiegel.* John Geiler of Kaisersberg (d. 1510), a theologian and a preacher of Freiburg and then of Basel, even dedicated a separate essay on the symbolism of a mirror and its physical properties.[25]

---

20 *[Gottschalk Hollen]*, Praeceptorium domini Gotscalci Hollen de ordine heremitarum sancti Augustini, (Nürnberg: Anton Koburger, 1503), fol. 1r.

21 Falk, *Drei Beichtbüchlein*, 11–12.

22 Nicholas of Dinkelsbühl, "Von den czehen poten ain tractat," Karin Baumann, (ed.), in K. Baumann, *Aberglaube in Laien*, 2: 503.

23 Volker Honemann, "Zehn Gebote und Ägyptische Plagen," in vol. 10 of *Die deutsche Literatur des Mittelalters: Verfasserslexikon* (Berlin − New York, 1999), col. 1503–1510.

24 Thomas of Chobham, *Summa confessorum*, Frederick Broomfield, (ed.), Analecta Mediaevalia Namurcensia, vol. 25 (Louvain−Paris, 1968), 27–37.

25 John Geiler of Kaisersberg, "Der dreieckecht Spiegel," in Geffcken, (ed.), *Der Bildercatechismus*, 30–35. About the author, see: Herbert Kraume, "Geiler, Johannes,

Referring to the Biblical explanation of Exodus 38:8 and the God's order to Moses that he makes a basin covered with mirrors, in which those approaching the altar would wash away their sins, John Geiler discussed seven consecutive attributes of a mirror. The *Holy Bible*, and especially the *Decalogue* contained in it, should be a mirror which reflects the real state of our soul, with the good and bad deeds therein. However, the mirror, in order to fulfill its inherent functions, has to be clear and not dirty, Geiler stressed. Only a clear and unsoiled mirror is reliable and only in such mirror a man can clearly notice a truthful reflection, "die masen der sünden [...] und die gezierd der tugenden", and as a consequence, according to the God's commandments, separate the good from the evil.[26] The instructions referring to the conditions of the so-called good confession (*Condicio confessionis*) headed in the same direction: the good confession ought to be "full, and therefore sincere and complete, simple, and not wordy", as Matthew of Cracow explained.[27] The *Decalogue* facilitated the preparation for the confession and the examination of conscience. For mnemonic purposes, such instructions were drafted in a form of simple rhyming lines and translated into vernacular languages, including the Old Polish. We know many native records from the 15th century with Polish adaptations of such rhyming lines.[28] In *Tractatulus multum utilis pro confessionibus* from ca. 1450, manuscript 2213 in the Cracow Jagiellonian Library, it was emphasized that the confession should be *"tearful, powerful, obedient and also regretful"*.[29]

---

von Kaysersberg," in 2 vol. of *Die deutsche Literatur des Mittelalters. Verfasserslexikon* (Berlin–New York, 1980), col. 1141–1152.

26 John Geiler of Kaisersberg, *Der dreieckecht Spiegel*, 31.

27 Matthew of Cracow, "*De puritate conscientiae,*" in: Mateusz z Krakowa [Matthew of Cracow], *Opuscula theologica dotyczące spowiedzi i komunii* [Opuscula theologica regarding confession and communion], Władysław Seńko, Adam L. Szafrański, (eds.), Textus et studia historiam theologiae in Polonia excultae spectantia, vol. 1, fasc. 1 (Warszawa, 1974)), 248, 258–259.

28 Bracha, *Nauczanie kaznodziejskie* [Preaching], 385–386, n. 75.

29 "placzacza, moczna, poszluszna y tesz nasza zaluyącza", *Tractatulus multum utilis pro confessionibus,* Cracow Jagiellonian Library MS 2213, fol. 194r. A Latin archetype of this known formula of still uncertain sources, it names sixteen conditions, although in other versions the number of conditions is different:
"Sit simplex, humilis confessio, pura, fidelis,
Atque frequens, nuda, discreta, libens, verecunda,
Integra, secreta, lachrimabilis, accelerata,
Fortis, et accusans, et sit parere parata."
Thomas N. Tentler's analysis in *Sin and Confession on the Eve of the Reformation* (Princeton, New Jersey, 1977), 106–107. The formula is quoted by, among others, Thomas Aquinas, *Summa theologica*, Supplementum III[ae], qu. 9, art. 4, in *Sancti Thomae*

Johannes Geffcken, one of the first researchers of the catechistic literature of the late Middle Ages, in his discussion of the Ten Commandments distinguished three separate categories of texts (as per recipient's criteria): scripts serving as manuals for educated confessors, scripts for parish confessors and lower clergy intended for practical use, and manuals in vernacular languages, intended directly for believers.[30] They belong to a broad group of pastoral literature, together with discourses of rudimentary prayers mentioned by Pierre Michaud-Quantin (*Pater noster, Ave, Credo, Decalogus*) and collections of sermons (*sermones*), *distinctiones, exempla* and *artis predicandi* manuals.[31] Following Richard of Wetheringsett's explanation of *Summa* from the first half of the 13th century, Joseph Goering, on the other hand, classified them according to the twelve themes belonging to medieval pastoralia (Creeds, The Lord's Prayer, God's Gifts, Virtues, Vices, Sacramenta, The Ten Commandments and Two Evangelical Precepts, Work of Mercy, The Rewards of the Just and the Pains of the Wicked, The Errors of the People, The Things to be Avoided (*vitanda*) and to be Done (*agenda*), excerpting, among others, the *Decalogue* from the Old Testament and the Great Commandment from the New Testament.[32] The boundaries between them are not closed but permeable. Regardless of their destination, however, their didactic message makes them, as Dieter Harmening put it, "Gelenk zwischen <oben> und <unten>", that is, a kind of a cultural mediator.[33] Their liturgical purpose is a service, where a preacher *de cancella* teaches the individual commandments and explains their meaning to believers in the vernacular. The functional level, on the other hand, is the confession, where the confessor penetrates the penitents' consciousness according to the scheme of the Ten Commandments.

Here is how Jean Gerson defined the purpose and the target recipient in his *Opusculum tripartitum de praeceptis decalogi*, which was translated into Old German by John Geiler of Kaisersberg; this Decalogue commentary belongs,

---

Aquinatis doctoris angelici Opera omnia iussu impensaque Leonis XIII P. M., vol. 12 (Romae, 1906). Earlier by Peter of Blois, *Poemata. IV: De poenitencia*, J.-P. Migne, ed. Patrologia Latina, vol. 207, col. 1153–1156, where the author names 14 attributes of a good confession. In Robert Courson's manual, whose Summa edited in 1204 – 1208 directly influenced the shape of the Fourth Lateran Council, a good confession is determined by eight attributes: "vera, hylaris, morosa, propria et accusatoria, frequens et integra". Vincent L. Kennedy, "Robert Courson on Penance," *Mediaeval Studies* 7 (1945): 301. See also Thomas of Chobham, *Summa confessorum*, art. III, dist. 2, qu. Ia, 45.

30 Geffcken, *Der Bildercatechismus,* 29.
31 Michaud-Quantin, *Les Méthodes*, 79–80.
32 Goering, *Pastoralia: The Popular Literature of the Care of Souls*, 674.
33 Harmening, *Spätmittelalterliche Aberglaubenskritik*, 244.

according to the classification proposed by J. Geffcken, to the third of the above-mentioned categories.

"Because there are many who have not heard the words, or have heard badly or have not understood, I have edited the *Summa* with the presentation of the God's commandments as a compendium, which could be used as a mirror. The presented work could be read on holy days by a bishop to believers, so that they could determine what they should believe in, how they should behave, and what to renounce". Gerson dedicated his compendium to simple clergymen and priests, as well as all laymen and clergymen in general, children and youths and also church servants. For the superiors, continues Gerson, ought to counsel the parish priests, and they, in turn, ought to counsel the parents, so that they draw the attention of the superiors in schools to this duty. And finally, the rudiments of faith, including the text of the *Decalogue*, ought to be written down on tablets attached to church and school walls, or in holy places, with the division of the content according to the following order: about the God the Creator of All Things, about the damnation and the Redemption, about the *Decalogue* with a commentary, about the confession according to the seven deadly sins and about the art of dying.[34] Similarly, Gottschalk Hollen addressed his comprehensive commentary, known under the title *Praeceptorium*, both to the clergy and also to laymen: "perutile cum suo registro clero et vulgo deserviens studiosissime collectum".[35] Nicholas of Dinkelsbühl, in the already mentioned commentary *Von den czehen poten*, talked openly about the independence of laymen, as "dÿe ain yeds mensch, das sein sinn hat, wol erkennen mag von aygner verständikaÿt".[36]

Because of the textbook character of the *Decalogue* commentaries and because of their intended recipients, various *Praeceptoria* found their way directly to schools and parish communities, and they were copied there not infrequently. The Latin *Decametrum* ascribed to the Cracow preacher Paul of Zator was, for instance, recorded in the community of cathedral schools, and one of the copies was rewritten in the Gniezno cathedral school by a schoolmaster Simon.[37] Paul of Zator himself, as we know, was a rector of the school at the Cracow Castle. Next, in the St. Mary Magdalene parish school in Wrocław the

---

34 Jean Gerson, *Opusculum tripartitum de preceptis decalogi de confessione et de arte moriendi*, Johannes Geffcken, (ed.) *Der Bildercatechismus*, 35. Latin edition Jean Gerson, *Oeuvres completés*, vol. 7, Palemón Glorieux, (ed.) (Paris – New York, 1966), 193–206.

35 [Gottschalk Hollen], *Praeceptorium*, fol. 1.

36 Nicholas of Dinkelsbühl, "Von den czehen poten ain tractat," 503.

37 Paul of Zator [?], *Decametrum*, Cracow Jagiellonian Library MS 2141, fols. 559r–568r. See also below.

Decalogue was discussed in the light of Jean Gerson's commentary and rewritten in a local scriptorium by Michael Hünczpek.[38] Rhymed *Decalogues* in vernacular languages ought to be on the other hand included in the canon of school reading.[39]

*

The stormily developing, especially since the 13th century, literature of commentaries on the *Decalogue* is not an object of particular interests in medieval studies and still remains somewhat in the background, and the same can be said about medieval pastoralia in general. I use the word 'pastoralia' in this case not without reason, for it has been adopted from the genre's expert, Joseph Goering, but due to the presented reasons it has been poorly exposed.[40] We have had superb source repertories in our hands for a long time, starting from the classical ones by Johann Friedrich von Schulte, Pierre Michaud-Quantin, Morton W. Bloomfield and the most recent ones by Jiři Kejř, Richard Newhauser and Istvan P. Bejczy, as well as the Biblical ones by Friedrich Stegmüller and the predicatory ones by Johannes B. Schneyer.[41] German scholarly accomplishments, previously mentioned, stand out, starting from the above mentioned genre's classic Johannes Geffcken and his transliteration of

38   Wrocław University Library MS I F 691, fols. 154r–156r; Częstochowa The Pauline Archive on Jasna Góra MS H/30, fol. 110r. Cf. Krzysztof Stopka, *Szkoły katedralne metropolii gnieźnieńskiej w średniowieczu: Studia nad kształceniem kleru polskiego w wiekach średnich* [Cathedral Schools of the Gniezno Metropoly in the Middle Ages: Studies on Educating the Polish Clergy in the Middle Ages], Polska Akademia Umiejętności. Rozprawy Wydziału Historyczno-Filozoficznego, vol. 76 (Kraków, 1994), 176.

39   Ibidem, 176. Cf. Mieczysław Mejor, "Kanon lektur i komentarzy w polskim szkolnictwie XIV–XV wieku: Uwagi o cytatach" [The Canon of School Reading and Commentaries in Polish Schooling in the 14th – 15th Centuries. Observations on the Quotations] in *Septem artes w kształtowaniu kultury umysłowej w Polsce średniowiecznej (wybrane zagadnienia)* [Septem artes in shaping intellectual culture in medieval Poland (selected issues)], ed. by Teresa Michałowska (Wrocław, 2007), 137–148; Andrzej Dąbrówka, "Treści religijne w średniowiecznych podręcznikach i lekturach szkolnych" [Religious Content in Medieval Textbooks and Books for Required Reading] in *Struktury kościelno-publiczne* [Church and Public Structures], vol. 1 of *Animarum cultura: Studia nad kulturą religijną na ziemiach polskich w średniowieczu* [Animarum cultura: Studies on Religious Culture on Polish Land in the Middle Ages], ed. by Halina Manikowska, Hanna Zaremska (Warszawa, 2008), 459–497.

40   Goering, *Pastoralia: The Popular Literature of the Care of Souls*, 670–676.

41   See n. 6 above.

excerpts from the 27 Commentaries on the *Decalogue* published in 1855, including, among others, Henry of Friemar's (Freimar) *Praeceptorium* (*Tractatus de decem praeceptis / Expositio decalogi*)[42], John Wycliffe, Jean Gerson (with a foreword by John Geiler of Kaisersberg), Ludolph of Göttingen, Stephen Lanzkranna, Nicholas Rus of Rostock, John Ulrich Surgant and many anonymous ones; other German important contributions include Franz Falk's study from 1907, discussing, among others, a commentary by the Frankfurt priest John Wolff from 1478.[43] From the more recent ones it is worth to mention a two-volume monograph by Karin Baumann with the edition of a comprehensive *Von den czehen poten ain tractat* by Nicholas of Dinkelsbühl and a list of manuscript commentaries in Old German (by Henry of Friemar, Henry Krauter, Marquard of Lindau, Thomas Peuntner, Stephen of Landskron, Hieronymus Pollster, John Schlitpacher, Martin of Amberg, and many anonymous ones)[44]; also, Gabriele Baptist-Hlawatsch with a "Commentary" on Ulrich of Pottenstein's *Decalogue*[45] and numerous studies by Dieter Harmening and, from outside this circle, Joseph Goering, Joseph Anthony Slattery, Robert J. Bast, Bertrand-Georges Gyot, and recently Lesley Smith and Marta Bigus.[46] They depict a part of vast medieval literature on the *Decalogue* and are

---

42   Henry of Friemar, *Praeceptorium*, Johannes Geffcken, (ed.), *Der Bildercatechismus*, 20-29: edition of excerpts in German translation under the name of Nicholas of Lyra and Cracow Jagiellonian Library MSS: 297, 1196, 1229, 1675, 1676, 1685, 2141, 2211; Wrocław Univeristy Library MSS: I F. 116, I F. 194, II Q. 12, II Q. 40; Petersburg Imperial Public Library Lat. I. MS Q. 125 (it may be an excerpt from John Herolt, *De eruditione christifidelium*). Cf. K. Baumann, *Aberglaube für Laien*, 2: 130; Adolar Zumkeller, *Manuskripte von Werken der Autoren des Augustiner-Eremitenordens*, Cassiciacum, 20 (Würzburg, 1966), 147, no. 325; Robert G. Warnock, "Heinrich von Friemar der Ältere," in vol. 3 of *Die deutsche Literatur des Mittelalters: Verfasserslexikon* (Berlin, New York, 1981), col. 730–737; Wolny, *Z dziejów katechezy* [From the History of Catechesis], 205; Bloomfield, *Incipits of Latin Works*, no. 850; Aleksander Brückner, *Kazania średniowieczne* [Medieval Sermons], part 3 (Kraków, 1898), 16–19.

43   Falk, *Drei Beichtbüchlein*, passim.

44   K. Baumann, *Aberglaube für Laien*, 1: 128–197: a list of works and manuscripts; Nicholas of Dinkelsbühl, *Von den czehen poten ain tractat*, ed. ibid., vol. 2, 498–831.

45   Gabriele Baptist-Hlawatsch, *Das katechetische Werk Ulrichs von Pottenstein*, passim.

46   See above, n. 8 and moreover: Paul Spaeth, *Works of Saint Bonaventure (VI Collations on the Ten Commandments)*, (St. Bonaventure, 1995); "Les Collationes in Decem Praeceptis de Saint Thomas d'Aquin, edition critique avec introduction et notes," Jean-Pierre Torrell, (ed.), *Revue des Sciences Philologiques et Theologiques* 69 (1985): 5–40, 227–263.

192   Krzysztof Bracha

estimated to 14000 pages, only on the basis of the Bayerische Staatsbibliothek's collection.[47]

Apart from the general layer of catechesis, the commentaries on the First Commandment have been so far of most research interest because they contain criticism of relics of idolatry and superstitions and the magic folklore condemned in them comes to a large degree from experience and to a lesser degree from literary topos.[48] The state of research in Polish medieval studies is in comparison very meagre. We can just mention Jerzy Wolny's source instructions and Stanisław Wielgus's repertories with a short register of 16 manuscripts with a discourse on the *Decalogue*, out of which many are already non-existent[49]. Only the Polish rhymed *Decalogue*s from the 15th century have met with research interest, which we owe first of all to Wiesław Wydra.[50] The extremely interesting Bernardine confessional "Interrogationes de decem preceptiis" from the 15th century are also worth mentioning; they were obtained from manuscript 119 from the Polish Academy of Science's Library in Kórnik and discussed by Jacek Wiesiołowski.[51]

---

47 According to Harmening, *Spätmittealterliche Aberglaubensliteratur*, 244, 248.

48 Idem, *Spätmittealterliche Aberglaubensliteratur*, 246; Paul Pietsch, "Kleine Beiträge zur Kenntnis des Aberglaubens des Mittelalters," *Zeitschrift für deutsche Philologie* 16 (1884): 185–196; Krzysztof Bracha, "Pierwsze Przykazanie w katechezie późnośredniowiecznej w świetle Komentarzy do Dekalogu" [The First Commandment in the Late Medieval Catechesis in the Light of Commentaries on the Decalogue], in *Nauczanie w dawnych wiekach: Edukacja w średniowieczu i u progu ery nowożytnej: Polska na tle Europy* [Teaching in the Old Centuries: Education in the Middle Ages and at the Brink of the Modern Era: Poland in Comparison to Europe], ed. by Wojciech Iwańczak, Krzysztof Bracha (Kielce, 1997), 119–134; Émilie Lasson, Superstitions médiévales: une analyse d'après l'exégèse du premier commandement d'Ulrich de Pottenstein (Paris, 2010); Gabriele Baptist-Hlawatsch, Dekalog-Auslegung: Das erste Gebot: Text und Quellen (Tübingen, 1995). See also above, n. 8.

49 Wolny, *Z dziejów katechezy* [From the History of Catechesis], 205; Stanisław Wielgus, *Obca literatura biblijna w średniowiecznej Polsce* [Foreign Biblical Literature in Medieval Poland] (Lublin, 1990), 241–242.

50 Wiesław Wydra, *Polskie dekalogi średniowieczne* [Polish Medieval Decalogues] (Warszawa, 1973); idem, "Średniowieczne polskie dekalogi i modlitwy codzienne z rękopisów i inkunabułów jasnogórskich biblioteki oo. paulinów" [Polish Medieval Decalogues and Daily Prayers from the Jasna Góra Manuscripts and Incunabula from the Pauline Library], *Slavia Occidentalis* 59 (2002): 183–198; Stanisław Wielgus, *Średniowieczna literatura biblijna w języku polskim* [Medieval Biblical Literature in Polish] (Lublin 1991), 24–30.

51 Jerzy Wiesiołowski, "Problemy społeczne klienteli bernardynów poznańskich na przełomie XV/XVI wieku" [Social Problems of the Poznań Bernardines' Constituency at

The commentaries on the *Decalogue* from the late Middle Ages are worthy of a greater attention, the more so because they are sources that can prove interesting for many disciplines within the humanities. Some examples of the most important writings from the Polish collections (please note that some attributions require a final confirmation and deeper research) are the following: *Dicta super decem precepta Domini* by Nicholas Wigand, *Decem praecepta (De modo confitendi)* by Matthew of Cracow, *De decem praeceptis* by Henry Bitterfeld of Brega (Brzeg), *Expositio super decem praecepta* by Nicholas Kozłowski, *Opus de decem praeceptis* ascribed to Francis of Brega (Brzeg), *Notulae de praeceptis* by Matthias of Łabiszyn and the above-mentioned *Decametrum* vel *Decalogus* ascribed to Paul of Zator.[52]

The same is true of the texts of Latin sermons from the 15th century which contain discussions of the *Decalogue*, which we know for example from the Postilla *Sermones dominicales et festivals* from the MS. 3022 at the National Library in Warsaw, where rhymed, Old Polish-sounding commandments interspersed in the text of the Latin sermon *De decem praeceptis*[53] provide the basis of the commentary.

---

the Turn of the 15th Century], in vol. 1, part 1 of *Zakony franciszkańskie w Polsce* [Franciscan Orders in Poland], ed. by Jerzy Kłoczowski (Lublin, 1982), 349–358.

52 Nicholas Wigand, *Dicta super decem precepta Domini*, Wrocław University Library MS. I Q 94, fols. 2v – 150r, 295v – 304r; Paul of Zator [?], *Decametrum vel Decalogus*, Wrocław University Library MS. IV Q 104, fols. 57 – 68v; Cracow Jagiellonian Library MS. 2141, fols. 559 –568; Nicholas Kozłowski, *Expositio super decem praecepta*, Cracow Jagiellonian Library MS. 1287, fols. 3–144; Francis of Brega [Henry of Friemar?], *Opus de decem praeceptis*, Budapest University Library MS. Lat. 108, fols. 198–231; Matthew of Cracow, *Decem praecepta (De modo confitendi)*. Władysław Seńko, Adam L. Szafrański, (eds.), Textus et studia historiam theologiae in Polonia excultae spectantia, vol. 2, fasc. 1 (Warszawa, 1974), 302–313; Matthias of Łabiszyn, *Notulae de praeceptis*, Cracow Jagiellonian Library MS. 2231, fols. 400v–408r. Cf. Magdalena Papuzińska-Mill, "Henryk Bitterfeld z Brzegu" [Henry Bitterfeld of Brega/Brzeg], *Przegląd Tomistyczny* 4 (1988): 178–190; Marek T. Zahajkiewicz, "Teoria duszpasterstwa" [The Theory of Ministry] in *Średniowiecze* [The Middle Ages], vol. 1 of *Dzieje teologii katolickiej w Polsce* [The History of Catholic Theology in Poland], 238; Wolny, *Z dziejów katechezy* [From the History of Catechesis], 197, 199; Stopka, *Szkoły katedralne* [Cathedral Schools], 177; Bożena Chmielowska, Zofia Włodek, "Maciej z Łabiszyna," *Materiały do historii filozofii średniowiecznej w Polsce* 3 (14), (1971): 29, no. 60.

53 *Sermo de decem praeceptis*, Warsaw National Library MS. 3022, fols. 91rb–95va and Częstochowa The Pauline Archive on Jasna Góra MS. II 39, fols. 60r–66v, furthermore *Sermones de decem praeceptis*, Kielce Higher Seminary Library MS. 31, fols. 88vb–90vb. Cf. Krzysztof Bracha, *The Ten Commandments in preaching in late medieval Poland: "Sermo de praeceptis" from the MS. 3022 at the National Library in Warsaw* [in print].

The commentaries on the *Decalogue* used the glossator's method. The scholastic method became in this way an attentive tool of didactics and practicism within the pastoral literature trend, which like no other performed the function of a cultural keystone.

The universal character of the content of the *Decalogue*'s commentaries from the late medieval period as well as their media character encourage speculative postulates, for they give us an unusually colourful, polyphonic, intercultural account of religious life, as well as of pastoral and specialist functions of people of the Church.

"Spiritu ambulate", id est racionis ductu.
Fifteenth-Century Latin Glosses on the Apostolic Letters[1]

Agnieszka Maciąg

The Institute of the Polish Language,
Polish Academy of Sciences, Cracow

The practice of supplying the text of Holy Scripture with explanatory passages and inserted glosses (marginal as well as textual and interlinear) has a long tradition and plays an important role in the biblical exegetical literature. The great medieval collection of biblical annotations, called *Glossa ordinaria,* attributed now to Anselm of Laon[2] and his followers, originated in the early twelfth century in a cathedral school. Anselm,[3] one of the famous French theologians of the Middle Ages, is said to have been educated at the abbey of Bec, under St. Anselm of Canterbury. He returned to Laon around the end of the eleventh century and founded a school for theology and exegesis, which became the most famous in the Western Europe. *Glossa ordinaria* was one of the great intellectual achievements of the Middle Ages, because it showed a new kind of learning by presenting patristic and earlier medieval interpretations of individual verses of the Scripture in a readily-accessible and easy way. *Glossa ordinaria* and *Magna Glosatura,* glosses for the Pauline epistles elaborated by Anselm's pupil Peter Lombard, greatly influenced Western European Christian theology and culture, and became in time the norm for biblical exegesis.[4] Commentaries of a similar kind were subsequently composed by, *inter alia*, Hugh of Saint-Cher, the author of a monumental work *Postillae in sacram scripturam iuxta quadruplicem sensum, litteralem, allegoricum, anagogicum et moralem*, by Nicholas of Gorran, who wrote his *Postillae in Bibliam* ca. 1280, by Thomas Aquinas, who composed a continuous commentary to the four gospels called

---

1   This research was partially supported by research grant from the Polish National Science Centre: *The 15th century translations of the New Testament – the Old Polish electronical concordance. Online database* (nr 2011/03/D/HS2/00859).

2   Before the twentieth century the *Glossa* was credited to Walafrid Strabo.

3   Cf. Michel Bur, *Histoire de Laon et du Laonnois* (Toulouse: Privat, 1987), 73, Cédric Giraud, *Per verba magistri. Anselme de Laon et son École au XIIe siècle* (Turnhout: Brepols, 2010).

4   Cf. Frederick F. Bruce, "The History of New Testament Study." In *New Testament Interpretation: Essays on Principles and Methods,* ed. I. H. Marshall (Carlisle: The Paternoster Press, 1977), 28–29.

Catena aurea, and later by Nicholas of Lyra,[5] a Franciscan in the convent of Verneuil-sur-Avre, a doctor at the Sorbonne by 1309, who devoted his life to exegesis. In the second prologue to his work, *Postillae perpetuae in universam S. Scripturam*, he deplored the state of biblical studies of his times. He agreed with St. Jerome that the text should be corrected from the Hebrew codices. Nicholas utilized all sources available to him, including Hebrew and rabbinic commentaries. His clear and concise explanations and logical interpretations made *Postillae* the most popular manual of exegesis until the sixteenth century.

In the mediaeval Poland, the University of Cracow was the main centre of biblical studies.[6] Most of the commentaries on the Scriptures were composed by professors of the Faculty of Theology, who were giving lectures on the Bible. There were also numerous cathedral schools, but their scholarly achievements were less significant. One should notice, however, that it is difficult to assess the value of Polish biblical scholarship, since most of the sources are still in manuscripts and have not been edited; consequently, they have not been yet studied.

One of the most important scholars composing glosses and biblical commentaries in the period up to the mid-fifteenth century was Mateusz (Matthew) of Cracow.[7] He studied and taught at the University of Prague. In 1397, he arrived in Poland and helped to organize the Faculty of Theology in Cracow. For many years he lectured and educated students, becoming one of the greatest scholars of his time. He wrote numerous commentaries on the Scriptures, for instance *Commentaria in Cantica canticorum, Commentarium in Matthaei Evangelium, Commentarium in Epistolam Pauli ad Romanos, Postilla solemnis*; sermons, for example *Sermones dominicales* and *Sermones de tempore*, as well as many other works. Matthew's texts were filled with quotations from famous ancient and medieval writers, but they were by no means of a compilatory nature. They are original intellectual works, in which he formulated his own opinions and interpretations. Jan (John) Isner[8] began to study theology under Matthew ca. 1382. After graduating, he accepted a Chair

5   Cf. *Nicholas of Lyra: The Senses of Scripture,* eds. Ph. D. W. Krey, L. J. Smith (Leiden: Brill, 2000).
6   Cf. Stanisław Wielgus, *Średniowieczna łacińskojęzyczna biblistyka polska* [The Medieval Latin Biblical Literature of Polish Autors] (Lublin: KUL, 1993).
7   Adam L. Szafrański, "Mateusz z Krakowa, Wstęp do badań nad życiem i twórczością naukową." [Mateusz z Krakowa. Introduction to the Research on His Biography and Scientific Work] *Materiały i Studia Zakładu Historii Filozofii Starożytnej i Średniowiecznej* 8 (1967): 25–92.
8   Jerzy Zathey, "Jan Isner," in *Polski Słownik Biograficzny* [Polish Biographical Lexicon], vol. 10 (1963), 434–436.

of Theology, which he held to the end of his life in 1411. Nicholas of Lyra's texts served as a model for his works. Under the influence of Nicholas' *Postillae* and commentaries of other great theologians of the time Isner composed his *Glossa super Novum Testamentum,* which was used in the education of young scholars at the University of Cracow. Franciszek (Francis) of Brzeg was Isner's pupil,[9] who, having obtained the degree of Doctor of Theology in 1409, lectured on the Bible until his death in 1432. He wrote, *inter alia, Collationes epistolarum et evangeliorum, Quaestiones circa Evangelium Matthaei* and *Glossae marginales et interlineares in Nicolai de Gubin Commento super Evangelium Matthaei.* Łukasz (Luke) of Wielki Koźmin[10] began lecturing on the Scriptures in 1410; his teaching was influenced by Anselm's *Glossa ordinaria* and Nicholas of Lyra's *Postilla.* He composed his own *Postilla* and wrote numerous *notae* on margins of his manuscripts. Mikołaj (Nicholas) of Kozłów obtained the degree of Doctor of Theology in 1425 and since then worked at the university. He is the author of *Glossae super Novum Testamentum* and *Glossa marginalis* on an anonymous commentary on the epistles for the Holy Mass at Christmas. He gathered one of the largest collections of books in Cracow at the time and donated over 150 codices to the university. Paweł (Paul) of Zator,[11] who was a cathedral preacher in Cracow for almost 40 years and who became famous on account of his sermons, composed *Glossa seu expositio in evangelia dominicalia per circulum anni, Glossa super epistolas per annum dominicales* as well as *Sermones de tempore* and *de sanctis.* St. John of Kanty[12] wrote *Glossa marginalis et interlinearis in Novum Testamentum.*

There are many other works of this type,[13] almost all available only in manuscripts. Catalogues of individual professors' libraries, frequently donated to the university, demonstrate works, which were read and commented in class. Besides commentaries of Anselm of Laon, Peter Lombard, and Nicholas of Lyra, also treatises of Thomas Aquinas, Anselm of Canterbury, Hugh and Richard of St. Victor, Isidore of Seville, St. Augustine, St. Bernard, Beda Venerabilis, and other authors were used in teaching.

---

9   Zofia Włodek, "Franciszek z Brzegu." In *Filozofia w Polsce. Słownik Pisarzy* [The Philosophy in Poland. Biographical Lexicon] (Wrocław, 1971), 87–88.

10 Maria Kowalczyk, "Łukasz z Wielkiego Koźmina." *Materiały i Studia Zakładu Historii Filozofii Starożytnej i Średniowiecznej* 4(15) (1971): 3–40.

11 Marian Zwiercan, "Paweł z Zatora" in *Filozofia w Polsce. Słownik Pisarzy* [The Philosophy in Poland. Biographical Lexicon] , 211.

12 *Cf.* Marian Rechowicz, *Święty Jan Kanty i Benedykt Hesse w świetle krakowskich kompilacji teologicznych z XV wieku* [St. John of Kanty and Benedict Hesse in Light of the Cracov Theological Compilations] (Lublin: RW KUL, 1958).

13 Cf. Wielgus, *Średniowieczna...* [The Medieval Latin...].

Glossa super epistolas per annum dominicales is found in a codex written in Latin and Polish, dating from the mid-fifteenth century. It was published in 1880 in *Sprawozdania Komisji Językowej Akademii Umiejętności.*[14] The codex contains a copy of the text and was produced sometime between 1457 and 1468, while the original was written in 1447 (the date has been established on the basis of historical information included in commentaries). *Glossa* consists of excerpts of the Apostolic Letters (of Paul, Peter, James, and John) which were read on Sundays (*epistolae dominicales*). There are 53 commented passages, arranged in the order of the liturgical year beginning with the Sunday of Advent. The author is not yet known; all we can say is that *Glossa* was probably composed by an educated Polish Dominican of the time. The author of *Glossa* did not copy any known work, but composed a skillful compilation, largely based on the *Glossa ordinaria* and Nicholas of Lyra's *Postillae.* The anonymous author knew also works of the Church Fathers and ancient writers such as Aristotle, Cicero, Ovid, and Seneca.

We can distinguish three types of glosses in the *Glossa super epistolas per annum dominicales*: (1) Polish and (2) Latin interlinear glosses; (3) shorter or longer comments on a fragment of a letter. Here is an example of Latin interlinear glosses:

> Epistle to the Romans: 13, 13
> **Sicut** *gl.* sicut decet
> **in die honeste ambulemus: non in comissationibus** *gl.* superfluis et luxuriosis conviviis,
> **et ebrietatibus** *gl.* inmoderatis potacionibus,
> **non in cubilibus et impudicitiis** *gl.* luxuria, que de nimio potu venit et cibo,
> **non in contentione et aemulatione.**

There are also Polish glosses written over the Latin text:

> Jako zależy poześliwie w obłojstwach, w żarłoczstwach... nie w miękiem a w długiem leganiu, w nieczystych myślach z o<p>witego picia i jedzenia, nie w swarze zwadliwem, w zazdrości.

And a part of a commentary:

---

14   Edition and introduction: Władysław Wisłocki, "Glossa super epistolas per annum dominicales. Kodeks łacińsko-polski z połowy XV^go wieku." [Glossa... The Latin-polish Codex from the Middle of the 15th Century] (Kraków, 1880), 1–141. Wisłocki's edition contains the text of Latin and Polish glosses, but without the Latin commentary. The manuscript, which originally belonged to Dominicans in Lwów, is currently in the library of Zakład Narodowy im. Ossolińskich in Wrocław, ref. 413, (available online http://www.dbc.wroc.pl/dlibra/docmetadata?id=5753&from=&dirids=1&ver_id=&lp=1 &QI=).

Debet esse sobrietas in plebanis et alijs sacerdotibus, qui deuota mente debent insistere spiritualibus officijs. Nolite ergo inebriari vino, in quo est luxuria, quia inebriari velle non solum est pecatum, sed eciam aliorum pecatorum principium. Exemplum de illo, qui post ebrietatem voluit opprimere matrem et occidere patrem etc.

We can distinguish several kinds of glosses:[15]

1. grammatical or grammatical–synonymous, used to explain difficult parts of a sentence to a novice student, in which frequently pronouns and conjunctions are explained, e.g.

Epistle to the Romans: 8, 23
non solum autem illa *gl.* creatura,
sed et nos ipsi *gl.* apostoli
Galatians: 4, 1
Dico autem: Quanto tempore heres parvulus est, nihil differt a servo, cum *gl.* quamvis **sit dominus omnium.**

2. synonymous, used to explain difficult or incomprehensible terms, often emotional in nature, e.g.

Romans: 6, 19
Humanum dico *gl.* leve et in nullo onerosum preceptum do
propter infirmitatem carnis vestrae. Sicut enim
exhibuistis *gl.* voluntarie preparastis
8, 18 **Existimo** *gl.* veraciter scio.
8, 20 **vanitati enim creatura** *gl.* id est homo seu humana natura

Corinthians I 11, 25
naufragium *gl.* id est navis fraccione **feci.**

James 1, 26
Si quis putat se religiosum esse *gl.* id est verum et perfectum cristianum scilicet per opera fidei.

1 Peter 2, 15
quia sic est voluntas Dei, ut benefacientes obmutescere *gl.* id est silere.
4, 9 **hospitales invicem sine murmuratione** *gl.* id est hilariter.

3. glosses which provide more profound (often allegorical or anagogical) explanation of the discussed passages; their aim is to help to understand the faith inherited from the forefathers, e.g.

Romans: 6, 19
immunditiae *gl.* peccatis carnalibus

---

15 Cf. also Mariusz Leńczuk, *Staropolskie przekazy kanonu Mszy Świętej. Wariantywność leksykalna* [The Old Polish Witnesses of Holy Mass Canon. Lexical Variation] (Warszawa: IBL, 2013), 72–77.

et iniquitati *gl.* peccatis spiritualibus
6, 21 **Nam finis illorum mors!** *gl.* sc. eterna.

Galatians: 5, 17
Caro *gl.* id est sensualitas

Ephesians: 5, 2
et ambulate *gl.* vivite, crescite **in dilectione**
5, 19   **in psalmis et hymnis** *gl.* hymnus est laus Dei cum cantico,
et canticis spiritalibus *gl.* qui de eterno gaudio sunt,
cantantes *gl.* sc. voce **et psallentes** *gl.* sc. opere

4.   longer periphrastic and emphatic comments, e.g.

Romans: 6, 21
Quem ergo fructum habebatis tunc *gl.* cum eratis servi peccati, id est in illis
turpitudinibus et peccatis
8, 20 **subiecta est, non volens** *gl.* id propter peccatum Ade quod non est
voluntarium.
8, 23 **redemptionem corporis nostri** (in addition: in Cristo Jesu domino nostro, *gl.*
id est per virtutem passionis domini nostri Jesu Christi)
15, 5   **Deus autem patientiae et solacii** *gl.* sc. Deus, qui est doctor paciencie et
solacii, prebet vobis consolacionem in omni turbulacione.

Corinthians I 10, 10
Neque murmuraveritis, sicut quidam eorum murmuraverunt et perierunt ab
exterminatore *gl.* ab angelo, qui eos percussit extra terminos terre promissionis.

Glosses which explain Latin terms, especially these which were written in the vernacular language, frequently reveal the glossator's thinking and show his level of education of the author as well as the sources he used.

The complex and elaborated character of the *Glossa super epistolas per annum dominicales* proves that the text was intended for students, other friars, or young priests working with the Polish people, and could serve as an aid for preparing sermons. I think the *Glossa* is worth further studying.

Warsaw Studies in Classical Literature and Culture

Edited by Mikołaj Szymański and Mariusz Zagórski

Vol.   1   Maria Grazia Iodice / Mariusz Zagórski (eds.): Carminis Personae – Character in Roman Poetry. 2014.

Vol.   2   Mieczysław Mejor / Katarzyna Jażdżewska / Anna Zajchowska (eds.): Glossae – Scholia – Commentarii. Studies on Commenting Texts in Antiquity and Middle Ages. 2014

www.peterlang.com